Advance Praise for
Dispatches From the Kingdom of Outsiders

"Tim Sommer is a throwback to when people writing about music wrote whatever they wanted, took shocking takes not to garner social media attention but because they really believed in them, and did not worry about industry repercussions. Tim Sommer writes because he has to, not because he's trying to impress anyone and his takes — on the Beatles, Glenn Branca, Kent State and just about anything that pops into his brain — are refreshingly disinterested in scoring social media points. He is mildly insane, charmingly irresistible and American original. This is a truly original document of the kind of smart, free, joyous writing we so rarely find anywhere today."
—Geoff Edgers, national arts reporter, *Washington Post* and author of *Walk This Way: Run-DMC, Aerosmith, and the Song that Changed American Music Forever*

"Tim Sommer goes deep on a whole century of rock and pop culture, from Bowie to Buddy Bolden, Spike Milligan to Taylor Swift, and everything in between. Punk was always a state of mind as much as a sound or a look, and this book is punk AF." —Billy Idol

"It's entirely fitting that Tim Sommer's college radio program was entitled Noise The Show as it's the SOUND, the NOISE, the music of the city that he was so enchanted by; music and noise signified the magic dynamism of his reality. Initially it's the urban cacophony of punk and hardcore which inspires Tim to stage dive headfirst into its communitarian clutch but eventually it would also be the experimental sounds of the avant-garde intriguing his rapacious receptors. Whether we heard Tim shouting out the latest Necros single on air, or read a think piece of his on Alan Vega or Mia Zapata, there would always be gleaned an intellect of considered and conversational gravitas. It was the pleasure of noise, be it from the margins or from the mainstream, that inspired Tim to pontificate so excitedly. While his "dispatches" are modestly critical and discerning they are essentially informed by joy, an aspect of shared dialogue utterly welcoming and one the world necessitates now more than ever."
—Thurston Moore

"*Dispatches From the Kingdom of Outsiders* is a non-stop roller-coaster ride through the mental and physical lives of Tim Sommer, and the lives of all of us who lived through the evolutionary trajectory of music and culture that he chronicles from the late 70s to the present. Speaking of the present, Sommer has emerged as one of the most creative, no holds barred, writers about contemporary rock and pop. Get this book!"
—Joseph LeDoux, neuroscientist, musician and author of
The Four Realms of Existence and the forthcoming *Starting Over: A Neuro-Emotional, Cajun, Rock'n'roll, Memoir*

In a 1994 interview, asked how he came to sign with Atlantic Records, John Lydon of Public Image Ltd. said, "They're the only ones that would pay me. Tim Sommer got me the deal. I like him. He tries hard. But the poor sod is going to have to try a hell of a lot harder. I don't think he knows what he's taken on. Or maybe he does. Then more power to him."

DISPATCHES FROM THE KINGDOM OF OUTSIDERS

WRITING ON MUSIC, CULTURE AND MORE 1979-2025

BY

TIM SOMMER

TROUSER PRESS BOOKS

Cover photograph: Gregory Crewdson, Untitled, 2003-2008, Digital pigment print, image size 57 x 88 in. © Gregory Crewdson

Cover and interior pages designed by Kristina Juzaitis

Lyrics to "Kill Yr. Idols" quoted by permission of Thurston Moore

ISBN 979-8-9990487-3-8

Library of Congress Control Number: 2026934207

Published by Trouser Press Books
Brooklyn, New York
First publication August 2026
LS262
Distributed by Publishers Group West

www.trouserpressbooks.com https://
www.hopp.bio/tpbooks

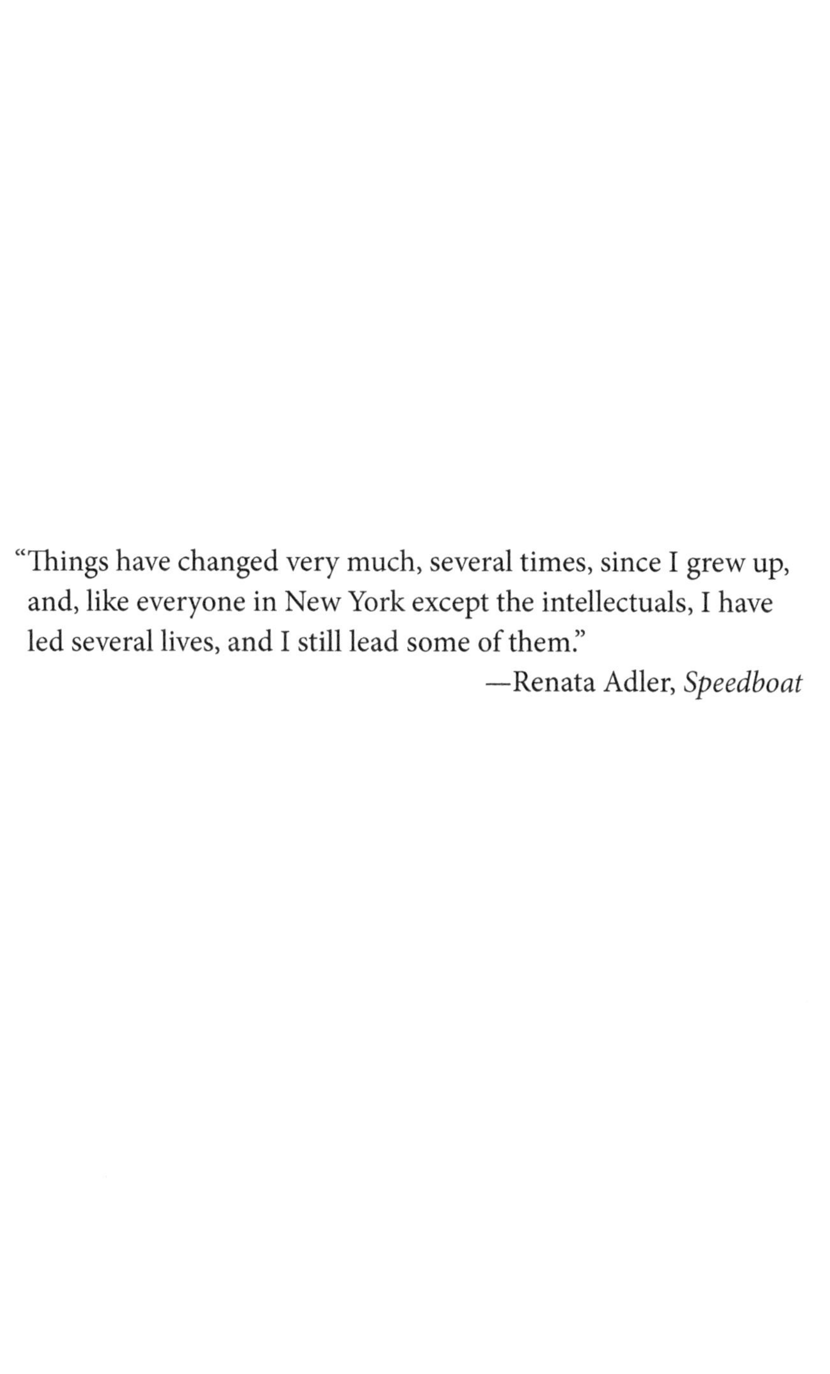

"Things have changed very much, several times, since I grew up, and, like everyone in New York except the intellectuals, I have led several lives, and I still lead some of them."

—Renata Adler, *Speedboat*

CONTENTS

Introduction

By the time I was 15, I knew exactly what I wanted to do with my life.

I wanted to write about music.

I did not want to make music (though I would do that one day); I did not want to produce other musicians or work for a record label (though that would come in time, too); I did not want to be a DJ on the radio or in nightclubs (though just a few years later I would find myself doing plenty of that).

I wanted to write about rock and roll and make people as excited about it as I was.

Truly, that was my mission: not to criticize, not to snark, not to meet rock stars (though that was certainly fun), *but just to get you so excited you would understand what I felt.*

The origin of this goal (of which I was bizarrely certain, in the same way that someone who is tall knows "I am tall") was quite straightforward: starting around the time I was 12 or 13, I got very excited telling people about the music that I loved and telling them gorgeous, corny and oblique facts about artists or records. I literally couldn't shut up about music. The friends who knew me as someone who — until very recently — had been obsessed with baseball or *Monty Python* found this new me quite tiring.

Other contemporary music journalists that I avidly read (no, *studied*) — namely, Caroline Coon, Nick Kent, Ira Robbins, Jim Green, Scott Isler, Dave Schulps, John Rockwell, Robert Christgau and Tim Page — had this same kind of effect on me. Their words made me excited to discover and listen; their words made me almost unspeakably happy to be sentient in the age of rock; their words made me go out and buy records; and their words described a remarkable clubhouse called the Kingdom of Outsiders. I, too, knew that's where I belonged, and I wanted to tell its story.

And the final, probably most important, piece was this: I didn't want to do this "when I grew up" (or even when I finished high school). I wanted to do it now. *Now.* I couldn't see any possible reason why I shouldn't. Anything else that happened concurrently — 11th or 12th grade, flawed and aspiring romances, college and so forth — would have to happen *alongside* this goal.

So, sometime in the spring of my sophomore year at Great Neck South, on the North Shore of Long Island — I would have just turned 16, being one of those kids who was always a year younger than everyone else (not due to skipping a grade or anything like that, I had just gone in a little young), I called my favorite music magazine, *Trouser Press*, to ask if they needed an office boy. An extraordinary stroke of luck intervened: the woman who usually answered the phones, who almost certainly would have responded to my request politely but negatively, was away from her desk. *Trouser Press* co-founder Ira Robbins picked up the phone instead. And he said, "Sure! Come on in and we'll talk."

With 11th grade just behind me, I began working for *Trouser Press* in the summer of 1978 ... and 47 years later, here we are. (Some more of my early adventures as a teenage *Trouser Press*-er in the heart of 1970s Times Square are detailed herein).

A few words about what follows: I have always wanted to pass on the magic blue fire that music lit inside of me, to tell the stories of the unique monsters and angels who drove our heroes — famous, infamous and hardly known at all — to create. Just as importantly, *just as importantly,* I wanted to try to describe why we were so drawn to this culture and investigate the shared history of desire, thwarted desire, frustration, ecstasy, grasping and dissatisfaction with the status quo that made so very many of us not only obsessed with music but residents in the Kingdom of Outsiders. As a journalist, I always had relatively scant interest in how so-and-so made their guitar sound such-and-such way on this-or-that album; I am much more interested in the why, and the fact that the same thing that inspired John Lennon to, say, put his guitar through a rotating Leslie speaker or Dave Davies to eff up his guitar amp was probably the same thing that drove Buddy Bolden to invent a century through his cornet … and that all these motivations are somehow connected to something magical about our world and the way our souls move through it.

Seriously: All I ever wanted to do was translate the magic of rock and roll into words, to somehow use language, limited as it might be, to say what it all meant to me; to say to you, the reader (as I might say to a friend sitting across a table), "This real and fake starlight, these shabby cities full of pale princes and princesses, these crumbling rialtos full of sticky floors and blue lights; this line from Bowery to Beale Street to Bourbon Street to lonely and broken Route 66 and motel-slung Airline Highway; it has moved my heart, it has changed my life. Here are some words where I try to explain that."

I'm not just writing about artists. I am writing about us and artists.

To quote Billy Idol, "I just want to give the feeling rock and roll gave to me" … and *that's* why I write. As simple and even naïve as that sounds, I'll stand by it: if Frank Sinatra's *Watertown* or a performance by a middle-aged Adam Ant moves me to extremes, it's my duty to try to explain to you why that is, and why it might matter to you.

We will note there is a slightly weird time frame (or is that time lapse?) to this collection. That's because I worked very actively — constantly, really — as a professional music journalist from mid-1978 until roughly mid-1984. Around that time, because I was beginning to actively forge a "new" self-identity as a musician (first with the Glenn Branca Ensemble and then Hugo Largo), and due to the reality that my "day job" at MTV News was taking up a great deal of time, I eased back significantly (though not completely) on the journalism. I didn't really start writing regularly again until 2013, when I had a chance encounter on a street in Brooklyn Heights with the amazing John Loscalzo, who asked me to contribute to his *Brooklyn Bugle* site.

This book is divided into seven sections. At the beginning of each are a few words explaining my logic in why I put these specific pieces in those particular places. Likewise, before most — but not all — of the individual articles (after the headline, but before the original text), there's a short introduction establishing some background and context for the original publication. These new introductions are always in italics to distinguish them from the body of the piece as originally published. Very occasionally, there's a new postscript and, even more occasionally, a new comment within the piece; these are always in italics and brackets.

Nearly everything here was previously published. The date of publication (or, in the cases of the unpublished pieces, the date of authorship), plus where it originally appeared, can be found immediately after each piece.

There is no need to read anything in sequence; I encourage hunting and pecking. However, there is some logic to the organization, let's just leave it at that.

Finally, although this anthology may say a lot about how I think about and love music, it is not remotely an overview of my tastes, preferences or prejudices as a listener, music critic, occasional music-maker/producer or music fan. In all these pages, there isn't one word about three of my five favorite musical acts: Neu!, Hawkwind and Kraftwerk. Two of my other top five, the Beach Boys and Wire, are mentioned only tangentially. Nothing in this book details how my entire musical perspective was altered by the Cure's "Carnage Visors," or that I have an almost unhinged attachment to the first Boston album and/or Dio-era Sabbath. Likewise, although there are autobiographical elements in some of these pieces, this anthology by no means tells my story; for instance, there's nothing here about Hootie & the Blowfish, whose career I am linked to in a profound and public way (I've already written a whole book about that); and there's only passing reference to Hugo Largo, whose recordings and performances between 1984 and 1989 I consider one of the creative highlights of my life.

Rather, in deciding what to include in this collection, I've tried to select pieces that had interesting perspectives; recounted remarkable, noteworthy or amusing events; or had (what I hope) was writing that was worth sharing.

So.

About the Title

A few words about the title of this collection.

Maybe 15 years ago, I found myself frequently using the phrase "The Kingdom of Outsiders." I used this in my writing, in conversation, in social media posts, etcetera. I used it casually; I used it intently.

It had a fairly specific meaning for me. Primarily, it meant us.

I felt the Kingdom of Outsiders was a powerful descriptor of the land of music, art, books and film where I had found shelter and comfort at the precise moment I was shuffling, shivering and sluicing through the agony, mystery, wonder and terror of puberty. I also felt it was an excellent way to describe the ephemeral land which housed the artists we discovered when we thought there was no one who could possibly understand us.

Did an artist's image or music make you feel heard or seen, or make you sense that you might be different from the larger adolescent world around you? Did an artist speak the words you wished you could say? Did just knowing they were there, and that other people liked them, too, make you feel less alone?

This was the Kingdom of Outsiders.

To me, the Kingdom of Outsiders was a passport-less nation of the lonely, bookish, bullied and sensitive, a congress of misfits and dreamers, a parliament of anti-jocks and prom no-shows. And even if it wasn't exclusively that — after all, many of us did go to our proms and have friends, and some of us were even bullies — we lived in a land adjacent to the Kingdom of Outsiders; it was a place that made sense to us in a way the world of mainstream 1970s (or 1980s) culture did not. All around you, people were saying that these were the best years of your life, but you knew this was a fetid lie. It frequently occurred to you that things would never get any better.

Do you remember that feeling?

Like many adolescents, maybe you felt alone, unloved, never to be kissed; you considered your own body, this rage of pimples and continuous trash-fire of desires, a stranger, an enemy. But then…

…taped up on a locker or on the front of a T-shirt, you saw a Schiele-like face and stick-figure sexbody. Who was this rooster, aflame, with an impossible jaw and alien eyes? Perhaps you were in 9th or 10th grade. Something stirred inside of you. Before long, you realized that there was a secret Kingdom of Outsiders, an army of anti-jock heretics, and it was beckoning you.

Maybe it wasn't Bowie who made you feel there might be a place for you in the world. Maybe it was Laura Nyro; or Frank-N-Furter; or Rita Mae Brown or Blue Öyster Cult; or the *National Lampoon*, or Tommy Tune on some variety show, or the magic Boticellian curls of Marc Bolan; or even the snark of Tom Snyder at 12:40 in the morning on a school night; or Patti Smith, this mysterious androgyne glimpsed in a black and white picture in a magazine only carried by that one newsstand. Maybe you saw *A Chorus Line* and stepped out of that theater and suddenly felt like there was a new world for you to explore. Or maybe it was the film *Cabaret*, or that utterly new, goosebump feeling you felt when you saw Michael York shirtless; or perhaps it was Lance Loud, tossing his hair like he was the Queen of a New World, in *An American Family* — you had never seen anything like that, but somehow he felt familiar, and you knew you belonged to the same nation as him.

Throughout America during the 1970s and early 1980s, a Kingdom of Outsiders was forming. But we did not necessarily know it. Without the unifying factor of the internet, this unmapped Kingdom existed largely in isolation. A nation, a whole nation, was forming in bedrooms scarred with scotch-taped pictures of cult heroes and icons, in which we studied Vonnegut, Brautigan, Ginsberg, even *New York* magazine, *Rock Scene*, *Trouser Press*, *The New Yorker* and *Esquire*; it was forming on long solitary walks when we dreamed of the glitter, glamour and dirt of the City and in suburban dens where overheated tube televisions were tuned to *Masterpiece Theatre* or *Monty Python*;

it was forming in high school auditoriums where teenagers experimented with camp or whispered rumors of Fosse; it was forming in lonely and cold train station newsstands which carried a British music weekly; it was forming under the smoky ceilings of crumbling old vaudeville theaters where glamorous new British bands made noise. The evidence, the semaphore signals we were sending, were the pictures in our lockers, the T-shirts we wore and the names scrawled on our notebooks.

To know this feeling: to be 13 or 14 and sitting cross-legged on the floor of your den, alone in a good way (it's good to be alone) and alone in a terrifying way (will I always be alone?), with Liptons in your bald tummy and ten hours until the too-cold-to-dream silence of the bus stop, and to watch *The Naked Civil Servant* and think: *someone else out there is watching this.* Somewhere, another never-kissed teenager who gym fills with terror is watching this, and they might be my friend.

A hope blinked on in you, like a light. You were certain someone else, somewhere, was feeling these things, too. How do I meet them? Where is my Kingdom?

So, by accident and by intent, we outsiders began to collect outsider things. (I don't need to reiterate that list, you know what it is.) Information was not always ubiquitous, once it was knowledge, yes? Knowledge was precious, knowledge was identity. Knowledge was grains of sand, luminescence from the sea foam; it was exotic, it was not everything at your fingertips and inside your head in an instant. Knowledge was precious, and it could be acquired to arm yourself against loneliness or, even better, to acquire an identity which might one day attract another seeker, another nonconformist in the age of pukka and peasant blouse.

Music was a mirror of our restlessness and curiosity. But it did not mirror us fully. We were full of dreams and words, and music was just one of the flags we would wave. My god, to leaf through *Steal This Book* or *The Whole Earth Catalog* or an older sibling's copy of *Fear of Flying* and feel connected to something beyond the dissonance of homeroom!

Only in an era when information was precious, when just a handful of artifacts could give you the pride of identity, could the

Kingdom of Outsiders thrive. Once upon a time, you made a friend for life just because they had also heard of Klimt or *The Goon Show*, Marshall Efron or Don DeLillo, Sylvia Plath or Syd Barrett, Robert Klein or Anne Rice and Todd Rundgren; there were a thousand and another eight thousand clues to be found in libraries and record stores, PBS and dusty volumes about silent film. We were spelunkers, gathering the stalactites of identity!

Have you seen this, heard this, read this, felt this?!?

Information was glee, information was the currency of identity.

Information, mundane or exotic, was once the esoteric language of lonely children.

We collected it because it made us feel less alone.

We collected it in the hope that it would allow us to send up a flare: We are here.

We were all poets, but our poetry was not built out of words; it was our sense of otherness.

There was nothing as sexy as finding someone who had read the same books as you.

"Straight off the boat — where to go?"

This book is very much about a lifetime spent drawing a map to the Kingdom of Outsiders; discovering clues and fellow explorers; continuing that search even as we age; and spreading the same sense of joy these discoveries provided when we first found them and realized we were not only *not* alone, but that a whole nation also existed who were a little like us — and just different enough.

Part 1: I Was a Teenage

I have long believed there were, generally, two types of teenagers. (I use the past tense because I suspect teenage life has changed so markedly in the last few years that I can only speak of the experience of the generations who went through adolescence before smartphone ubiquity.)

There were those who accepted the notion that these were supposed to be "the best years of your life" and sought to fit in or achieve status within that peculiar notion and there were those who were always looking outwards and beyond and merely saw high school or middle school as a necessary and sometimes unpleasant waiting room for the real world that lay beyond.

One sort is by no means better than the other, and often the two types overlapped.

I was most adamantly the latter type. Even during my early/mid-teenage years — *especially* during my early/mid-teenage years — I did not remotely understand the notion that this time was somehow a sort of apex or ideal of freedom, joy or social engagement. I just wanted to get out and get on with my adult life as soon as possible. In fact, it was my intention to begin my adult life concurrently.

I did not have an unpleasant time in high school; not at all. I wasn't really bullied, and I did have friends. Nor did I have a particularly negative attitude towards my contemporaries who embraced the traditional experiences and ideals of high school. It just wasn't for me. By the time I was 14, in my mind — and in many of my actions as well — I was preparing for a life entirely outside of high school and, to nearly every degree possible, attempting to actually live that life. Others might be thinking about sports or academic achievement or the party on Saturday night; I had, quite literally, not a single concern about anything regarding high school life — not the academics, not the social scene (though maybe a little about the spring and autumn musicals). Even if I was still physically in school six or seven hours a day, my spirit had already left. I did not think, "I will be this or that one day." Instead, I was quite certain, "This is what I already am, I just happen to still have to go to classes at Great Neck South five days a week until the first possible and practical moment I can stop."

The pieces in this chapter fall into five different yet complimentary categories: the music, media and personalities that obsessed and formed me while I was in high school and middle school in the mid- and mid/late-1970s; some thoughts on the way teenagers engage with music; how music creates both a mnemonic and a template for a lifestyle; the artists who had (and have) particularly adamant constituencies amongst teens; and accounts of my own experiences and encounters while I was still a teenager. In addition, this section includes a handful of pieces I wrote while still, technically, a teenager. These reflect teenage naïveté, teenage passion, the curious ambience, tastes and underground trends of the time and — perhaps most of all — the peculiar opportunities and luck I manifested for myself before I turned 20.

Times Square, 1978

I began working at Trouser Press *magazine as an office boy in the summer of 1978. I get asked a lot about working in Times Square at the very zenith — or is it nadir? — of its, uh, Times Squareness. In 2017, I put some of my memories of the district, and the era, into words for the* New York Observer.

In the summer of 1978, when I was (barely) 16 years old, I was hired to work as an office boy for a pioneering alternative rock magazine called *Trouser Press*. Our office was at the exact northeast corner of 42nd Street and Broadway, the geographic and spiritual center of the mossy, briny, sepia- and piss-colored arcade of faded, flaking and for-sale sin that was Times Square in the late 1970s.

Listen, this isn't a sexy piece about my adventures in the Deuce. Rather, these are some thoughts about a year and a half spent working in a part of New York City that has vanished so thoroughly that it might as well have been an Iron Age settlement. For a darker and more picaresque portrait of Times Square at that time, I strongly recommend the work of Nik Cohn, Josh Alan Friedman and Samuel R. Delany, each of whom expressed the beauty and shock of the district in graceful and magical words. For me, it wasn't the Deuce. I was a teenager who worked in Times Square, went to the Nathan's in Times Square, went to the Baskin-Robbins in Times Square, went to the Post Office in Times Square. So, I will call it Times Square.

At the time, I did not attach any real drama to the idea of working in Times Square. However, New York City felt special, unimaginably special; it was the logical destination for any of us who, spurred on by loud and limp-wristed art rock and a gnawing sense that the suburbs would kill us, sought a place in the Kingdom of Outsiders. Times Square was just another piece of the Kingdom.

True, it was a particularly shabby place in a shabby city; that's the word that occurs to me again and again when I think of Times Square circa 1979: shabby.

And shabby is not a bad word.

Shabby means over-lived-in and under-polished. It is a word that reflects a living community, a place where people work and play and shop and drink and hang out and sit on the stoop and laugh and shout and listen to loud music. If a place is full of life but not full of money and not dominated by outside financial interests, people tend to label it "shabby." And Times Square in 1979 felt shabby.

Let me also note that the idea of memory was different then.

See, in 1979 we went through the world without an outboard translator, without the internet telling us precisely what a location was going to be like before we got there and how we ought to interpret it after we have been there. And we did not have these wonderful devices to photograph every possible object of interest from every conceivable angle, to freeze in amber or aspic any potential memory. You probably already know this: to a large degree, memory has become what we see on our phones, not necessarily what we actually find in our brains.

So, I look back on my experience as a 16-year-old working in Times Square with pure memory, with only my brain as a resource. Without photos, memory is sourced by all my senses. What I summon is scraps of motion, swaths of color, bursts of noise, acrid smells. It is an impressionistic picture. It is not a crossword, already two-thirds finished, assembled out of the grins and red eyes of old Facebook posts.

I never considered Times Square sleazy, and I still don't. To me, sleazy is American Apparel ads or Terry Richardson or big-titted clickbait hovering on the left side of your Facebook page. The Times Square that I knew may have been shabby, lovable but unloving, and absolutely slathered with urine and disinfectant (this smell hung over the district like fog hangs over Santa Monica in the mornings), but the word sleazy does not occur to me.

The sheer density of porn culture and commerce was extraordinary (even the most lurid panoramas don't do it justice), but that's not my strongest memory of the area. What I remember most is the noise: the constant babble of the drug peddlers, hookers and three-card monte dealers, the rhythmic hollers of people selling shoeshines and salvation and hot dogs, the constant click and clack and cough of the barkers trying to get you into their strip bars and massage parlors. I wish I had a tape of all that, because that noise, more than any picture, would capture the time.

My other dominant instant memory is the overall color of the district during daytime. A dull bleached yellow — I'll call it VA Hospital Yellow — pervaded the whole area. Honestly, it's the first thing I see in my head when I think of Times Square in the late '70s. It seemed to be everywhere, underneath the movie marquees, on the strips of wall between the endless rows of cigar shops and porn palaces and juice stands and arcades. This dull, disused, joyless industrial yellow could not be shouted down by the lights, and even the posters advertising the porn films were leeched and infected by that color.

Was Times Square dangerous?

Let me note that as a white male (as young and naïve as I may have been at that time) my experience in Times Square Classic is going to be profoundly different then the experience of a woman or a person of color. I understand this, so I'll rephrase the question: As a white male in his teens, did I feel that Times Square was a dangerous or threatening place?

Absolutely not. I have no hesitation in saying that.

This was due to two factors. First, I presented myself as neither a threat nor a customer. If you weren't a threat or a customer in Times Square, you were pretty much invisible. Secondly (and more practically), I kept my eyes to myself. If someone were to ask me what my primary trick was for staying safe in Old School Times Square, I would tell them, "I didn't make eye contact with anyone ever, and just as importantly, I didn't march around as if I was deliberately *not* making eye contact." I was just a person going from one place to another, I wasn't buying, taking or selling. Via instinct, common sense or just because I was humming a rather distracting Jam song in my head, I minded my own business, but not in such a manner that I appeared arrogant or challenging.

That's not to say that I didn't feel vulnerable. One of my regular tasks was putting the subscription copies of *Trouser Press* into envelopes and then loading all those envelopes onto a large hand truck which I would roll from our office on 42nd and Broadway to the Post Office on 42nd Street between Eighth and Ninth Avenues. In other words, this stroll took me directly through the throbbing, suppurating, blinking, Peepland-ing heart of Times Square. I did this errand often, delicately steering the over-filled hand truck (the tower of envelopes usually coming up to eye level) through the sidewalks crowded with precisely the sort of characters you would imagine 42nd between Eighth and Ninth being filled with in the late 1970s. I have often wondered why someone didn't pick me off out of curiosity, wondering what kind of stash I was carrying. But it never happened.

Before I seem too blasé, let me note that there were two places that freaked me out in a major way, pretty much on a daily basis: I have never experienced anything like the Times Square subway station in the late 1970s. You descended into a hot hell of fierce noise, banging, angry gamelan chatter and desperation. It was a city within a city, a city unto itself. It seemed lawless. I was certain there were people living there, working there, scamming there, dying there, who never saw the light of day. Whatever was happening above ground was happening at twice the density and four times the volume beneath the streets. This was further compounded by the labyrinthine nature of the station itself, which expanded and contracted and spun out in filthy, clattering, echoing confusion. I spelunked into the Times Square station daily, and every single time I noticed a donut shop which advertised, in rusty tangerine neon, "DONUTS BAKED ON PREMISES." Each damn time I saw this sign I thought to myself, wouldn't it be better for business if it said, "DONUTS DEFINITELY NOT BAKED HERE"? Why would someone boast that their baked goods were actually made in the sigmoid colon of the world?

There was one other place that seriously spooked me: a vacant lot on the southeast corner of 42nd and Eighth, directly across from Port Authority (maybe it was a parking lot, I don't recall). If the sidewalks of the district were an open market where sellers looked for buyers (and vice versa), this lot was the waiting room for all the sellers, the departure gate for the predatory class. I still think of that small plot of land as the worst eighth of an acre I have ever known in New York City.

I will note that the primary visible product of the district did not particularly engage me. At the age of 16 I kept my nose peculiarly clean. I was a pale and over-dramatic thing and my thoughts about love and desire were very much wrapped up in the idea of the unattainable fox in the peasant blouse who should be worshipped to impractical, impossible and wholly idyllic degrees.

Nearly 40 years later, I am left with frames of memory, the memory of memory, the chalk outline of memory; and I think I like it that way, because I am *feeling* what I remember, instead of remembering a picture. Think: When we have a picture of an event, from that moment on the mention of that event will likely bring back the picture, not the memory.

So, I can only access my memories by reaching inwards and backwards, and other random scenes emerge: I recall a cynical feeling that came over me when I realized that the marquee of a lower-rent porno palace near our office merely scrambled the same words on the marquee each week — Horny, Lesbo, Deep, Hot, Love, Action, Slave, Teacher, Throat — to give the impression that they had new movies. And I remember staring at the amazing old McGraw-Hill Building, sea green and foamy with dirt and curved like an old chorus girl. In the days before they dressed the old, smashed theaters in Disney clothes and decked the area out in shiny Shinjuku and glass, she hovered over the proceedings like a wise aunt, soiled yet proud. Today she is just invisible.

Nearly every city on the planet has a sordid center to its social heart, a place where desire meets commerce. This is beyond normal, and these places are the core of our entertainment and social culture stripped of their frippery and pretense. See, add layer upon layer of money and marketing to an old Times Square live peep, and you have *Keeping Up With the Kardashians*. Really. I appreciate that Manhattan is always moving, always inconstant, but I still miss Old Times Square; and I feel so fortunate that, during my time as a teenage office boy at the best rock magazine in the world, I got to experience it.

2017, *THE NEW YORK OBSERVER*

America Underground

To my great excitement, in 1979 Trouser Press *offered me the extraordinary opportunity to take over the monthly "America Underground" column, the part of the magazine devoted to covering independent 45s released in North America. Very soon, I expanded the column to include slightly more in-depth coverage of specific scenes, fanzines and interviews with noteworthy independent artists.*

This is one of these columns in its entirety. It appeared in Trouser Press 60, *cover date April 1981. The piece begins with an interview with the extraordinary Walter Lure, co-leader (along with Johnny Thunders) of the Heartbreakers; this was done at a time when he was actively trying to create a career identity separate from that of the erratic Thunders. The second part of the column discusses some fanzines that had come across my transom. It reminds us of a peculiar time when it was sort-of miraculous to find out that Lawrence, Kansas had a punk/new wave scene, and there were some of us who would get excited about anything that had Secret Affair's name on the cover.*

The Heartbreakers, like their direct predecessors the New York Dolls, were always *the* New York band. They were loud, dirty, sooty, reeked of the five boroughs and couldn't possibly have been from anywhere else. They lived the classic rock and roll "lifestyle" — a self-destructive myth of junk, women and clothes — and played music inspired (or smothered) by same. They were an essential part of the NY scene, but the Heartbreakers never earned their due. It always seemed sad (or at least ironic) that audiences, press and record industry chose largely to ignore what was perhaps the purest rock band around. The uncompromising roar of 1977's *L.A.M.F.* album shamed most contemporary punk records; onstage, the Heartbreakers were, despite their erraticism, at their best unsurpassable.

In 1981 the Heartbreakers are little more than a shadow, a sloppy and deteriorating reproduction of their former selves. Original drummer Jerry Nolan is long gone; bassist Billy Rath's position is in jeopardy; heroin-riddled guitarist Johnny Thunders is incapable of doing anything new; and guitarist Walter Lure sees the band as a ball and chain around his ankle.

Heartbreaker co-leader (with Thunders) Lure sits sipping a beer in a friend's room in downtown Manhattan. His tired eyes, patched-together clothes in a wide array of designs and colors (the HB's never went for black and white chic) and hair of uncertain style and shade mark him a typical Heartbreaker. But appearances can be deceiving: Lure is an intelligent, literate and articulate college grad. The first thing he makes clear (and restates again and again) is that the Heartbreakers are dead.

"The band isn't a band; it's just four guys playing a bunch of old tunes. It's like a copy band, even though we're playing our own songs. Sometimes the shows are great — when Johnny's together we can be as good as we were in the early days — but it's the same songs, nothing new. I can enjoy it when I'm onstage, but I realize it's going absolutely nowhere. It always amazes me that these kids come and pay their eight or ten dollars to see this group that can barely stand up playing songs they've heard a hundred times already. It's mostly Johnny, I guess; people come to see him die onstage, I suppose."

Lure responded to the artistic collapse of Johnny Thunders and the Heartbreakers' stagnation by forming the Heroes in early 1980. The Heroes are made up of three-quarters of the Heartbreakers — Lure, Rath and Billy Rogers, the Heartbreakers' steadiest drummer since Nolan — and Richie Lure, Walter's younger brother, on guitar and vocals. They pretty much pick up where the Heartbreakers left off three years ago: loud, fast, traditional rock and roll, similar to that of Rockpile, early Stones or early Flamin' Groovies. The Heroes sound a bit cleaner than the Heartbreakers, but then they don't have Johnny Thunders' sleaziness to contend with.

"As much as I like the Heartbreakers or love John," Lure says, "it's been going nowhere for the last three years. We just kept on doing these monthly rent party gigs at whatever club would have us. Finally, Billy and I decided that if we started a group on our own that we could control, it would be a lot better, rather than hope Johnny can stay straight one day to play a show." Because of the Heartbreakers' spotty reputation and New York's trendy refusal to accept straight-ahead rock bands, the Heroes don't have the local following or support they should. Their audience is growing steadily, however, and a 45 in the near future will help. They'd undoubtedly create a stir in Britain, but they don't have the money for the trip. So, the Heroes play on, one of New York's top unsung bands, and one hopes they can triumph.

"It's hard to get away from the Heartbreakers, because I do need the money," Lure explains. "I've got to pay the rent. But as soon as I get the Heroes to a point where it's viable — a record deal, a tour or something like that — the Heartbreakers will be long gone. You can't sit back and put your arms around a memory, as someone used to sing."

Ah, the long-promised fanzine rundown, to be updated when and where space allows.

Idol Worship, the self-proclaimed "Home of Lucy and Ethel Journalism," is definitely one of the best new fanzines of the past year. It's relatively weighty at 28 pages and well put-together, filled with fine photos, neat graphics, ace articles and that all-important blend of fun and fact. By covering new British bands ignored in the bigger mags (Stiff Little Fingers, Modettes, Secret Affair), *Idol Worship* recalls the spirit, humor and inherent professionalism of early *Trouser Press*, *Bomp* or *ZigZag*. Clearly above any of the other 'zines I've received in the last couple of months.

OP, the print organ of the Lost Music Network, will tell you more about underground music in the U.S. than any other paper in America. This large-format, professional-looking 40-pager is crammed with information about clubs, labels, fanzines, records and bands all over the country. To quote editor John Foster, *OP* exists "so that everyone can find out what everyone knows about everything." *OP* does an amazingly comprehensive job of just that. Editorial comments on discs, clubs, etc. are brief but to the point. Features — usually concise Q&A interviews — are also very good, but too understated.

(Overall, *OP* is far too modest.) This mag is doing a wonderful job of keeping us informed about what's happening off the big time — the true paper of the America Underground.

Top Rankin', "The Fanzine of Reggae and Third World Music," is ambitious, well realized, vastly informative and readable, cornering the market on UK, U.S. and Jamaican reggae, roots, ska coverage. It covers its chosen field very well, with emphasis on an American reggae scene I barely knew existed. Interesting and entertaining, even if you've never skanked in your life — good graphics, informative discographies and helpful in understanding just why reggae is so important.

Talk Talk, "The Midwest American Rock and Reggae Magazine," offers a different perspective: how the British scene looks from Lawrence, Kansas. It's a small (5½" x 8½"), neat 30-pager, covering a broad range of bands and genres. The writing is somewhat introspective and self-indulgent, but the authors clearly know their stuff and have a keen sense of what's happening; there's coverage of new UK developments not even NY has caught on to yet.

1981, *TROUSER PRESS*

A Weird Little Story About Tim and the Clash (Am I the Gump?)

I considered putting this one into the section titled My Weird Goddamn Life *but decided it made more sense here, since it describes something remarkable that happened in the course of my work as a happy teenage office grunt for* Trouser Press *magazine and probably only could have happened when I had the peculiar fearlessness I had when I wasn't yet old enough to vote. It takes me a little while to get to the "whaaatthefuck" payoff of this tale, but setting the scene felt like an interesting journey to go on.*

I was 16. All I wanted to do was leave the suburbs and live on the same tiny island that held both Tom Verlaine and John Lennon. I did not consider this desire either a challenge or a fantasy: it was a simple necessity.

I was fleeing Great Neck, in Long Island, a place I demonized far more than necessary; I found nothing warming in its dull, mostly kind suburban sun, and I was utterly uninterested in the conformity of taste and style that I perceived as being essential to cultivating high school relationships. I left Great Neck South halfway through my senior year, in January 1979. I truly did not look back — which was a shame, I think. But it seemed like a good idea at the time. I chalk this up to well-intended misanthropy. I did not hate my peers, I merely considered them unenlightened; I lived on a cloud of superiority, lifted there by an empowering obsession with punk rock and all things British.

This is well before the plurality of alternative culture, and I think that's important to remember: only three of us children in that entire massive, squat, red-brick building known as Great Neck South Senior High School owned a Sex Pistols record.

Now, fast-forward to today — or, rather, the other day. I sat down to a vegetarian enchilada plate in a Mexican restaurant here in New Orleans. At the next table sat a girl of about 11 or 12 with her family; she appeared a bit sullen but otherwise was fairly normal looking.

She was wearing a Ramones T-shirt.

And I thought to myself: "We won. I guess we won." And this is what I meant: I was in high school between 1976 and 1979. Kids wore Kansas shirts and ELP shirts, and you might espy a sensitive lout in a Billy Joel shirt. But if I had told any of my classmates that 25 or 30 years from now kids would be wearing Ramones shirts, the howls of laughter would have followed me all the way to Syosset. As it happens, this all may have been a fairly hollow victory, but that's another story entirely.

But back to Great Neck. Every now and again I recall an energetic young teacher, or the thin-lipped half smile of a peach-colored Semitic Venus who was trying to get me to notice her, and I think of opportunities lost; I also recognize that I had it pretty good. But having worked fiercely to identify myself as an outcast, I wasn't going to let reality intrude (even if it came in the form of female attention that I was so certain I didn't deserve). You see, it's the difference between rebels and freaks; I was merely a rebel, not a freak, and I could have attracted some kind of positive energy during my years as a lucky whelp on the North Shore of Long Island if I had wished to. But I had no interest in impressing the locals; magazines and record stores had given me the idea that somewhere out there I might find a peer group of the like-minded.

Fortunately, I didn't have very far to go to reach the promised land.

Manhattan in the late 1970s was a gold dark hole, a slinky, sticky stinktown of slanted buildings and dirty subways, simmering on a slow, hazy burn at the end of the [mayor] Abe Beame years … and it was barely half an hour away from Great Neck via the Long Island Railroad. Waiting for me in this incredible city, peeling yellow and cavernous during the day, steamy and blue-black at night, was a terrific job: the previous summer (the summer of 1978), I had begun to work as an office boy/columnist/factotum for an ultra-hip rock magazine called *Trouser Press*. For all intents and purposes, it was the first non-fanzine American publication to focus purely on new music and British rock, and it was immensely, immeasurably important. Where else in the 1970s, other than in some secretive fanzine or some hard-to-find UK weekly, could you read about Syd Barrett and Magazine, the Motors and Shoes, Sparks and Brian Eno? Bram Tchaikovsky was not invented by recent compilation producers, you know; he was a living, breathing British musician that you could read about in *Trouser Press* and virtually nowhere else. This was quite exciting at the time. We could barely hear this stuff on the radio, we certainly couldn't read about it in *Rolling Stone*, but we had *Trouser Press* to gather around. The lovers of new music made up a delicious clique in those days, and each of us felt a kind of pride and sense of identity.

I am reluctant to say that Manhattan was a more approachable and accessible mistress in those days; this is a conclusion I certainly want to jump to, but who am I to say what Manhattan in 2005 looks and feels like to ambitious teenagers eager to live there and anxious to realize their fantasies on that particular canvas? I suspect that Manhattan is always Manhattan in the eyes of artsy, wide-eyed and ambitious refugees from suburbia. I do, however, believe that the Manhattan that embraced me in the latish 1970s is gone, and I am probably not fit to judge or even identify what replaced it; I am not 16 or 17 or 18 anymore and cannot look at a city through those eyes, those needs, those lusts, those hopes.

But I do know that you must, for a moment, imagine Manhattan when it was cheap, truly cheap; when it was not actually dangerous but very dirty, and huge swaths of the town were shrouded in silence and mystery; when enormous strips of downtown, today completely blighted and bedazzled by neon and glass, were still lit by the pale blue of loft light, and factory windows bedecked with flaking gold Hebrew lettering still looked down over lower Broadway.

Mostly, I remember a Manhattan that welcomed the (fairly) poor and (fairly) unemployed artist. True, true, true: once, you could actually live on this Manhattan island and still be a poor, hopeful artist type. You could find a huge apartment on Eldridge Street for $150 a month; a perfectly acceptable flat at Spring Street and Sixth Avenue for $175; a brilliant garret at Bleecker and MacDougal for $125; a livable, ground-floor apartment on Avenue B for $60 a month; an entire floor in Soho for $600 a month. Think about it for a moment: this changes everything, you see. There wasn't a shop or a restaurant in every doorway, but it was still a brilliant city. It was the Kingdom of Outsiders, as opposed to what it is today: a kingdom of insiders.

Contrary to a belief very popular in New York at the moment, the artistic quality of a city is not determined by the number of successful and wealthy artists living there; it's determined by the number of poor and not yet successful artists who can afford to live there. A town full of artists and musicians who can afford to do their work and remain poor is always healthier than a town that excludes the poor artist.

Trouser Press was staffed by a tiny but confident horde of enthusiastic music hounds barely in their 20s who were originally drawn together in the early 1970s by their love of the Who, the Move, Roxy Music and stuff like Robert Wyatt and Kevin Ayers. They eagerly accepted me as their Wire-adoring younger brother in short hair and an earnestly worn corduroy jacket. I could have passed for 18 or 19, or at least that's what I thought, and I don't remember anyone ever posing any serious challenge to my pretense. So, I guess I did look older.

During this time (the late 1970s and the cusp of the 1980s), every other week or so there was a great big punk or new wave type of show at the Palladium, down on 14th Street. Part of my job at *Trouser Press* was to cart boxes of the magazine down to that stained and trashed theater to be sold at these shows. This was during the glory days of that old vaudeville atrium: it had only recently stopped calling itself the Academy of Music — a name that still held the decaying echo and crumbling chalk outline of burlesque, Sara Bernhardt and Tammany Hall — and it would be a few years before it was remodeled and reborn as a popular, whacked-out, culturally useless disco. Sometime between these two eras — between the piss saints and donut hells of 14th Street in the 1970s and the reborn, Disneyfied downtown of the late '80s and beyond — lay the heyday of the Palladium, with its sticky floors, pale lights weakly tumbling through cracked, sepia-colored glass, haze of tobacco and pot smoke and ceiling so brilliantly high that it made me giddy. On a show night, all this faded, flaking glory would be seen through a fog of moisture rising from a thousand leather and suede jackets that were always damp from the long fall and wet winter.

(The other day, I was thinking of the enormous and strange neon sign that hung above the Palladium stage and was lit before shows and between acts: it advertised a cheap rosé called Mateus. Does anyone, I wondered, still drink Mateus? I remember the bottles were opaque and oddly shaped, ideally suited to having cheap flowers stuck into them. Do they still even make Mateus?)

When a new wave show came to the Palladium, I would cart two or three heavy boxes of *Trouser Press* from our office at 42nd Street and Broadway (and this is when 42nd Street and Broadway was 42nd Street and Broadway, full of endless-August creepiness and sloth and the hazy buzz of bud and porno) to the Palladium and drop the magazines behind a counter on the right side of the massive, creepily majestic, desiccated lobby.

I would do this toward the end of the afternoon, usually at the time that the headlining band was doing its soundcheck. It always amazed me how utterly simple it was to sneak into these things, and I came to regard soundchecks as brilliant little private performances just for me. In fact, you could barely call it sneaking in. Having dropped off my boxes in the lobby, I would walk straight into the auditorium, where, making no great fuss, I would sit myself down a few rows from the stage; once I ascertained that there was little chance of anyone objecting to my presence, I would move up to the first or second row. Often, I would even get up onstage and stand virtually amongst the band members. As you might imagine, this is unspeakably exciting when you're 15 or 16.

If the vibe was right (which it almost always was), I would approach the musicians, usually in an attempt to set up an interview for a fanzine that I had some affiliation with. I can picture myself now, exchanging words on the dimly lit Palladium stage with Ian Hunter and Paul Weller and Nick Lowe and John Cooper Clarke and the Boomtown Rats; I would give them a polite spiel and foist on them a copy of something called *Living in Paradise*. *Living in Paradise* was published, or, rather, xeroxed, if memory serves, by two enthusiastic ladies in Queens who had an inordinate fondness for the Stranglers. Even before *Trouser Press* published me — when I was still baffling the readers of my high school newspaper with essays about *Monty Python* and the innate superiority of Barrett-era Pink Floyd — this fanzine welcomed my contributions.

So... It is February of 1979. I am still living in Great Neck, commuting to the *Trouser Press* office in Times Square, and I am 16 years old (but just about to turn 17). Having delivered my boxes to the Palladium lobby, I stroll into the theater, where the Clash are preparing to soundcheck.

I settle myself in the front row, dead center.

The brilliant thing about the Clash was that they always looked exactly like the Clash; they were colorful and leapt about photogenically, just like the Clash; they held their guitars just like the Clash, dropped their lower lips and curled their top ones to snarl, just like the Clash; stomped their right feet and bounced on their left ones, just like the Clash. I saw the Clash many times, in every type of venue and from almost every conceivable vantage point, and they were always exactly like the Clash. I have never seen another band that performed so precisely like the band I pictured in my imagination. Every time I saw the Clash, it was like seeing a movie that I had high expectations for and finding that the movie was exquisitely, exhilaratingly, precisely like I thought it would be. They were a brilliant, bold, three-dimensional cartoon, everything the poster on the wall or the picture in the magazine had promised, each time, every time.

They were absolutely no different in soundcheck, playing with the same arrogance, twist, passion, snarl and hop with which they played every show. The highlight of this particular soundcheck was an extended, epidermis-ripping version of Bo Diddley's "Road Runner."

When the soundcheck ended, the members of the Clash stepped off the stage and into the auditorium. They had the sense of happy disorganization that I would later recognize was very common to this specific moment: the soundcheck done, you have yet to be corralled by the tour manager and told what to do next. This moment of easy purgatory — which might be some of the only unstructured time a band member has all day — could last seconds or hours.

Topper Headon, Paul Simonon and Mick Jones were standing fairly close to me, in the fifth row of the orchestra, leaning against the back of the seats in front of them. Joe Strummer was standing a little further down to the right, in the aisle. With a polite, practiced lack of assumption, I approached Topper, Paul and Mick. The key here was to look thoroughly unthreatening, like you might be a younger cat from their record label or a fellow awaiting a scheduled interview.

I was holding a copy of the first Clash album — the English import, I might add — but this wasn't what I offered to them. From inside the album sleeve (from which, for the sake of convenience, I had removed the actual album), I carefully removed a section of newspaper.

This was a partial copy of a recent issue of the *New York Post*. On the front page of this particular edition was an excited, premature and inaccurate story about a possible Beatles reunion. (All of the four primary Beatles were still alive then, you see.) Naturally, the story featured a large picture of the four Beatles in a classic '60s pose.

"Excuse me," I asked, deepening my voice and adding just a fleck of a mid-Atlantic accent, "would you mind signing this?" I gently nudged the Beatles picture in their direction, resting it on the cardboard album sleeve. At that moment in time, for some reason, I thought the single most brilliant thing to have in the entire world would be a picture of the four Beatles signed by the four members of the Clash. I was so excited by the idea I could barely contain myself.

Three-fourths of the Clash reacted as if they had just been handed a surprise Latin quiz; they looked quizzical and kind, displaying a collective raised eyebrow.

"Ah, yeah, well, I don't know," Mick Jones said.

"I can't see it, can't see doing it," Paul Simonon added.

"Let's see what Joe says," Mick Jones continued. "I'll do it if Joe does it. Hey, Joe!"

Jones shouted over his left shoulder, beckoning Strummer over. "This fella wants us to sign, uh, sign this picture."

Joe Strummer took it in his hands, examined it, parted his lips with distaste and shook his head.

"Nooh, nah, not that, won't sign that. We'll sign *that*, though," he quickly added, gesturing with his chin toward my album sleeve.

And they did. In thick black ink, the Clash scrawled their signatures in adamant fashion, more or less obscuring the green, white, black and red colors on the album sleeve.

That night, the Clash plastered their drum riser with copies of that *New York Post* front page; perhaps my odd, minor encounter inside an empty theater in downtown Manhattan inspired this decoration.

I am a little proud of this, I suppose; after all, how many people ever asked the Clash to sign a picture of the Beatles? More curiously, it's always been in the back of my head that maybe, *maybe,* just maybe, this little encounter inspired the line about "phony Beatlemania" in the song "London Calling," which was released about ten months later.

I'll never know, but my desire to apply my narcissistic standards to rock and roll history has been rewarded and confirmed on other occasions. While leafing through a book in a Borders in Metairie, LA, I stumbled upon the fact that Sonic Youth had written "Kill Yr. Idols" about me, and I have a rather amusing story about the day I turned down a chance to tour as the Beastie Boys' deejay.

But that's another story. [*Noted elsewhere, of course.*]

2005, *THE BIG TAKEOVER*

Lance Loud: The First Real Boy on the Sun

This piece is about the adolescent discovery that there was a whole remarkable world just beyond the status quo. What a powerful moment of awareness that was!

In the pre-punk 1970s, there were some extraordinary people who handed us a map to the Kingdom of Outsiders.

One of these was the amazing Lance Loud.

Not only did he hand us the map; personally, he may have been one of the first people to make me aware that such a place existed, before I even knew such essential miracles were possible.

In addition, Lance and his quirky, poppy and ahead-of-their-time alternative pop punk band, the Mumps, had a significant impact on the burgeoning punk and new wave scene in New York City in the mid- and late-1970s. The Mumps were formed by California friends Lance Loud and keyboard player Kristian Hoffman. The earliest days of their gestation was documented in the landmark reality television series, An American Family. *Filmed in 1971 and 1972 and aired on PBS stations in early 1973,* An American Family *was a pioneering 12-episode documentary series tracing the daily life of a "typical" upper-middle-class American family in Santa Barbara, California (two middle-aged and successful parents and their five attractive and bright teenage children). This trope seems all too familiar now — ugly and tiring and even reactionary — but it was legitimately startling 55 years ago when director Craig Gilbert and cinematographers Alan and Susan Raymond began documenting the actual, real lives of an American family. The series drew over ten million viewers a week and became extremely newsworthy and controversial, both for its extremely novel approach and its content (also, it's one of the things that established PBS as a household fixture, along with* Sesame Street, Monty Python *and* Masterpiece Theatre*). Viewers soon realized that even a family that seemingly had it all could be beset by chaos, drama, depression and divorce. Perhaps most dramatically, eldest son Lance Loud — 20 at the time of the commencement of filming and handsome, charming, effeminate and articulate — came out, loudly and proudly, during the series. When he stepped in front of the camera, flipping his Ray Davies-blowsy hair and bending his wrist, he made America face the gorgeous fact that queer children were not only in your backyard, but they also might be the best thing in your backyard. Barely 36 months after Stonewall, Lance Loud was suddenly, delightfully, in the living room of every home in America.*

And then Lance and his best friend Kristian formed a band, largely based on the model of their musical heroes: the Kinks, Sparks, Roxy Music, the New York Dolls and a happy pile of obscure British and American garage pop groups. Shortly after An American Family *aired and turned Lance Loud into one of the most visible and notorious gay men in American history, Kristian and Lance relocated the Mumps to New York, where they served as a powerful inspiration to many of the young people just beginning to discover the new wave and punk scene exploding in the city in the mid-1970s.*

Lance Loud died in 2001 at age 50.

In 1973, I was inarguably a child, arguably pre-sexual and extraordinarily curious about the world around me. I was also constantly aware that I was being conned. I knew that the people I saw on television were strangers; not just strangers to my way of life (full of the usual oppressions, limitations, disenfranchisements and handicaps of pre-pubescence), but also strangers to reality: these characters, these Bradys, these Partridges, these summertime replacement sketch comics, they were caricatures that reflected reality no more — and often far less — than cartoon characters did.

Very few 11-year-olds are free. Not only are they almost completely dependent on family and parents, their worldview is defined by available and accessible media (and their generational peers vomiting up the same). At that age, in any era (not just the rotary phone/terrestrial television world of the early 1970s), even in *this* era, young people are a grotesque and addlepated mofungo of their environmental influences; we don't know who we are, but we try to form an image of ourselves based on the slivers and shards of a thousand funhouse mirrors the world throws all around us. In fact, virtually none of these mirrors reflect our actual selves in any functional or useful way. Each child is full of great depth, in many ways the same depth they will presume and assume as adults, yet we have to construct a world out of the largely one-dimensional residue of what adults presume to be our usefulness as consumers.

The list of the fears that shadowed my 11-year-old world was long and common: the end of the world; the mortality of my parents; the thick shadows of the bullies or the lock-jawed disapproval of the teachers; the terror of lifts home from Hebrew school that never came — not to mention the foreshadow of sex, mysterious almost to the point of being otherworldly. Honestly, not a single minute of any television show spoke to any of these issues, yet television *was* our world, our refuge from screaming families and fall-out drills and all the aforementioned everyday terrors.

I was aware when I watched anything *except* for the news (Vietnam! Spiro Agnew! John Lindsay! Mario Biaggi! The Colombo Family! Joan Whitney Payson! Aristotle Onassis!) that I was not watching reality; I was not watching anything that told me about who I was and who I might become.

Into this world, this world of fear and fakery, stepped Lance Loud.

He was light, he was beautiful, he was an angel and he was utterly unlike anyone I had seen on television (being lonely, strange and chubby, I watched *a lot* of television). The world to him seemed to be a suitor to be charmed with a flip of your hair and a sly comment. Even within the documentary format of the show that featured him, *An American Family*, he seemed hyper-real, like the birdsong heard for only eight seconds that is more beautiful than any recorded composition.

I immediately fell in love, even though I knew nothing yet of sexual desire, much less the mechanics of homosexuality. I fell in love with his joy, his lithe, rubbery spirit, this person who seemed free and real and so strange yet so utterly familiar; he was the dreams I had not yet had. What was most important about Lance Loud *wasn't* that he was the first openly gay person on television, but he was the first utterly real person on television, the first person who reflected us at our most sensitive, at our most truly silly, at our most casual and cavalier and intense and introspective, at our most flippant or flirtatious. He, alone of anyone on the Empire of Television, seemed to understand that we might dance in front of a mirror and be someone we never could be (or precisely the person we would become!). He alone seemed to understand that while riding a bike down a suburban street we might pretend, for 48 seconds, to be the king of an empire that had the same name as our street. In other words, he was the first person on television with an interior life.

When I looked at Bobby Brady, I saw no interior life. When we are children, when our lives are full of the most beautiful secrets (mostly the secrets of our *strangeness*, for every child is strange, for one minute an hour, or one hour a day, or for one year of a life, until the strangeness is hyper-normalized out of them!), when our lives are full of the belief that the world is full of infinite possibilities and infinite miracles and a million ghosts and a million stars, we are ALL interior life. Lance Loud, long and grinning with lips that split the screen, clearly not only had an interior life, his interior life looked like ours *and he wore it on the outside.*

Now, that's just my personal perspective. In a more universal sense, let me state this clearly: Lance Loud was the first announced gay man on American television. Do you *know* how fucking huge that was? He was Jackie Robinson, he was Louis Armstrong, he was Neil Armstrong, he was Chaplin, he was Crosby, he was *that important*. In our revisionist perspective, we see the world of the 1950s and '60s as being full of visible gays: but not only were these gays unannounced, they were often broad caricatures, easily dismissed, objects of fun or ridicule. Paul Lynde, Liberace, Truman Capote: these gentlemen were caricatures, deliberately ridiculous, the source of ridicule. If they waved *any* flag, it was the flag that their sexual predilection was like the name of a Hebrew god, not to be spoken aloud, and thereby easily denied and easily mocked.

But here was Lance Loud. He might have been gay, but he was also our brothers, our sons, our neighbors, our schoolmates; he was a part of us (and if we were deeply a fantasist, like so many of us were, he was *most* of us, he was the best part of us!), he was gay, he was on television, he was real, he was not a figure of fun or ridicule, he was gay and on television and more realistic than any boy next door; which is all to say that Lance Loud wasn't just the first gay on television, as deeply important, indeed historic, as that is; he was also the first real boy on television.

He was complicated, shaded, confused, arrogant, funny, tragic, he was everything we suspected a *sensitive soul such as ourselves* might be, but we had never seen one before outside the shadows of our own hopes!

He also carved the idea, somewhere in the willing, supple and soft balsa-wood of my brain, that our fantasy self, our fantasy *I*, so private, so lonely, could one day be a *we*, we might meet others like him, like us, we might meet Morrissey or Michael Stipe or Dean Johnston. He instilled the idea that *we* were not overly sensitive, but appropriately sensitive; not overly artistic, but appropriately artistic; not overly bookish, but appropriately bookish; not overly fey, but utterly beautiful in our own true boy skin.

Lance Loud was the first true boy on the sun, which is to say, he was *real*, he reflected the hopes and flaws and realities and shades of masculinity, and the sun was the television, beaming his brightness all over America.

2015, *THE BROOKLYN BUGLE*

The Well-Tempered Frye Boots: *Saturday Night Live* Turns 40; Tim's Visits to the Show Turn 38

The curious events I recount here didn't seem particularly strange or daring at the time. They truly didn't. They just felt like what I "had" to do. They felt like everyday life to me, and I believe the fact that these undertakings felt so normal to me was what fueled the nerve to make these things happen in the first place. There is no nerve like nerve fueled by certainty. "Of course, I'll walk through that door. Why wouldn't I?"

This one was written about Saturday Night Live's *40th anniversary special, which aired in February 2015.*

When I watched the occasionally thrilling circus of self-congratulation that was *SNL 40*, more than anything, I saw myself. I'm sure a lot of us did. When we revisit old episodes of *Saturday Night Live*, we flash back to where we were and who we were when we first saw these actors, these sketches. I found myself entirely conscious of how I reacted to the show when it was a bright, sassy miracle that suddenly appeared on my TV during the dreadful years when Junior High was preparing to end its reign of humiliation and cruelty.

Circa 1975, there were essentially two models for non-sitcom television comedy: the American and the British. The American model involved light satire, broad sketches, musical burlesques and guest stars, and was typified by (the wonderful) Carol Burnett, Sonny & Cher, Tony Orlando & Dawn and a large stack of forgettable summer replacement shows. It had fairly direct roots in the vaudeville format omnipresent in the earliest days of television variety.

The British model involved high-concept and frequently absurd sketch comedy, acute topical satire, an ensemble cast and minimal guest stars; it was typified by *Monty Python*, *The Frost Report*, *That Was The Week That Was*, lesser lights like the *Two Ronnies* and *The Goodies* and many brilliant (but unknown in America) shows like *Not Only but Also*, *At Last the 1948 Show*, *Do Not Adjust Your Set*, etc. It had direct roots in the cool, crisp satire of *Beyond the Fringe* and the Dada hysteria of *The Goon Show*.

These two branches did not meet, at least not in any real or lasting way, until *NBC's Saturday Night* came along in 1975. *NBC's Saturday Night* (I am deliberately using the show's original name, which was not altered until 1977) was the child of three very distinct but compatible bloodlines: *The National Lampoon* (from which it drew the heart of its writing staff and its acidic attitude — also, a chunk of *SN*'s original cast came from the *Lampoon* stage shows); Toronto's Second City Troupe (which gave *Saturday Night* some cast members and, more importantly, the general skill-set and acting style of its performers); and *Monty Python* (whose ensemble style, penchant for absurdity and non-punchline based sketches was possibly the most visible influence on *SN*). Put the three together and throw in a soupçon of *Don Kirshner's Rock Concert*, and you had the DNA for *NBC's Saturday Night*.

If you were sitting in front of a television set in late 1975 or early 1976, this bizarre, beautiful, feisty, fluid object startled you. It was, quite literally, like nothing on American television. The unsubtle and unpredictable sketch format felt vaguely familiar to those of us who were already Pythonophiles, and the language and attitude of the new show had a resonance if you were acquainted with the *Lampoon*. But, aside from that, it was an atom bomb. If you watched a lot of television and listened to a lot of comedy albums (and being a lonely, trivia-obsessed and highly curious 13-year-old, that would have been me), *Saturday Night* seemed to achieve the impossible: it was obnoxious, unpredictable, cocky British-format humor Americanized.

I instantly became obsessed. Starting with the third episode, I found myself glued to the TV every Saturday at 11:30. I would even carefully place my cassette recorder in front of the TV speaker and tape every new episode to aid the process of memorizing, analyzing and understanding this exciting new object.

I turned 14 in March of 1976; I grew a few inches, lost the baby-fat-bursting face and yam-shaped body so permanently memorialized in my bar mitzvah photos, and I suddenly found myself somewhat confident in my abilities to actually achieve the goals that my obsessively nerdy mind had latched on to. In the long term, this set me on a course to insert myself into the world of British and American punk rock; but more pertinently, I recognized that Rockefeller Center was only a short ride away on the Long Island Railroad. By the autumn of 1976 and the onset of *Saturday Night*'s second season, nothing was going to stop me from trying to investigate my obsession firsthand.

So, I did.

Now, this story isn't going to involve sex or drugs or even encounters that are particularly anecdotal or remarkable. This story just is, well, what it is.

Throughout the second and third season of *Saturday Night*, I began regularly going to 30 Rock on show days. Sometimes I waited on the standby line, a few times I actually had tickets, but the most interesting times were when I just snuck in. I found that if I put on my older brother's tan corduroy jacket and wore his well-tempered Frye boots (which supplied me with a somewhat jaunty, adult step), I could basically look like someone who might belong in Studio 8H. I can't recall the precise method I used to slip past security, but it wasn't too hard. I think the trick was to keep your head up (if you keep your head down, it's fairly obvious you're trying not to be noticed; keep your head up, and you look like someone who isn't trying not to be noticed, therefore you belong there); to move smoothly but not rapidly; and to have that slight angle to your shoulders that says "Hey, hold that elevator!" I am quite damn sure it wouldn't be that easy now (though I will note that I did do this trick again in 1996 to visit a friend working on that week's show). I really think it was the corduroy jacket that made it so easy; the other fans hovering about wore down or denim, and it seemed like an inordinate amount of the staff wore corduroy.

When I would get up to 8H, I would find a spot in the hallway adjacent to the big studio and just lean against a wall and try to stay invisible. I wasn't pretending to be a writer or a musician or whatnot; rather, I just wanted to pass for someone who had some small but not intrusive reason to be there (maybe people would think I was the younger brother of a cast member, or the guy who had just dropped off an important prop). Sometimes, if I felt exposed, I would look at my watch and glance around with a small frown on my face, as if I were waiting for someone to hand me something that hadn't come yet.

I didn't talk to anyone. I wasn't there to engage; I was there to observe. The only person I revealed myself to was one of the writers, Alan Zweibel. I was very curious about his craft, and for some reason he seemed approachable. He could not have been nicer. Seriously, I will always recall that this busy, brilliant man took the time, on a show night no less, to be kind to a wide-eyed 14-year-old passing as a devil-may-care 18-year-old. I also talked a little bit (on different visits to 8H) with Dan Aykroyd and Laraine Newman, both of whom were nice, especially Newman. Again, I am grateful for her unnecessary kindness.

Not very exciting, right?

But it was hugely exciting to be 14, to be captivated with the process of television, to be utterly obsessed with this exciting new show, and to just be able to lean against a wall and watch the incredible, beehive-like buzz of frantic activity and visible tension as the live show unfolded in the hours and minutes before it aired. Who needs anecdotes when you had a front seat?

Somewhere along the way, in the nearly 4/10ths of a century since then, I lost the Frye boots, the corduroy jacket and the cockiness that would allow me to just stroll past security at a live network TV show. But I had it once; it served me well on those nights and many other times, too. Nothing bad happened to me because I did such ridiculous things — some kind of inner compass of common-sense counterbalanced my nerve — and I just followed my dreams onto a train from Great Neck to Penn Station.

2015, *THE BROOKLYN BUGLE*

PiL: Riot at the Ritz

In early 1981, Garry Bushell, then the editor of the English music weekly Sounds, *contacted me out of the blue and asked if I would be interested in becoming the New York correspondent for the paper. For an Anglophile like me, raised to read and cherish every word of the three primary English music weeklies, this was absolutely a dream come true. He paired me with an extraordinary young photographer named Laura Levine, and for roughly the next two years, I contributed weekly news, reviews, features and gossip to* Sounds. *Odd to think that I hadn't even turned 19 yet; I had no sense of being "young," I really didn't, just a sense that this felt right.*

I solidified my position with Sounds *— and my bona fides with Bushell — in May 1981 when I happened to be in the right place at the right time (largely thanks to a close friend named Patty Marsh who worked at a downtown Manhattan music hall, the Ritz) and caught wind that Public Image Ltd., still a mysterious and artistically sparkling and extreme entity, would be playing a surprise show at the venue. PiL's performance that night — and the riot that ensued — has become legendary, and thanks to Patty, I had unique access to the event.*

Here, in full, is my report of that performance, which Sounds *ran as the cover story of the issue dated May 30th, 1981.*

Any way you look at it, rock is theater, because it doesn't usually make that crossover into real life, real threats and influencing and directing real actions.

We have grown accustomed to seeing great bands on a stage, within a frame, within a setting. They can be great within this frame and setting; they can be threatening and energetic and violent and even terrifying within that setting, but that ends where the frame ends, where the box of their stage ends.

On Friday May 15th, Public Image Ltd. performed at the Ritz nightclub in New York City and obliterated those boundaries between theater and real life, between the mock violence and the implied threat of the Dead Kennedys or the Sex Pistols and the real desire of an audience to destroy a band and everything they stood for, and the encouragement of the band for them to do so.

It's the first time I've ever seen a performance leave the stage/frame and the control of the performer (and the controlled reactions of the audience) and enter the gut; by doing what they were doing, in front of who they were doing it in front of, PiL knowingly created a performance/theater that reached into that spot right below the chest and just above the stomach, that spot where you feel fear and terror before you feel it anywhere else.

It is also the first time that PiL has actually done what they've always said they were going to do, actually lived up to and acted on everything they claim to stand for and have stated that they wanted to achieve. In this sense, May 15th's show was really the first true Public Image Ltd. performance. It just so happened that PiL chose to debut in the wrong place at the wrong time.

The events leading up to the May 15 show were swift and, above all, surprising. On Wednesday, May 13, Bow Wow Wow suddenly pulled out of a long-hyped and anticipated two-night weekend stand at the Ritz; according to some sources, McLaren and Bow Wow Wow never had any intention of coming over to the States to tour in the first place, and the whole thing was just another big publicity stunt — but that's unconfirmed (to say the least).

In any event, this left the Ritz in a lot of hot water. On such short notice, they would have a great deal of trouble finding an act that could top or equal Bow Wow Wow; in any case they would have barely a day to promote the gig, and it would be too late to get any ads in the papers or stick any posters up.

That anything came together at all was the [work] of mastermind Michael Alago, a slight, pretty and effeminate man who books the Ritz. In the hectic offices of the cavernous, gaudy art-deco ballroom-turned-rock-club, Alago explained the chain of events that led to

PiL's appearance. This conversation took place a few hours before the doors opened for the show.

"I found out through the grapevine that Keith (Levene) was in town," Alago states over a cup of fruit salad which he seems only too happy to offer to me, "and I said, 'You have to bail me out.' Within 40 minutes he was down here, and the band arrived the next day." (Thursday) By way of explanation of what was going to go on later that night, Alago simply said: "Yes, a lot of people are going to be surprised, but it's art, and it's sound and vision."

By "band," Alago means Keith, thin and wiry, hair newly cropped to a short and spiky crewcut and restored to its original brown color (in fact he looks almost exactly as he did when he formed the Clash five years ago), John Lydon (complete with flaming red hair) and Jeanette Lee, who does anything and everything and is definitely to be taken seriously as the third member of the band/corporation. They would also be helped out by a 60-year-old overweight white jazz drummer named Sammy, who they had found playing in a New York City park the day of the show, and Eddy Caraballo, an American friend of the band who would coordinate the video part of the performance from the Ritz's high-tech state-of-the-art video booth.

Obviously, this lineup wasn't going to get on stage and run through "Careering" or "Low Life" or "Death Disco," etc. For one, in effect there would only be two people — John and Keith — on stage who knew the songs or were conceivably prepared to play them. And what were they to do? Would John sing while Keith played drums, or would John play drums and sing while Keith played guitar and synths, or would Keith play bass and John play drums...? So, obviously there was no intention — or even the means —for PiL to get on stage and "play a gig."

"I hope no one's been misled. No one said it was a gig," states Jeanette Lee, curled up and cross-legged on the floor of the Ritz's video booth. It's about 8:00 p.m., two hours away from the doors opening and about five away from the show itself. Lee is, in a word, adorable: small, big brown eyes, a wonderful yellow party dress. She could quite literally pass for eight or nine. She's also a joy to talk to and wants to be as helpful and as informative as possible.

Lee continues: "It wasn't supposed to be advertised as playing.

There are instruments up there, and we will be up there, but there will be no playing. If you had told us a week ago that we would be here doing this, we wouldn't have believed you. We weren't even positive that we were actually going to go through with this until 9:00 o'clock this morning, and we still don't know what we're going to do when we get up there. Everything is actually going to be done live, there's no preparation. The band will be live, the video will be live, it's all spontaneous. It happened so quickly, and I'm too interested in what we can do in a day — that's the exciting part. The whole thing about this corporation is spontaneity, and that wasn't the story on the last tour. We did that really because we wanted to come to America."

She makes a broad gesture that includes the video booth and all of its equipment, the hall and the stage, which is obscured entirely by a gigantic video screen, behind which Lydon is pounding out the "Flowers of Romance" drum riff, accompanied by Keith's synthesizer blurbs and belches. "This was a perfect opportunity to use a visual thing with video and noise added. I hope no one's been misled."

But what if they are?

"People should know what to expect, or what not to expect, out of this corporation. They should know that we're not going to get up there and play songs. We've said that in so many interviews and it bores me to death to say it again. This is so much more interesting than going to a gig and hearing what you've already got on record. This has so much more to offer." John's reply to the same queries is far less explanatory and far more blunt. "Haven't you sussed it out yet?" he says, speaking from a nearly pitch-dark corner of the ballroom. "Why don't you just hang out and wait for it all to happen, baby?"

Okay, a little about what PiL intend to do, and what they intend to do it on: John, Keith, Jeanette and Sammy are going to be up on stage, but they plan to spend the show completely behind a 20-foot by 20-foot video screen, which covers the entire stage except for half-a-foot at the bottom and about five feet at the sides. Behind that screen the set-up almost looks normal — sparse, modern but almost normal. There's a drum kit, a synthesizer bank, a few guitars and basses, two video cameras and a record player.

A massive array of lights and spots situated behind PiL will throw their silhouettes onto the screen — the closer PiL are to the screen, the more defined the silhouette. The video cameras will project whatever it is PiL is going to be doing back there onto the huge screen and over the silhouettes. And, finally, pre-recorded videos of PiL will be shown on the screen and over the shadows, presumably mixed in with a live relay of what PiL will be doing behind that screen, which still remains a complete mystery. They could play records, play white noise, make shadow puppets, tell jokes, even, for all we know, play a set. But the key thing seems to be that from no vantage point out front will anyone be able to see any of PiL in the flesh.

Near the front of a large line outside of the Ritz a blond-haired teen punk, complete with dog collar and Sex Pistols T-shirt, tells me that PiL is his fave band, he's excited about seeing them in a smaller place, he saw them last time and he thought they were great and, no, he wasn't going to come back on Saturday night, but he did have tickets to see the Jam later in the month. He and about 500 others have been waiting in a line that started forming outside of the Ritz at about 12 o'clock in the afternoon. By about 7:00 it's begun to pour and it'll continue to rain very hard all night.

When the doors open at about 10:00, these people — and about 1,500 others — will have paid $12 and waited in abominable weather for hours and hours to see and hear Public Image Ltd., the band. Nearly all of them expect a show pretty much along the lines of what PiL gave them last time at NYC's Palladium: a more or less straightforward traditional rock show, perhaps a bit more spontaneous and unpredictable (this *is* PiL) and a bit more intimate (this being the Ritz, an unseated ballroom). No one has given them any reason to believe that neither will they be seeing PiL in the flesh nor hearing familiar PiL material. Do you sense a conflict of interests?

The doors open at 10:00 without real incident. Strangely, it takes a while before the place really fills up. The people who've been waiting outside all day are excited and very wet — the spiked hair becomes more spiked, the thrift shop clothing (or the expensive duds made to look like thrift shop clothing) has become a few shades darker and has occasionally fallen to pieces. But the mood amongst those who've waited for this — and now crowd to the front of the stage — is very high. In fact, the whole place seems to be electrified by PiL and the suddenness of it all. The staff of the Ritz is totally wired and galvanized: it's as if each and every one of them was going onstage that night. So much seems to be at stake, so much could happen, this thing has been pulled together so quickly and so tightly, it's very nearly as if the Ritz and all of its staff have become part of the corporation.

A Ritz employee: "Definitely, it's a performance for us, too. Everything could be blown; everything could go perfectly. John summed up our role better than anyone: 'If anything gets busted up, if everything gets broken, we can just catch the first plane out tomorrow.'"

The waiting starts, the ballroom fills up, the liggers mill around and the crowd on the floor and at the front gets packed tighter and tighter. An opening act, a Suicide-like two-piece, comes and goes with relatively little incident and abuse. More waiting, more crowding. An announcement that "Public Image will appear at one." At 1:00 a.m., with the ballroom lights still up, the stage and screen still dark and UB40 blaring over the PA, the immediately recognizable bass riff of "Public Image" (the song) comes booming out from behind the screen. There's no vocal, but the drums kick in pretty cohesively, and a complete drum-and-bass version of the tune is run through about three times in the next ten minutes. There's a lot of confusion — is this the performance or not?

Finally, about 1:20, the lights seemingly go down in earnest. Immediately, before anything has even happened, things had become scary — you knew that a threat was there, and whether it was going to be acted on or not was the question.

Oddly the first part of the program was a video of Shox Lumania, a New York theatrical rock/costume troupe somewhat along the lines of Shock — and nearly as miserable. This was followed by a silly but almost informative sketch on video of Keith, bound and gagged, being interviewed by a woman in a trashy dress sitting in a garbage can. This went on a bit too long, about 10 or 15 minutes. The technical and artistic quality (though not necessarily the intent) of the video was terrible, and much of it was inaudible, but some interesting things were said: basically Keith and his bizarre interviewer kept on reiterating that this wasn't going to be a concert, you weren't to expect the normal and don't be surprised when you weren't going to get it. But it was hard to hear, and no one really seemed to be paying all that much attention.

After a short but ominous silence, PiL was introduced by the same woman in the same garbage can, only this time in person and holding the top of the garbage can as a shield against the onslaught of bottles. "I told you they were weird!" she shrugged and squawked. "Ladies and gentlemen, here they are: Public Image Limited!"

What followed was pretty much what those who had been warned expected. Four distinct and pretty identifiable shadows against the screen, videos over it, audience confusion and derision. Keith then walked over to the side of the stage (this part I could actually see from my vantage point), flipped a lit cigarette into the audience and put a copy of PiL's "Flowers of Romance" onto the turntable, which PiL then lip-synched their way through. The audience seemed to quite like this, actually.

When that was done, things stopped being even vaguely musical and became a sort of a pantomime absurdity, accompanied by the live video, which took on the character of embarrassing but amusing home movies. They danced, they mugged, they laughed, they chatted, they made various noises, but they remained firmly unmusical and definitely out of the sight range of most of the crowd. The audience was getting a bit restless, an occasional beer bottle would sail through the air and hit the screen, but at this point it was still more or less amusing. Entertainment.

At about 1:40, much to our surprise, PiL gave us an actual song: about two-thirds of "Four Enclosed Walls" from the new album, Keith having temporarily relieved Sammy on drums and John singing. But that over with, the experimental stuff continued, and some of it was pretty good, though they never quite got the audio/sound part of it together. Visually it became quite curious, and often well-done and alluring.

Shortly after that (at about the 25-minute mark of the performance), the bottles and the catcalls started in earnest, the first sign of real and dangerous hostility from the restless crowd, the first realization by the audience that PiL had no intention of raising the screen and playing a normal set. Keith and John responded by hanging together over a mike and taunting the audience with "Oh, boo, boo, hiss, boo, they're cheating us, oh, boo, hiss, we're being cheated!" This of course was akin to teasing a soon-to-be rabid dog. Things became a bit more frightening, and John monotoned into the mike, "It's so nice to be here in your wonderful city."

For whatever motive, Keith then sat down at the drums again, and he and John ran through a fairly straightforward verse of "Banging the Door," followed by John's "Did you like that? Is that what you want?" and the resumption of the chaos. This is when things really began to fall to pieces. The show degenerated into Keith and John teasing and baiting the audience from behind the safety of the screen, and the audience responding in kind.

"Aren't you getting your money's worth?" John taunted. "Isn't this what rock and roll is all about, *maaan*?" At this point there was no turning back. A fuse had been lit, and it was only a matter of time before it blew; John and Keith's behavior certainly wasn't helping things. There was now a steady stream of bottles flailing against the screen, many missing and zonking people in the front, the rest just bouncing off the screen and smashing in the faces of the people in the first rows. Keith was also starting to get genuinely angry, though John's grin and sarcasm held through to the end.

"If you destroy that screen, you're going to be destroyed," Keith grimly deadpanned, without a trace of humor. "We have the power to destroy you — all of you!"

"You're not throwing enough bottles!" John shouted over Keith's shoulder. "Throw more bottles!" At 1:50, a chair was heaved from the balcony, hitting the screen dead center and smashing down on the stage. This was the signal for the true riot to begin. Suddenly Keith darted out from behind the screen, a truly possessed and angry look on his face. Who knows why he decided to appear? He looked set to kill. He made it about ten feet out from the wings, when a bottle swiped him on the forehead and a bouncer grabbed Levene and tossed him back behind the screen, possibly saving his life.

The audience — now a mob — surged towards the stage, lunging for the screen and the white tarp that all the equipment and lights sat on. In one swift and terrifying motion, all of PiL's lights and equipment went sliding into the audience, bouncers risking their lives to save what they could, the battered screen flew up, apparently a move directed from the video booth, and everyone and everything went quite insanely and horrifyingly berserk...

All the while, Lydon's taunting continues. He sings, "New York, New York, a helluva town...," and when he sees the video screen going up, his floor sliding out from under him and he realizes he's seconds away from certain injury, he quickly barks "This is the end of the show" into the mike and dashes off up the stairs and into the dressing room, where Jeanette and Keith have already fled.

From then it's a blurred two-minute flurry of fighting, bouncers attacking and being attacked, the mob grabbing for anything and everything they could, and that pervasive feeling of danger and threat becoming real. For about two-and-a-half minutes when things really went wild, you weren't sure if you were going to get out alive, if PiL had gotten out alive, if 30 or 40 people were going to die ... it's the sort of feeling you get when you think the elevator is going to fall, when you realize that you're likely to get the shit beaten out of you with nowhere to run. This was terror, pure terror, brought and nurtured knowingly by PiL. When the smoke cleared, it looked like everything was going to be alright and there hadn't been too many serious injuries, which didn't really make it any better. It could've just as easily gone the other way.

Up in the dressing room, John and Keith snorted coke and chatted with the injured who had been brought up there. They had performed, they had gotten a reaction, whether this was the reaction that was desired or expected is known only to them.

The show the next night was cancelled. PiL had wanted to do it, but the Ritz just couldn't take the risk.

At the risk of sounding scholarly, there are certain things about the show that really should be recapped and restated:

1. There truly were some moments when the combination of sound, video, shadow and chance was very effective.

2. Beyond a certain point the riot became a certainty, and PiL did nothing to forestall or divert this. Indeed, they went out of their way to encourage it.

3. After a certain point, if John, Keith or Jeanette had shown their faces in front of the screen, they — without exaggeration — would've been seriously injured, perhaps killed. This was scary, particularly the image of frail little Jeanette being ripped to pieces by the angry mob.

4. The fact that no one was killed or seriously injured, or the fact

that the riot didn't really blow, was pure luck. It just as easily could've gone the other way.

5. There was no excuse for PiL or the Ritz to have not gone out of their way to warn the audience that this was not going to be a gig but a video and noise presentation. That this was not done was a major show of gross negligence on the Ritz's part and gross arrogance on PiL's part.

Rock had stopped being theater, had become a real threat on our lives and the performers' lives. And not unintentionally, this was part of the performance. It's like the finale of Nathanael West's *The Day of the Locust*, when Hollywood goes berserk and all the anger pent up from living and watching a fantasy explodes into real anger and violence. The act becomes real. In a way, it achieved what the Sex Pistols always said they wanted to achieve: the destruction of rock and roll, the rape of rock and roll.

I'll never be able to see another show without being aware of it being fantasy and theater — the reality and genuine threat of the PiL show spoiled that game for me.

Near the front of the mob, just as things started getting out of control, some kid said, quite seriously: "I wish I had a gun. I'd just blow him [Lydon] away, bang bang, and I'd be famous just like those other guys. Bang bang!" This time no one had a gun.

1981, *SOUNDS*

Market Correction (coughing from 30 years of Camels and Canal Street exhaust)

This one wasn't meant to read like a poem; it just sort of came out that way.

Born of punk rock's rough and red womb, weaned at the rubbery leatherette teat of punk rock, wiped and diapered by wet-nurse punk rock, grim and fishnet'd;

Schooled on the linoleum floors and bleach-stink'd hallways of punk rock school;

Boiled in her Canal Street lunchrooms, bullied on her Bowery playgrounds and first-time fellated in her crumbling old ballrooms;

First job'd in her flyer-flooded cubicles and first-fired while slashed on acid in her briny toilets; rehired in narrow punk rock stairways leading up to low-ceiling'd Park Avenue South shrines and fired again in 2 AM Tompkins Square punk rock parks lit by lights yellow'd and joyless, casting squinting shade over our shadowed, Holiday high'd punk rock heads;

Aging fast, as punk rock pipe-glass crisply cracked underneath creeper'd feet in Eldridge Street punk rock doorways smelling of piss and hash; punk rock trash'd and punk rock shellacked as the '80s turned arty but still at a screaming Birthday Party.

Born in '76 a fully sentient infant knowing of no other language but punk rock, we believed, believed, believed, believed, through metal eras/errors and swelling bellies and punk rock babies and the shabby crow of nostalgia, replaced by the happy glow of nostalgia for punk rock, punk rock, punk rock; and we *had* to believe, because without belief we believed we would vanish; even as we strolled with put-on pride on the deck of our mid-life Titanic, clutching deflated life-vests labeled with the (lie) 50isthenew40 and (lie) 60isthenew50 and so on, denying that we were finally our own sad dads, we *had* to believe in *our* punk rock, we *had* to believe we had witnessed Trinity in the Second Avenue Desert, we had to be able to boast that *we were there*

We were there!

We were there

so we shrieked, coughing from 30 years of Camels and Canal Street exhaust, exhausted were we but still *we were there* at the Zero Hour in the Lower Manhattan Project, *our* bar chord sun was brighter than a thousand others!

Yes. But. It was all a lie, I mean not a mean one, I mean not a bad one. See, we all ache for the wheel to be reinvented, it is essential to our myth that *our* lives, *our* time, our *era* is more important than anyone else's; so, every grown-fast suburb-sick teen calls *their* age 18 *Year Zero*, and it's true, every newly free (eight)teen is the pilot of the Enola Gay (or just curious), every newly free eight(teen) feels Shiva-rock was unleashed for them and them alone; and, necessarily, we believe *not* in Mendel's peas but in Eve's apple: *we alone* discovered sin, *we alone* discovered lust and drugs and girl drummers and dive bars.

Who wants to admit that they are just another consumer, subject to just another market correction?

We, the Sentient Babies of '76, did not know that to *every* wide-eyed and wide-lipped teenish, *their* time under the heatless city moon is the *hottest time* under the heatless city moon:

See, every teenager is Vicodin'd Columbus discovering the Kingdom of Outsiders and the Kingdom of Night-Rockers, every teenager is their own and only Vasco de Gabba-Gabba-Hey, saiing *their* ship around the Cape of Godless & Horny and sighting natives underneath the Manhattan Bridge; every teenager of any era *believes* that the lowscrapers and old Polish rooms and new model barrios were built *only* for them to discover and colonize, and that they are the *only* midnight children with a life so bright and sweetly dark and too fast and full of love crouched in cabs (and every single one of them doomed one day to be *they*). *But anyway* —

We, the sentient babies of '76 (and '82, and '80, and '84) believe that *we* came upon St. Marks Place a midnight dreary and *we* invented the wheel.

But we didn't. So *appalled* were we, Watergate cynical an' lonely an' dreaming of Loud and Kinks, each of us made so lonely by the high school hallways full of blown-dry boys and peasant-blous'd foxes on the run humming "Dust in the Wind," so distressed and shut out by *Saturday Night Fever* were *we* that we saw 1976 and *insisted* it was 1776.

We wanted to believe we were part of a revolution, but it was only a market correction, alas, at last.

The frippery of the second half of the '60s and the slow-burn indulgences of the '70s left the Teen Soundtrack corrupt, lousy with wilted flowers, sodden with sitars and sibilant horns and shitty songs about money and the suede-vested high-life; so we shot at the Tsar (but only damaged his car), and we wanted Stalin (but only got the New Deal), we wanted revolution but all we got was a Market Correction, layers of winter clothes and Commander Cody hair left on the dorm room floor and pissy fringes given away to Love Saves the Day.

The *lie* was that it was revolution; it was just evolution.

I mean, so thrilling it was, it was our lives, *our lives,* but just a market correction.

One of many.

But this was actually as it was supposed to be.

We, the newly free grown-fast children of suburb-sick, eternal, never aging, regenerating always and forever, never crossed the same East River twice; and we would not recognize the next incarnation, and nor would we be young for it; and we did not want to admit that no river that ever slashed through the Kingdom of Outsiders ever stopped flowing *just* for us. No river in any city, Camden Town to Chapel Hill, Aylesbury to Athens, Brighton to Brooklyn to Brookline, ever halted its inexorable, inevitable and majestic march from the continental divide to the sea; no river stopped and proclaimed that *we* were the *only* colonists in the Kingdom of Outsiders. See, we were tourists, for a while happy tourists, replaced by the next army of the newly free grown-fast children of suburb-sick.

Perpetually replaced by new seekers of the eternal chord,
Nourished at the maternal breast
of the evolving punk rock mother
who stroked the hair, dyed and knotted and fair, of every new
incarnation of eternal seekers of egg creams and 4 AM plates
of French Fries.
And this mother calls us by one of our 108 names,
And each of the named is convinced that they invented the wheel,
and that the echoes of their name will fill the chiliochosm,
Each one certain that they are the only janitors of lunacy.
But each is only a version of the other,
each one is loud and artful and beautiful,
Part of a collection of one trillion solar systems,
each positive that the universe exists for them alone,
and that they alone invented sex and open tuning and late-night
trips to Wo Hop.

And we embrace the moving river, and we say
Hey Ho Let's Go, go, go
Gone, gone, gone beyond, gone completely beyond, enlightenment.

Long live evolution.

2014, *BROOKLYN BUGLE*

Part 2: My Weird Goddamn Life

This book is not to be mistaken for a memoir; it is a collection of articles, nearly all previously published. True, these may draw a sort-of chalk outline around my life (a very trod-upon outline with enormous gaps, and one that certainly says more about my biases than my experiences); the pieces I have included were not selected to tell my story, but rather to describe a curious life spent exploring and enthralled by pop and rock music.

If this archival work reveals anything about me, that's because it reveals different facets of my obsession with music and the Kingdom of Outsiders, and my experience as a constant observer and occasional participant in this remarkable world.

However, at different occasions over the years — usually on the anniversary of some event, or at the request of an editor, or just because I felt like telling a story — I wrote pieces about something (presumably) interesting or distinctive that had happened in my own life, or that I witnessed. I suppose the pieces in this section comprise scenes from an autobiography.

All the strange stories in this chapter are true. Very true, actually. They are in roughly chronological order, except for the exceptionally peculiar true tale that opens this section.

I Watch in Awe and Terror While Johnny Depp and Evan Dando Nearly Kill Themselves

Once upon a time, there was a music industry. Now there's just music, and it flops around the universe, sort of like the fish in that Faith No More video. It has shiny sides and it gasps for breath in terror, yet it looks ever-so-slightly sexy with its mouth open. But this is another story.

It did exist, yes it did, and I bet it was just like you imagined! Gentlemen just south of middle age (or just north of college radio glory), their slightly-too-long curls oiled perfectly, sat in large offices with cream-colored walls splashed with gold and platinum records. When no one was watching, these youngish men would stand in front of these records and see their reflection in the faux silver and gold. They would adjust their hair, check for boogers and feel just the right amounts of pride and decadence. Their business was making, breaking and stealing dreams — and alternately underestimating and overestimating the cultural intelligence of the Republic.

Their offices had enormous glass windows that looked out over Beverly Hills, sloping south from Sunset Boulevard under improbable palms; others had a view north to the Hollywood Hills, an anthill of dreams spotted with adobe-roofed bungalows, the pointed eaves of steroidal Tudors and glass spaceships at the end of endless driveways. Occasionally, these windows even looked out over the old deco profiles and golden bricks of Rockefeller Center or the shuffling ant-canyons of Madison Avenue.

These men — and women, too — worked very hard, and they didn't work at all. They charged $408 sushi dinners to their expense accounts; they would imagine that the precise left-speaker panning of an acoustic guitar could affect whether a song would be a hit or not (and sometimes they were right); they would scream jovially at superstars over the clattering of plates in loud, late-night delis; they would crawl though low clubs battered by yesterday's noise claiming to be today's; and most of all, *most of all*, they would consider this, so perfectly stated by Bertolt Brecht in 1942: "Every day to earn my daily bread I go to the market where lies are bought; hopefully, I take my place among the sellers."

For a while, I was one of these people.

In the early autumn of 1992, I was just beginning my career as an A&R person at Atlantic Records in Los Angeles. Atlantic had a couple of floors in a Brutalist bone-white box of a circa-1960 building on Sunset Boulevard, exactly at the point where the Sunset Strip bent into Beverly Hills. It was about a quarter past 7:00 in the evening, and I was scribbling details on some receipts. I suspected I was the only one left on the entire eighth floor. Outside my window, the skies were turning from bright blue to ash blue, and the orange and red lights of the sushi gardens, video and liquor stores and nightclubs of the Sunset Strip were just beginning to blink on.

I became aware that two figures were standing in my doorway.

I then became aware that Evan Dando and Johnny Depp were standing in my doorway.

Some backstory: circa 1992, Evan Dando (with his band the Lemonheads) was a rising young star on the label. I was already a little friendly with Evan: we first met in the mid-1980s when a band he played in opened for my band in Cambridge, Massachusetts; in addition, his A&R person was a close friend of mine. Also, you could still smoke in office buildings back then (!) and Evan knew I smoked, so when he visited the label, he sometimes stopped by to bum a cigarette.

On this evening, in a vaguely serpentine way, Evan and Johnny slid into my office — really, they more poured than walked. Steadying themselves on the backs of the two chairs in front of my desk, Evan murmured, "Can we bum a smoke and listen to some music?"

They dissolved into the chairs, Marlboros were exchanged and ignited, and Evan waved a cigarette at the fellow seated to his left. "This is my friend John." Weak handshake followed.

It was common knowledge at the time that Johnny and Evan were fast pals.

The room quickly filled up with a pale blue fog of cigarette smoke and the mesmeric, ecstatic music of Stereolab. If any words were exchanged, I don't recall them. Evan was frequently an indifferent conversationalist; it was as if he was functioning with half a brain, and you never knew if you were going to get the working half (which was charming and agile) or the non-working half (which was duller than the third hour of a seder when your grandparents make you do the whole thing). At this moment, he and Johnny were giggling, slumping into their seats, wearing Cheshire Cat smiles, nodding gently to the music and occasionally raising eyes, marble-blue and pinned, to stare at me, at which point they would break out laughing. Johnny was going through a decidedly fleshy phase; his face was round and soft, like a Teddy Bear that someone had wrapped in well-kneaded white bread.

This went on for about 20 minutes.

At some point, Evan leaned forward and quietly informed me, though narrow lips that barely moved, that he and Johnny were in the midst of a "trip." The eyebrow I raised upon hearing this news may still be etched onto my forehead.

Not too long after that, Evan and Johnny flounced/poured out of the room, bouncing through the doorway like puppets on an unseen psychotropic string.

For the next 88 seconds or so, I raised clasped hands to my lips and stared straight ahead — the last yellow sobs of light were cutting their way west from the sea and filling the office with a dull, calming glow — and I thought to myself, "Well, you don't see that every day. This will make a fine anecdote in 24 years."

But I was snapped out of my reverie by a peculiar sound.

This would be a good place to note this fact: at the time this story takes place, the top two floors of 9229 Sunset Boulevard (floors eight and nine) were wrapped with scaffolding; some kind of major exterior renovation was going on.

This odd noise sounded like horses thumping down a track, or fat kids running up the diving board at the pool, or people charging into a general admission concert when the door opened. *Whumpa-whumpa-thwump-thump, whumpa-whumpa-thwump-thump* — and the sound was getting closer. It was completely unidentifiable — I really had no bloody idea what it could be — and it was coming from *outside* the building.

The rumbling/thumping got nearer.

I looked out the window and saw Evan Dando and Johnny Depp, their brains scattered, smothered and covered by who knows what, running around the eighth floor of the building, *on the outside.*

Somehow, they had found an opening to the exterior scaffolding and had crawled through, and now they were *running laps around the outside of the building.* Here they come, laughing their heads off … *whumpa-whumpa-thwump-thump* … there they go, and the sound gets quieter, and it vanishes … and then it starts getting closer again, and HERE THEY COME AGAIN!

After Dando and Depp did three complete orbits of the building, I lifted my jaw off of the floor and tried to get a handle on the situation. Here's what went through my head:

1. One of the label's Bright New Voices *and* a Rising Hollywood Star are running around the outside of the building on rickety scaffolding, 104 feet above Sunset Boulevard, supposedly under the influence of a powerful, uh, something. Heck, I once took two Benadryl and nearly walked out a window, so I did not have great faith in Evan and John's chances.

2. I am, apparently, the only human being who knows this strange event is taking place.

3. The likelihood that one or both of these young icons will imminently plunge to their ugly and newsworthy deaths appears to be at least, oh, 50/50.

4. Do I call the police? And how exactly would that play out? I ran that simulation in my head a few times and didn't like what I saw.

5. Since I was new to the label and hadn't made a mark yet, I felt fairly certain that if — rather, *when* — these famous gentlemen plummeted to their deaths, it would not reflect particularly well on me, no, not at all. I know this seems unimportant in the scheme of things, but... "How's that Sommer guy doing?" "Well, aside from killing Evan Dando and Johnny Depp, he's working out fairly well."

6. I considered going out on the scaffolding to try to reel in Evan and Johnny, but I realized that if I tried that, it was entirely likely I

would be the first to taste the bittersweet lips of eternity. Oh, Calgon Take Me Away, I thought.

Then it occurred to me that, since I was apparently the only person who knew that Johnny and Evan had visited me, listened to some fine motorik rock tunes, smoked roughly three Marlboros each and then crawled out onto the scaffolding, it was likely that *if* I left the office right now without telling anyone I had been there no one would know my role in this whole mishegas. Evan and Johnny would be scraped off the sidewalk later that night, paparazzi flashbulbs and police car dome lights would blaze away and people would probably think the two of them had just snuck past the security guard downstairs.

So, I poked my head into the hallway.

I called out a firm "Hello?" two or three times to confirm that I was alone on the floor, then stepped, coolly, into the elevator, took it straight down to the garage (thereby bypassing any security guy), got in my car and pointed it east down Sunset Boulevard.

I lived only about eight minutes away — six with no traffic — in a little house tucked behind the Canyon Store on Laurel Canyon. I arrived, walked in, lit another Marlboro and simultaneously put on the TV news and a news radio station, expecting to see or hear a bulletin regarding the rather bizarre defenestration of two young men from a building on Sunset Boulevard.

Nothing happened.

I watched and listened for at least an hour.

Nothing.

And only a day or two later, once I confirmed that both Johnny and Evan would continue to walk the wide, rapid and *Koyaanisqatsi*-perfect streets of Los Angeles in a definitively unsplattered manner, did I begin to tell some close friends, "Something very strange happened to me the other night…"

2017, *THE NEW YORK OBSERVER*

December 6, 1980: Bono and the Edge Give Mike and Tim a Private Concert

In December of 1980, I was 18-and-three-quarters years old. My (apparently) precocious journalism career — I did not think of it as precocious at the time, it simply seemed that I had things to say and people were willing to publish those thoughts, it all felt very ordinary and natural to me — was reaching its first peak. I was also going out to clubs four or five nights a week, almost always to see bands. Honestly, aside from the occasional party, it would not have generally occurred to me to go out "just" to go to a bar, though I certainly stopped for cocktails on the way to and from different music venues (though after a gig, it was more common that I'd go to a West Village diner or an East Village Ukrainian restaurant). I also had a very healthy social life, largely revolving around my NYU dorm, the Weinstein Center for Student Living, on University Place between Eighth Street and Waverly. Since it was a very musically tuned-in dorm, and NYU was a place where in any given class you would see the same faces you had seen at Max's Kansas City, Hurrah or the Ritz the night before, there was a lot of commingling between my college and my late-night social lives.

In the last month of 1980, several new British bands I was excited about were set to make their NYC debuts. These included the Skids, the extraordinary Scottish group who played ringing, singing, charging, clicking-clacking anthemic music that balanced on the knife's edge of punk, post-punk, prog and some kind of Celtic stadium punk, and the Ruts DC, who were the new ideation of the extraordinary, musically masterful punk-meets-metal-meets-reggae group the Ruts, whose vocalist, Malcolm Owen, had died seven months earlier.

In addition, at the end of the month, Gang of Four would be making their first visit to NYC as headliners, and Killing Joke would be making their American debut.

I was also intrigued by a new Irish band called U2, who had released a handful of very distinctive 45s that were (significantly) influenced by some of my favorite contemporary acts, like PiL, 154*-era Wire and especially the Skids, to whom this young Irish act owed a great debt.*

In early December of 1980, U2 were coming to New York to do some press in advance of the release of their first album.

These relatively common causes and conditions led to one of the most curious anecdotes of my whole career as a journalist.

This is what we did in 1980: we saw bands and we interviewed bands. What a treasured and fortunate existence. I was 18, and through a combination of deliberate calculation, proximity to Manhattan, good timing and happy accident, I found myself deeply embedded in the alternative and Anglo-import music scene in New York City. I was working as a journalist (for *Trouser Press*, a UK weekly called *Sounds* and a few other major and minor publications) and (very) regularly interviewing bands for a show on WNYU called *MusicView*.

[*WNYU was — and is — NYU's college radio station; at the time, due to a quirk in transmitter placement, it had a signal nearly as strong as most area FM stations and could be heard in three states. Curiously, because of this peculiar transmitter placement — the transmitter was at NYU's original Bronx campus — the station could be heard everywhere except the downtown NYU campus, where the signal was blocked by the high-powered radio tower at the top of the Empire State Building.*]

This story is about an interview I did at the Gramercy Park Hotel on December 6, 1980.

Almost all the visiting bands I spoke with — for my printed interviews or WNYU — stayed at the Gramercy Park or the Iroquois, though some of the thriftier ones stayed at the Seville or the George Washington (two places that were, essentially, SROs). Very occasionally, I interviewed a group big enough to stay at the Plaza, the Sheraton or the Omni Berkshire.

On December 6, I would be going to the Gramercy to interview two members of U2: Paul "Bono" Hewson and Dave "The Edge" Evans. Their debut album, *Boy*, wouldn't be out in the U.S. for another four months.

In fact, on this day I was set to interview Bono and the Edge twice: once for a small feature for *Trouser Press* and a second time for WNYU. My friend Mike Dugan would be running the reel-to-reel recorder for the WNYU interview. That evening, the band would be making their New York City debut, playing a somewhat hastily set-up show at the Ritz on 11th Street, where they would be co-headlining with a workmanlike hard rock act called the Jesse Bolt Band.

I was already familiar with U2. A few months earlier, my friend Arthur Brennan had summoned me to his dorm room to play me a few new import 45s. This was 1980, and this is what we did. Some people cheered sports, gathered in coffee shops to discuss Scorsese or cruised the aisles of NYU's Bobst Library for hushed and rapid encounters in the closed-off study hutches. Heck, some people even studied. But this is what we did: we sat around our dorm rooms and played each other new import 45s. And on this particular day, Arthur was especially keen to play me "11 O'Clock Tick Tock" by U2. Arthur knew that I was very responsive to the open, click-clack landscape of post-punk, and that I was especially fond of the Skids, whose chiming, Celtic/martial sound had clearly influenced this new act.

Although I found the band Arthur played me inferior to the Skids, there was clearly something aspirational going on here. I use this word very intentionally. On "11 O'Clock Tick Tock," you could hear something that *aspired* to the dynamics, the thunder and lightning and far away gazes, of classic rock. This was notably different from other post-punk acts we admired (like the Au Pairs, Pylon, Delta 5, A Certain Ratio, etcetera) who seemed intent on establishing their own genre, built out of the shards of punk rock. But although U2 were clearly working with the same tools as the Skids, PiL and *154*-era Wire (to name the three acts who were, very obviously, U2's prime influences), it felt like they very much wanted to build a house that could stand alongside, say, Dire Straits, Pink Floyd or the Moody Blues.

Leading up to the interviews, I had been listening to U2's debut album, *Boy*, a lot (even if it wasn't released in the States yet, it had come out about five weeks earlier in the UK). It sounded (here's that word again, but it works) aspirational. True, other newish alternative acts were integrating classic rock guitar tones and techniques into their sound (namely the Skids, the Ruts/Ruts DC, Killing Joke, *Go for It*-era Stiff Little Fingers and Generation X, especially on their second album, *Valley of the Dolls*). But U2 seemed to be reaching for something larger, something that both looked backwards — to Thin Lizzy, Sensational Alex Harvey Band and Floyd — yet had a keen sense of the space and stardust of the artier end of post-punk.

On the sidewalk in front of the Gramercy Park Hotel, early on the afternoon of December 6, 1980, a young man, barely a year older than me, with a fantastic puff of dark hair. extends both his hands, greeting me like an old and treasured friend. His name is Bono, and this is his first day ever in New York City.

And this was something else that was different about this band. Bono was only 20. U2 were one of the very few bands I had interviewed who were, more or less, the same age as me, of the same generation, and this felt quite radical. I was used to everyone being five or seven years older — even Ian McCulloch was three years older than me — and that seemed like a *lot* at the time. While I admired and identified with acts like the Soft Boys, the Damned and the Stranglers, they felt like an entirely different generation.

Bono seemed excited to meet me, and immediately after we were introduced, he pulled me aside to share a story. In the early afternoon daylight — the sky was high, bright and whitish blue, what my old friend Tom Carolan used to call a "College Football Sky" — Bono told me about arriving in New York City late the night before. Excited at having landed in a place he had heretofore only known in books, films and magazines, he had headed out to explore. "I walked around in Greenwich Village. I mean I had been hearing about the Village my whole life," Bono explained, grinning. "So, I wandered into a pub. It was absolutely packed. I looked around and realized there was nothing but blokes in there! I had never been in a place like that in my life."

I did not attach any particular rock star vibe to Bono and the Edge. In fact, I can say that the whole encounter felt distinctly less "monumental" or rock star-ish than my encounter with the Boomtown Rats, who I had interviewed not long before at the same hotel. And, honestly, I cannot recall that much of the interviews themselves, aside from the fact that Bono projected an intense, almost joyful sincerity, and he looked me in the eye. I remember that.

What was most remarkable was what happened after both interviews were finished.

As Mike Dugan and I were saying our goodbyes in the Gramercy Park lobby (the WNYU interview had been the second one), Bono suddenly and excitedly said, "The Edge went to 48th Street this morning and bought us some new acoustic guitars. We haven't tried them out yet. Do you guys want to come to the room and hear a few songs?"

Mike and I said yes. I would love to say that we thought, "Ohhhhh damn, Bono and the Edge are going to perform just for us," but it wasn't anything like that. It really wasn't. U2 just were not that well known yet, not at all. I will be bloody honest and say that Mike and I were probably more excited when (following *his* interview at WNYU) Andy Partridge had shown us how to make a Möbius strip and how to effectively design a paper hat (he really did that).

We followed Edge and Bono through the lobby, dripping with faded class, and up the gilded, ever-so-slightly shabby elevator. We went to the room they shared.

The Edge and Bono sat down on their respective beds, facing each other, each cradling their new guitars. Mike and I found spots on the floor; I put my back against the wall, wedging myself between a radiator and a TV. I distinctly recall thinking to myself, "You better remember this *really* clearly, in case they become the biggest band in the world, because if that happens, in the future this will make for one hell of a story." I really did think that. Those thoughts actually went through my head.

Alas, I don't remember a single song that U2 played during the four-song concert they performed in their hotel room for two NYU students. I do recall that none of the songs were on *Boy*, and for some reason I remember that one of them had some lyrics about wheels on a bus, or something like that. That's pretty much all I remember, aside from the fact that it did actually happen.

And that was exactly 40 years ago. Of course, John Lennon was assassinated two nights later, just 64 blocks north of our dorm. And that was one of those mnemonics, a giant one, one of those moments when we say time stops, even though we know it doesn't. And 40 years before that, I mean precisely 40 years before that, Hitler approved plans for Operation Barbarossa, the Reich's invasion of the Soviet Union, and in the United States, *The Philadelphia Story* and the Marx Brothers' *Go West* were released. And exactly 40 years from now, well, who knows. Because life, you see, is like going to a really exciting movie and falling asleep pretty quickly, and you wake up at the beginning of the closing credits. But you remember a little of what flashed before your fluttering eyes. And you think, you know, this is what we did in 1980: we saw bands and we interviewed bands. And Bono and the Edge sat on their beds in a hotel room and played some songs for my friend Mike and me.

2020, *Rock and Roll Globe*

U2, 1980: "There are enough little groups around playing little sounds… We wanted a big sound."

…and here's the article I wrote for Trouser Press *based on the interview I did with Bono and the Edge on December 6, 1980 (it did not appear until about six months later). We note that in the adamant and obnoxious manner which was my general modus operandi when I was in my late teens and early 20s, I lobbied* Trouser Press*'s editors for a significantly higher word count on this piece than I ultimately got; I distinctly recall pleading — okay, whining — "I have a feeling this band is going to be really big." But then again, I would have said the same thing about Bram Tchaikovsky (which tells you a lot about the very early 1980s).*

New music requires new classifications. Or is it no classification?

U2 is the sort of band that prompts the above riddle. The Irish group's sweeping and majestic music is "rock" in one sense but simultaneously transcends all genres.

U2's uniqueness is probably due to the emotional depth charges they detonate live and on record. Their debut album, *Boy*, is a glorious roar of hope, drenched in emotion. The band has a wonderful ability to find the musical correlatives to the ideas stirring in their young hearts and minds.

U2 singer and main songwriter Bono, 20, projects warmth and openness from the moment you meet him; when introduced, he grasps your arm with both hands, making you feel immediately at ease. He's quick to pick up on a comment that *Boy*'s images and aural wash are startlingly vivid.

"What we were looking for in *Boy* was a sort of cinema sound, a Panavision — really textured and big, like a huge screen in a cinema. The lyrics are very picturesque; they don't tell a story as such; they're just various images in the album that link together to form one big picture. There are enough little groups around playing little sounds, very unimportant. We wanted a big sound. We're using a three-piece format — bass, guitar and drums — like the three primary colors. We're mixing them, trying to get the most out of them."

It works well. The Edge, U2's guitarist, lays down thick chords here, dreamy tonal support there, even a straightforward solo now and again just to bring it all back home. Bono's expressive tenor is always in control; Larry Mullen's drums, with Adam Clayton's bass, make a solid foundation, no matter the dynamic shade. For all that, the music fits into a pop format, as full of hooks and memorable melodies as deeper moments that make you mull over — or just appreciate — what you're hearing.

U2 stands for hope — another singular trait. A lot of groups represent some form of nihilism, escapism or despair; how many can honestly state the opposite case?

"It is a celebration," Bono says. "'Shadows and Tall Trees' on the album begins in a pensive mood, as the character — who is me — looks around him. He sees this pattern developing, the repetition of everyday life. It really gets to him, really irritates him, as he realizes 'Mrs. Brown's washing is always the same.' I was listening to housewives talking; in Dublin there's this expression — 'I *know*, I *know*,' they say to each other, 'I *know*' — but I realized that's very beautiful in many ways. It's often the everyday things that are beautiful.

"We chose the name U2 to be ambiguous, to stay away from categorization. People who work in print tend to tidy things up a bit — put a stack of bands in that way, a stack of bands in here. People don't fit into boxes. We all smell different, we all eat different, we all *are* different. There's a huge audience out there of individuals."

1981, *TROUSER PRESS*

Wherein Tim Plays a Small Part in the Birth Pangs of the Beastie Boys

On a few occasions in my life, I have found myself having significant encounters with artists before they were particularly well known but sensing that attention must be paid.

I can't say this was something I actively tried to do; it just so happened that in the last quarter of the 20th century my sensibilities seemed to be tuned to a particular frequency, and when you combine that with being in the right place at the right time and having a good network of music-loving friends, it just sort of happens. It was this peculiar reputation for being "early" on artists that led Danny Goldberg to hire me in 1992 to scout and develop bands for Atlantic Records. But that's a different story and please feel free to buy THAT book. (Danny was — and is and always will be — an enormously respected music manager and former record executive; in the early 1990s, he took on an executive role at Atlantic Records, and shortly thereafter hired me to do A&R for the label.)

This piece is about one of those early encounters with an act that would go on to become very famous. In fact, of all the times I saw, engaged with or was excited by an artist before most of the rest of the world knew about them, this was possibly the "earliest" encounter, taking place before the band had even played a proper gig.

The difference between 19 and 17 is enormous. Do you recall? And not just that, we're talking *almost* 20 and *barely* 17. When I was *almost* 20, two high school students requested a meeting with me, and now these two wiry young men, both with hair shorn to the closeness of suede, sat on a low bed in my NYU dorm room, looking up at me with expectation of the wisdom of experience I would most surely dispense.

They had found me through my radio show.

At the time — it was the autumn of 1981 — I was hosting a rather feral weekly radio show on WNYU-FM devoted to the more extreme forms of punk rock, and I had gone out of my way to play, book and advise local bands. It was not at all uncommon for young bands to seek me out for advice or to needle me for a favor. (I was regularly DJ'ing at local clubs and assisting these venues with booking nights devoted to punk and hardcore music.)

For a few weeks prior to this meeting, someone had been calling the studio during my show shrieking a song request (literally shrieking, as it happens). That wasn't unusual; I would normally get 50 or more phone requests in the half-hour I was on the air. What was unusual about these multiple requests is that none of us in the studio — not me, not my engineer, not anyone else hanging around the little studio on LaGuardia Place — had heard of the band. But these calls kept coming, no matter how many times we countered that the band being requested apparently didn't exist.

There was something else different about these calls, too. Whoever was yelping and screeching on the other end of the line was *funny*. Not hostile, or pleading, or supplicating, as song requesters usually were, but genuinely funny.

I was usually too busy spinning records to actually speak to the people who called in, but something about this felt different; so, after my show one evening, I called one of the persistent mystery callers back. (I gathered there were two of them who had been making the calls.)

When I reached them, I quickly got them to admit that there really weren't any records, or even a cassette, by a band called the Beastie Boys. The band was, shall we say, in development (although they had played at a few very informal parties and done some "open" rehearsals in front of friends). But whoever these kids were, they had a relentless charm, some kind of underlying sweetness, and it made me want to meet them and offer whatever wisdom an almost 20-year-old college DJ who was spectacularly full of himself could offer.

So, I summoned Adam Yauch and Michael Diamond to my dorm room.

I explained that there was one surefire way for a band that was almost a real band but not quite a real band to actually become a real band: book a gig. Even if you're not ready, even if you don't think there's any way you can possibly be ready, if you actually book a show, you get yourself ready. So, I volunteered to book them a gig. If I did that, I rationalized, they would actually have to get their act together. Because, surely, once you saw your name in a newspaper ad, with a date and place attached to it, you then had to show up and play, or we would all look like asses.

Michael and Adam nodded respectfully.

I picked up the phone. There was a strange little place on Sixth Avenue and Ninth Street called the Playroom (the former Trude Heller's). It wasn't an A-list club by any means, but they did punk rock shows, and I knew there was one coming up that I was actively hyping on the radio show. So, I easily talked the club into allowing a new band called the Beastie Boys to play third on a bill, opening for the far-more battle-tested Reagan Youth and the legendary Bad Brains.

There were two halves to the Weinstein Center for Student Living, on University Place between Waverly and Eighth Street. My room was in the back half. My sixth-floor window overlooked a courtyard, through which all manner of reasonably happy, reasonably horny, reasonably stoned, occasionally studious young scholars and lovers and drug addicts and music geeks passed, hurrying from class to room and room to cafeteria and cafeteria to date.

It was a perfectly normal late afternoon in New York City. Ronald Reagan was in the White House, the Los Angeles Dodgers were about to beat the Yankees in the World Series; MTV had been on the air for three months and, far away in Sweden, just two weeks earlier, the first public cellular phone network had gone into service. If anyone had told me that with my phone call a tiny cog in the great timepiece of music history had just turned in a significant way, I would have said you were high, then I would have asked you where I could get whatever it was you had smoked/sniffed/swallowed.

Slightly to my surprise, the band got their shit together and showed up to play the show at the Playroom. They climbed onstage, and Michael Diamond stepped to the microphone. "This is for Timmy Sommer," Michael snapped, in that weird yapping voice he used onstage, "who doesn't believe we exist."

These were the first words the Beastie Boys ever said onstage.

2014, *BROOKLYN BUGLE*

I Was Almost a Temporary Beastie Boy

After my initial encounter with Mike Diamond and Adam Yauch in the autumn of 1981, I maintained a friendly relationship with the Beastie Boys. It is fairly well documented that I was the first person to play the band on the radio, when I debuted their original demos on Noise the Show *(in fact, excerpts from* Noise the Show *are used as a framing device on the Beastie Boys' album* Some Old Bullshit, *and my distinctive "radio" voice is sampled at the end of the Beasties' song "Heart Attack Man" on the* Ill Communication *LP).*

In 1982 and 1983, in a yet-to-be-related development, I started spending a significant amount of time with Rick Rubin, who also lived in Weinstein Dormitory. Rick shared much of the same social circle as me and many of the same musical interests (we both spent a lot of time at 99 Records, on MacDougal Street); we passed many, many hours scheming how we were going to change the music industry. In fact, in 1983 when Rick and Russell Simmons formed Def Jam, I was asked to become their third partner in the then-theoretical label. I declined the offer, to the great, booming, resounding laughter of the universe. (I was in the early stages of theorizing and forming my avant-pop band, Hugo Largo, and explained politely to Rick that I wanted to devote my energies to that. He told me I was making a big mistake. This is an utterly true and ridiculous moment in my history.)

I have been told that I was the person who introduced Rick to the Beastie Boys, but I don't recall that, though it's certainly possible. In any event, as Rick became involved with the Beastie Boys, he would regularly use me as a sounding board for plans and concepts for the band and other Def Jam projects. (My small but not entirely insignificant role in the conception of the Run–DMC/Aerosmith collaboration "Walk This Way" is partially documented in Geoff Edgers' excellent book, Walk This Way.*)*

The piece below details this time when Rick was regularly bouncing his extraordinary ideas off me. It is an account of another fascinating missed opportunity in my curiously Zelig-like life.

Hold your forefinger and your thumb this far apart. A paper clip turned sideways would fit neatly in that space. Raise it up to eye level for a better look.

That's how close I came to being a temporary member of the Beastie Boys.

One of the magical things about memory is that it puts a pin in the unspooling film of time. Memory stops the frame and lets you look around.

Think about the moon landing (if you are old enough to recall that). You don't just see a dislocated, free-floating TV picture hanging against some grey fog of brain matter, do you? No. You see the heavy edges of the giant Zenith console TV, almost as big as a refrigerator and the color of milky espresso, with all those edges that beg to be nicked, banged and scratched. You taste the SpaghettiO's you had for dinner that night. You look down and you see the burn on your fingertips from the Mattel Creepy Crawlers bug-making oven you and Gordon Platt were playing with the afternoon before. You think about Ron Swoboda and Jerry Koosman, who were in the news those days almost as much as Armstrong, Aldrin and Collins. Rheingold Extra Dry Beer! How can a beer be extra dry? Isn't it completely wet in the first place?

This is the location pin of memory.

So, I remember exactly where I was when Rick Rubin asked me to join (temporarily) the Beastie Boys.

In early 1985, I was working at MTV News as a writer/producer. I was almost 23, which felt terribly grown up, as anyone who was ever 23 will surely remember. It was a fairly small department contained within one medium-sized room crowded with word processors, monitors and big old 3/4-inch tape machines. John Norris and I had adjoining desks facing one of the newsroom's sea-grey walls. I had known John for half a decade; we had been friendly when we both lived in NYU's Weinstein Dormitory. Another friend from Weinstein, Martha Quinn, was a popular VJ. Our job was collecting entertainment news, and since a lot of it came out of the West Coast, John and I almost always worked late. Every evening at 7:00, we turned our chairs around so we could watch *Jeopardy!* Both John and I took *Jeopardy!* very, very seriously, and much adamant fist pounding and shrieking was involved. On this particular evening, I had a slice of pizza in front of me. Mariella's, who produced one of the great sloppy, floppy, thick and greasy slices in the insular city of the Manhattoes, was just a few doors down from our office on Broadway and 58th.

My phone rang, interrupting both Double Jeopardy and my pizza. Rick Rubin was calling. This was not a rare occurrence. Rick and I talked, often multiple times daily, and had been doing so for years. Rick was another Weinstein alum. In fact, my roommate in Hoboken at the time, Mike Espindle, had been the singer in Rick's proto-stoner sludge punk band, Hose.

Like me, Rick trafficked in ideas and conceived of surrealistic yet sensible seismic cultural events. Unlike me, he made many of these a reality (I mean, I'm responsible for a few, but we will discuss those at another time).

Rick and I had been discussing a Beastie Boys television series. We wanted the show to utilize corny video trickery so that giant heads could appear on tiny bodies. "Sometimes these heads will pop off the neck, spin in the air and land on someone else's body, because that's always funny," Rick had noted. Rick was also going through a stage where he was earnestly studying the work of ultra-nationalist Jewish activist Meir Kahane, who advocated Jewish repatriation to Israel. In that spirit, we were considering assembling an all-Hasid, Kahane-indoctrinated hardcore punk band to be called, simply, the Jews. Another time, Rick and I devised a cunning plan to release a version of the Led Zeppelin concert film, *The Song Remains the Same,* with all the music parts cut out, leaving *only* the confusing fantasy elements (note to self: this is a *fantastic* idea). [*Why hasn't someone done this yet?!?*]

But this evening, Rick wanted to talk about something serious and timely. He asked if I could meet him immediately at a Chinese joint he favored on University Place.

Rick ordered General Tso's chicken and got down to business. The Beastie Boys, a band Rick worked very closely with (and whom I had been friendly with since their inception about three and a half years earlier), were about to embark on their first high-profile tour. They would be opening for Madonna on her first major arena swing, the *Like a Virgin* tour.

Now, this may be difficult to imagine, but Madonna was once considered fairly damn hip. She had taken the style and flavor of various deeply insular underground scenes in the fascinating night-land that was New York City, and she had moved them into the national mainstream.

Because she had her pulse on the paper-cut edge of the underground, Madonna had chosen the Beastie Boys — who were still a year away from releasing their scene-changing *License to Ill* album — as her opening act. At the time, the Beastie Boys were a hot and innovative downtown rumor who were virtually inventing a new genre, some kind of mad, whining, dynamic cross between Brooklyn Friends School, the Paradise Garage, A7 and the Bowery Boys in *Spook Chasers*. [*My god, what a good description of the Beastie Boys.*] Even if they were barely known above 14th Street, they were clearly one of the most charismatic and original bands in the world, and Madonna had noticed this.

The tour was going to start in a few weeks.

At the time, Rick was not only producing the Beasties but also DJ'ing their live performances. Between bites of food, he explained that he would not be going on tour with them. He went on to say that the band was young and immature and needed someone on the road who could keep an eye on them and make sure they did not screw up this massive opportunity. It was also important, he explained, that this "someone" should be a person they knew, liked and trusted.

I quickly surmised that Rick was going to ask me to drop my MTV job for a few weeks and tour manage the Beasties. I figured I could handle that. By 1985 I had spent a considerable amount of time on the road as a member of the Glenn Branca Ensemble, and due to my work as a journalist, I had been hanging around bands, buses and backstages since I was 16.

But what Rick asked me next surprised me. *Really* surprised me.

"I usually would be the band's DJ, but of course I won't be there," Rick stated. "So, you'll be doing that, too."

"You mean I'll be onstage with the Beasties, behind the turntables?"

"Uh-huh."

"Rick, I've DJed in clubs, but I've never done the two-turntable/scratchy thing. I really don't know if I can do that."

"I can teach you everything you need to know in an afternoon," Rick cheerfully assured me.

"Really? An afternoon?"

"Actually, an hour. Not a problem. And we will give you clothes to wear, and we'll come up with some kind of DJ name. You are perfect for this. The guys like you, but they will also listen to you, and I totally know you can handle the DJ thing."

Every 23-year-old has a dream of going on a big rock and roll tour. I had certainly tasted a tiny bit of that with Branca, but the *Like a Virgin* tour would be old-school *Hammer of the Gods* stuff! I virtually floated back to the PATH train station on Sixth Avenue and Ninth Street.

Of course, I had no idea how taking six weeks off work would affect my job. The head of MTV News was a very nice fellow named Doug Herzog. Since Doug had been kind enough to allow me a week or ten days off here and there to tour with Branca, I thought he might be amenable to working something out, especially since Madonna basically *was* MTV at this time.

The next day, I spoke to Doug. His office was attached, via a glass wall, to the main newsroom. Doug listened to my shpiel patiently. Now, I was making about 25 grand a year at MTV News — a lot of money for a musician living in Hoboken in the mid-1980s who paid $225 for his share of a railroad flat — and I quite liked my job.

Doug, sensing my confusion, said, "Look ... this sounds like a lot of fun, but I just cannot guarantee you'll have this job when you come back. Maybe you will, but it's entirely likely we will have to replace you. Plus, Tim, I want you to remember..."

He paused for effect...

"There are no Xerox machines on a tour bus."

With exquisite timing, Doug then held up my most recent carefully honed piece of hoaxery, which I had produced on one of the office's Volvo-sized copiers: a picture of a baseball team, each face deftly replaced by the image of porcine child star Mason Reese. This bizarre, hellish — why, almost Boschian — vision was accompanied by a fake memo asking people to join the MTV softball team. After creating this, I placed it in the mailbox of every MTV Network employee. I did this sort of nonsense at least twice a week.

I called Rick and declined his offer.

2018, *REAL CLEAR LIFE*

NOTE: *Okay, since the smallest part of you — that voice inside your head that isn't quite as loud as the part that wonders if you're running out of Half and Half and is very slightly louder than the part that wonders if Elizabeth Montgomery had more fun playing Serena than Samantha (of course she did) — wants to hear that "Walk This Way" story, here is a very short version:*

One evening in early 1986 — maybe it was late 1985, I have no hesitation in confessing I am utterly awful with dates, I am a miserable archivist and have never kept a diary — Rick Rubin phoned me at home. In that very matter-of-fact/let's-talk-business way of his, he announced — and I do literally mean announced — "Tim, we've finished recording the new Run–DMC album. It's fantastic but it's missing something. We need something that's going to cross them over to white rock radio. So, I need some very familiar rock song that we can rework as a rap song for them to do." (He really did say this as straightforward as this.)

Rick and I bounced ideas back and forth, singing various riffs and lyrics to each other. I noted that the truly obvious song for Run–DMC to cover was AC/DC's "Back in Black," since that was basically already a rap song, and Rick agreed, but since the Beastie Boys had used the guitar riff from "Back in Black" about a year earlier on their song "Rock Hard," that was out of the question.

After about 20 minutes, Rick announced, "I've got it! 'Walk This Way.' It's perfect." He then began to sing the riff and rap the lyrics, and I agreed it was a great idea.

But then I chimed in: "Rick, this only really works as a true mega-crossover hit if you get Steven Tyler and Joe Perry to play on it."

"They won't do that," he said quickly. (At the time, the division between legacy white rock artists and rappers was enormous.)

"Oh, yes, they will," I countered. "Their reunion album [the just-released Done With Mirrors, *their first, commercially unsuccessful, "comeback" album] hasn't done well, and the press and the ticket sales haven't been good." (I knew all this because of my position at MTV News; I was very aware that the industry had high expectations for the Aerosmith comeback, and that these hadn't been met.) "In fact," I continued, "I'm positive they'll do it."*

Rick still wasn't sure.

"Honestly, Rick, I know two things: first, this track will really blow up if you get Perry and Tyler involved, and secondly, I am about 88 percent sure they'll say yes."

He said he'd try to reach them.

So, that was my role in "Walk This Way." For the record, another close friend of Rick's and mine — the wonderful Sue Cummings, who was then an editor at Spin *— claims that she also (independently) suggested Tyler and Perry become involved with the track, and this is entirely possible.*

Now, let me tell you about turning down a date with Morrissey.

Actually, we'll save that for Volume II.

How I Became the "Yr." in "Kill Yr. Idols"

Sometimes it occurs to me (often when I see the phrase on a T-shirt or used as a generational touchstone) that I am the "Yr." of the Sonic Youth song "Kill Yr. Idols." Not only does it bring a little shimmer of pride, it also reminds me that "Kill Yr. Idols" is, generally, extraordinarily good advice.

The origins of that advice are rooted in my past. And the past is a stranger with whom I share a hard drive, a corrupted hard drive. Whole summers are missing, entire arcs of experience have been reduced to fractured zeros and ones, two semesters of college are completely unrecoverable and the entire unit has a big sticker on it that says: "For Amusement Purposes and/or Self-Loathing Only."

Nevertheless, the past sometimes sends me postcards.

This postcard tells a story that begins in June 1982. Jack Rabid, the legendary concierge and chronicler of punk rock, and I had been walking north on the Bowery; we had just made the right turn onto St. Marks Place. We were both 20 at the time and visited St. Marks Place nearly every day, usually landing at a spectacular record shop called Sounds, halfway down the block.

On the southeast corner of St. Marks and Third Avenue, a fellow was sitting on the sidewalk behind a blanket that held a strange assortment of possessions. Amidst the toasters, cowboy boots and 8-track tapes was a bass guitar (a very reasonable Fender Jazz imitation made by Carlo Robelli). It cost $100.

Jack was the drummer in a reputable local punk band called Even Worse. A few nights earlier, during a gig at Irving Plaza, Jack's entire band had quit onstage (which would be tragic if it weren't so funny). Jack may dispute this account, but my version makes for a prettier postcard.

Jack turned to me and announced, "If you buy that bass, you can be in my band."

I had done a DJ gig at the Mudd Club the night before, so I had enough cash on me.

Despite the fact that I really couldn't play the bass, I handed over the hundred bucks without hesitation.

As soon as I took ownership of that bass, I was a member of a band.

There is nothing like that first realization that *you* are now *in a band*. Why, only seconds ago, you were a *normal person* who *listened to things* and *argued about B-sides* and *ate at Blimpies* and *hoped people would notice that Artaud book sticking out of your backpack.* But now, you — yes, you — are in a band! You had been reading about bands and seeing bands and listening to bands and fantasizing about bands for as long as you can remember, and now you are actually in one.

In my entire life in the music industry [*40 years at the time this piece was written*], the only thing that compared to that feeling — that fever-on-the-inside/grin-on-the-outside/scream-in-your-heart awareness that you are now in a band — was the first time I learned that an act I was working with had achieved gold record status.

I set about teaching myself the rudiments of punk rock bass guitar. Over and over and again and again, I played along with the first Ramones record, the first Clash record, PiL's *Second Edition* and the Clash's *London Calling.* I did this pretty much for a week straight. I hereby apologize to my roommate at the time (sorry, Kevin). It did the trick and, honestly, I still recommend this as a way of learning the instrument.

A few days later, Jack and I were walking down MacDougal Street, on the way to another one of our standard hangouts, 99 Records. A small but amazing import and independent record store, 99 Records also boasted its own very influential label. As we were approaching the store, a boyish, very tall and very blonde fellow was climbing up the steps out of 99. Jack said to me, "That's Thurston. I'm going to ask him to play guitar in the band." I had some familiarity with Thurston Moore, since I had seen him perform multiple times as a member of the Glenn Branca Ensemble, and I also knew of his relatively new (and, at the time, well under the radar) art-rock band, Sonic Youth.

Thurston did indeed join Even Worse, along with two pals from NYU's Weinstein Dormitory, vocalist Ken Temkin and second guitarist Steve Waxman.

Thurston and I quickly became fast friends. We were both record geeks with a penchant for the more extreme ends of hardcore punk and metal, and we both saw an overlap between hardcore punk's grind and the tripping, droning harmonics of avant-garde music. We went to a lot of shows together, mostly stuff like Motörhead, Black Flag, Meat Puppets, Iron Cross, things like that.

Thurston and his owlish girlfriend Kim Gordon lived in a shattered, smashed corner of the Lower East Side, what was then a no-go zone except for the heartiest and most intrepid pioneers. I remember that their flat was pale blue, long and trapped between lightless tenement airshafts. They had terribly interesting friends who made odd films and strange, skeletal music.

Thurston never seemed to have any money, and since I was actively working as a journalist at this time, I would occasionally hire him to transcribe my interviews at the fairly generous rate of ten bucks a cassette side (which seems steep, even now). (BTW, Thurston, you still owe me a Mick Fleetwood transcript.)

Simultaneously with our time in Even Worse, I was writing a great deal for the *Village Voice*. My editor at the *Voice* was the legendary Robert Christgau. He was very generous with his time, wisdom and skill. I would often tell my friends how fond I was of him. This seemed to especially annoy Thurston, since Christgau had given a negative review to Sonic Youth's first EP.

In its early years ('81–'83), Sonic Youth was pretty much the world's greatest rock and roll band, a raucous, chanting, shrieking subway-screech meets refrigerator-drone blend of Branca's apocalyptic, scraping guitar and hardcore punk's thrash and rumble. Live, their sound was often so feral that it was reduced to nothing more than gorgeous, courageous and ridiculous rhythm and noise.

They were also pretty unpopular in those years; the contemporary rock critic cognoscenti despised their disorganization and anti-pop, and they usually played in front of tiny audiences. At the time, I was virtually the only mainstream music journalist writing anything positive about Sonic Youth.

Sometime in mid-1983, Sonic Youth debuted a new song called "Kill Yr. Idols."

I remember being startled when I first heard it: it began with a woozy, clipped two-chord guitar sequence; at that time, it was by far the closest thing Sonic Youth had recorded to a traditional rock guitar riff. It seemed almost like a rockist parody, but I could tell it wasn't: Sonic Youth was trying to shoehorn the sibilant, slapping riffs of SS Decontrol, Minor Threat or even AC/DC into their own smothering, steamrolling, lug-nut-shitting sensibility. It seemed like an enormous leap forward for the band.

I was so blown away by this musical development that, bizarrely, I missed what was staring me right in the face in the first verse of the song:

"I don't know why
You wanna impress Christgau
Ah, let that shit die
And find out the new goal"

I never talked about this with Thurston or any member of the band, but it was later confirmed by him that the lyric was inspired by, uh, me, and the fact that I had one foot in Sonic Youth's world and another in Christgau's sphere.

By early 1984, both Thurston and I were out of Even Worse. He moved on to an unusually credible kind of stardom (the sort reserved for people like Beck or Neil Young), and I moved on to the Glenn Branca Ensemble (where, ironically, I replaced Thurston Moore). Later in 1984, I formed my own avant-pop ensemble, Hugo Largo — which was inspired by the idol-killing spirit of Sonic Youth, Swans and PiL, but sought to shatter glass with whispers instead of screams.

Mind you, Sonic Youth was not using the phrase "Kill Yr. Idols" in any heavy duty philosophical, cosmological or spiritual context, but it does totally work in that fashion. And regardless of Thurston's somewhat purposeless attack on Robert Christgau, one of the most supportive, literate and intelligently provocative music journalists I've ever met, 30-plus years later, Kill Yr. Idols remains exquisitely sharp advice. By lovingly investigating the fact that not one of our favorite artists achieves perfection, by demolishing the myth of infallibility (even amongst our most sacred cows), we can truly appreciate the native and acquired genius of these artists. For instance, the Beatles, or the Clash, or certainly the Beach Boys et al. are an amalgamation of imperfections, rendered with invention and sweat; no person seeking perfection would have the courage to create something as startling as *The White Album*, or *London Calling*, or *White Light/White Heat*, or *Pet Sounds*, or *Pink Flag*. These works are all acts of extreme courage — which is to say each of these masterpieces, full of distortion and majesty, are about human and artistic flaws, rendered with energy, passion and creativity. In fact, the very definition of creativity is seeking perfection by taking imperfect roads. When you believe in the godlike infallibility of artists you love, you virtually demand that they deny the *human* qualities and the potential for exploration (brilliance is often the result of error) that leads to groundbreaking events and "genius."

Kill Yr. Idols. Or at the very least, recognize that not only is no one infallible, everything in life is suffused with impermanence, and impermanence not only makes all life possible (imagine a river that does not run, a blade of grass that does not grow, a sun that neither rises nor sets), impermanence, which is to say the quality of variation of influence and skill and the willingness to err, makes all great art possible.

I thank Thurston and Sonic Youth not only for making me the 'Yr." in one of their trademark songs, but also for helping teach me that idol-killing, when done with as much joy and as little pretension as possible, is a beautiful path to creativity.

2018, *INSIDEHOOK*,
with some material from a 2014 story in THE BROOKLYN BUGLE

Remembering the Glory Days of MTV News… and Revisiting the Meaning of MTV

In mid-1983, I was probably at the height of the first stage of my journalistic career. I was writing regularly for the Village Voice, *the* Daily News, *the fantasy/sci-fi/alternative culture monthly* Heavy Metal, Trouser Press, Sounds, Smash Hits *and a pile of others whose names have fallen into the lost luggage piles of my mind.*

If my journalistic career — and please recall I was barely 21 — was at its apex, my scholastic career had reached an irretrievable low point. After the spring semester of 1983 — in theory, it should have been my senior year at NYU, but I had barely completed two years' worth of credits — I decided to take the low road and climb, with unsteady shame, the shabby back fire escape down from the heights of academia (let's put it that way). I am not proud of my scholastic record, though I maintain that my time at NYU, and specifically at Weinstein Dorm, was profoundly formative; the filmmaker Adam Dubin, who was also in Weinstein around the same time I was, frequently says, "I didn't go to NYU. I went to Weinstein."

So, now, I had defenestrated from academia and was formally out into the "real world."

Although I was making decent money as a journalist, I was already getting a little bored with it, and I sensed that it might make sense to get a 9-to-5-ish job. At just the right time, two close friends — Stuart Cohn and the wonderful Merle Ginsberg (who went on to become a legendary fashion journalist) — came to me and suggested that I join them in the nascent MTV News department.

This piece was written to coincide with the 40th anniversary of MTV's debut.

I say this with all the earnest, tight-jawed, almost fevered pretension that you have only when you are in your twenties, when it seems like the night-blooming fragrance of a great city is opening up in front of you:

Those of us at MTV News in the 1980s thought of ourselves as the conscience of the network. We really did. We were the annoying over-chatty boyfriends of the nation, insisting on telling you about B-sides and Syd Barrett solo albums when all you wanted to do was enjoy your dinner.

MTV puffed its way into life one minute after midnight on Saturday, August 1, 1981. It is always worth noting the anniversary in some small or large way. From that moment forward, nothing was the same; it profoundly, irreparably changed the way people heard and saw music. In any compilation of the fundamental moments when the music industry went sailing off a cliff, Wile E. Coyote-like, and looked down and saw an abyss that was filled with nothing but peril and promise, we must include 2/9/64 (the Beatles' *Ed Sullivan* debut), 8/1/81 and the release of iTunes on 1/9/01. Other dates, of course, are profoundly significant — but few had such immediate and irreversible effects.

I was a part of MTV News, on and off, from 1983 until 1990. Despite the time I put in within those walls, my perception about MTV has changed enormously over the years. Back then, I believed that I was a Soft Boys-loving fly in the Journey-belching ointment, and I had some kind of childish, sophomoric detachment from the overall mission and power of the network. But I had that wrong. I have come to realize that MTV, regardless of the behemoth shadow it cast on music throughout the 1980s and most of the '90s, was an enormously positive force in shaping and broadening the musical tastes of the United States. It did not reinforce earlier biases and inaccuracies (as it may have appeared to us snobs), but in fact broke them down in an enormously positive way.

There are many examples of this. Alternative British and American music, which mainstream radio and media had considered virtually a non-starter prior to 1981, was given second, third and fourth life by MTV. Circa 1980, *Rolling Stone,* the major labels (with some small exceptions) and virtually all the major FM outlets were extremely satisfied with the Eagles/Mac old guard and effectively conspired to keep it that way. MTV changed this profoundly because it operated on the most fundamental revolutionary level: it took choice out of the hands of the corporations and returned it to the audience.

It did so for two enormously pragmatic reasons. First and foremost, in its earliest days, MTV had to build the programming for an entire 24/7 network out of available stock. When the channel blinked on its glowing nightlight, it found that British bands in general (and lesser-known alternative artists specifically) had made a lot more videos than older FM stalwarts. Secondly, when you flashed the cultural pop Rorschach at young people sitting in their dens and dorm rooms, they were going to be a lot more intrigued by Simon Le Bon and Cyndi Lauper than they were by the mancows in the Outlaws or the Atlanta Rhythm Section.

Within 18 or 24 months of MTV's debut, British acts previously relegated to large clubs, small theaters and college radio were playing arenas. A new die had been cast. When your dad prattles on and on about the Stooges and Big Star and all the cool bands *he* liked in the 1970s, you may get a very distorted perception of the 1970s. *It was* awful, and the mainstream was perfectly happy to keep it that way. People forget. We were so utterly subsumed by Dan Hill-ism and Steven Bishop-ry, not to mention turd-breathers like the Little River Band and conceptual monstrosities like Kansas, that when transparent near-mediocrities like the Cars and Costello emerged, we understandably greeted them like manna from heaven. My god, even the fucking Babys seemed like a relief. This, friends, is the "then" that existed in the United States before MTV altered the landscape.

Secondly (and more importantly), when the color line was broken at MTV in the mid-1980s, mainstream popular culture was impacted by a multi-ethnicity that was virtually unique in the pop industry.

Some backstory: In 1933, in order to help focus retail efforts more efficiently, the labels, retailers and the trade papers separated "race music" (that's the actual terminology used back then) from the other divisions of the pop, hillbilly and classical music they manufactured and promoted. From that moment forward, the public face of pop spun into a 50-year cycle of Jim Crow. The Jim Crow line that existed in the music industry between 1933 and 1984 was remarkably pronounced. African-Americans were sold music made by African-

Americans and Caucasians were sold music made by Caucasians, with radio, retail and media outlets and sources accordingly divided. Although MTV was late to the party (the degree to which this integration took place under duress is not something I will discuss here, though I have reason to believe that conventional accounts are not necessarily accurate), everything changed when MTV climbed aboard the rap/R&B train. *Everything.* The music industry (and the outlets it used to expose music to consumers) would never again be distinctly racially divided. Once half a century of pop Jim Crow ended, everything fundamentally and permanently changed — not just in record stores, but also in malls and high school hallways.

Which is all to say that even a pretentious old cynic like me thinks that MTV did far, far more good than harm. But it did not necessarily seem like that at the time.

I joined MTV News about halfway through 1983.

Merle Ginsberg was a good friend, and a pioneer of downtown arts and fashion journalism. She was a stalwart at the *Soho Weekly News* (which was a little hipper and more artsy than the *Voice*). She also had a very solid day gig writing for the newly created MTV News department, and along with another acquaintance, Stu Cohn, she recommended me for a job there. It seemed like an extraordinary opportunity, one that was adult and exotic. You would be in an office, and you would have health insurance and a rolly chair, yet you would also be working on the edge of the music and cable TV industry, at a time when there was still something ever-so-slightly strange, even naughty, about the 36-channel world of cable television.

In 1983, MTV News was a fairly straightforward concept. Once an hour, an MTV News logo would pop up behind the VJ's shoulder, and they would deliver about 150 seconds or so of music news. So-and-so has a new album coming out! Such-and-such just announced a new tour! Such-and-such just shot a new video, and we were on set, let's roll the tape! See, someone had to write that stuff. The small staff of MTV News writers were probably obscenely overqualified for this sort of work: Merle and Michael Shore, another *Soho News* vet, were pretty much top of their game; Stuart Cohn, another *Trouser Press* vet I had known since my mid-teens, was also first-rate; and the "new" guys were myself and an old friend from my NYU dorm, John

Norris. (John may have actually come in a bit later; dates elude me utterly, completely, and catastrophically, and entire years have sunk back into the fog of the loam, *Brigadoon*-like.) John served a very important function: he wasn't a college radio snob and therefore could throw himself into the mainstream and pop stuff with complete abandon and no smug detachment. Soon after, Kathy Levinsky, an extremely good-humored, wide-smiling young woman who shared virtually none of our hipster obsessions but tolerated our singlehanded pursuit of them, joined up. There were also some non-writer types there — people who produced video shoots, ran great, clunking armfuls of three-quarter-inch tapes all over the building and did all the other things that didn't involve talking on the phone to publicists and typing on enormous electric typewriters that could easily be used to kill a man or ballast a reasonably sized Hudson River garbage barge.

In late 1983, the boss of the small department was the second youngest person in the department (I was the youngest). That was Doug Herzog. Within a decade or two, Doug would be running some of the largest TV networks in the business (including MTV, Comedy Central and FOX), but back then he was just a pretty deep reggae/alternative rock fan who had some experience writing about entertainment for CNN. He was also unduly impressed by the fact that I played with the Glenn Branca Ensemble, and he very kindly gave me time off to go on brief tours with Branca.

We all really, really liked each other. Every single day felt like when you would go to dinner in the dorm cafeteria, and everyone would congregate around that one special table and try to impress each other with bad jokes and bits of arcane knowledge.

Our job was to generate eight or ten stories a day. Once written, our typed copy would be run — I think literally run — a couple of blocks west to the studio on the far end of West 57th Street (for most of my time at MTV, we were on Broadway at 57th, in an unshakable old wedding cake which some of you would know as the Coliseum Books building).

Finding these stories was a bit harder than it sounds. First of all, nearly all of it was dependent on getting phone calls returned, so if that didn't happen by 4:00 or 4:30 you might suddenly have to rearrange your whole lineup or go scrambling to fill stories that had fallen through. Secondly, you had to work within a framework of 60 to 125 words that could be easily read off a teleprompter.

Everything would be coordinated with our department head (at first, Doug Herzog, and then when he was kicked upstairs, Linda Corradina and Dave Sirulnick, all really magical humans). And then it was left to the VJs to present our stuff as best as they possibly could. I say, without hesitation, that the original VJs were, without exception, professional, able, capable and friendly. They never took our contributions for granted, and I especially single out Martha Quinn, Alan Hunter and Mark Goodman for really making the effort to make us feel like they were part of our team, and that we were one holistic news gathering operation.

An average day would go like this: you'd have a few leads about video shoots, album releases or tours coming up, and you'd start calling publicists. You'd get the info confirmed, you'd scramble for some graphic support and Bob's yer uncle. Sometimes, you would have to accommodate a larger MTV agenda. "Oh my god, Armand DaSilba of Violated by Geese was arrested after peeing inside a 7/11 in Dothan, Alabama!" "We can't run that, they are trying to get the Violated by Geese to play the New Year's Party." That sort of thing happened frequently. You generally couldn't say "Boo!" about Guns n' Roses or Michael Jackson without clearing it with about half a dozen people higher up the food chain. Honestly, we didn't get that worked up over that sort of thing. We basically knew we were working for MTV, not *Harper's* magazine.

This brings us back to what we thought we really did.

We thought we did our best work in the margins. Our *real* purpose, or so we thought, was to sneak the names and faces of our personal favorites onto the MTV platform. On any given week, each one of us would be permitted to slide in a story or two about some fave artist who could only tangentially be connected to someone on the MTV playlist. For me, this meant wedging in stories about, oh, R.E.M., old garage bands, Hanoi Rocks, the Bad Brains and so forth; for Michael Shore, it meant world music heroes like Fela Kuti or extreme jazzpunks like Sun Ra; for our boss, Doug Herzog, it meant Boston college radio faves and reggae stars; for John Norris, it meant promoting the leading edge of Britpop and downtown dance music.

We *lived* for this stuff, we *lived* just to get a sentence or even a half sentence on the air about some favorite act. Now, we usually could think of *some* legitimization for interpolating our bias; perhaps we would say, "While Sting was in Nigeria, he guested on a session with…" or "College radio faves the Frantic Eggs will be opening some dates for the English Beat next month…" That sort of thing.

I also believe that, in the 1980s, MTV News assumed the role of seers and prognosticators for the network, and the network respected and encouraged that. The great movements and artists of MTV's future — from R.E.M. to Run–DMC to the Beastie Boys and many more — first surfaced in blurbs on MTV News. We did not take this role lightly. Thankfully, circa 1985, the network was structured in such a way that we could actually say to a front-rank exec, "Pay attention to this act, you'll be hearing more from them."

I left MTV News for the first time at the very end of 1986 to go full-time with my art-rock band, Hugo Largo. When I returned in 1989, things had changed enormously. The VJs were no longer reading the news segments, and MTV News had a dedicated newsreader (the wonderful, grave and slightly smug Kurt Loder and, later, John Norris, Tabitha Soren and, to a very limited degree, myself). We also had a show called *The Week in Rock*. This allowed us a terrific platform to attain both credibility and branding for MTV News. Since, without exception, all of us were music geeks who took music history very seriously, we were able to find a really first-rate balance between the "obligatory" tour/video stories and other aspects that gave MTV News the veneer of being the Source of Record for music news. I think it is important to explain why this seemed so bloody important in 1989.

In the very late 1980s, we were still living in the Underdog Age of American Rock. So very many of us had been formed in the fire of music that stood apart from what was on the radio, covered in *Rolling Stone and* available for perusal at the local EnormoDome. Our social lives and our careers had been defined by a desire to tell that story, to find friends, to convert the townspeople. As late as 1989, the United States still had distinct outsider and mainstream music cultures (in the UK, Canada, France and West Germany, alternative sensibilities had been significantly infiltrating the mainstream since the late

1970s). Once upon a time, it seemed it might always be that way. As long as that was the case, we at MTV News felt we had an extremely vital function: we told the story of the alternative nation from within the halls of the temple of the mainstream.

The grunge era, which essentially mainstreamed music directly descended from the outsider communities of '77-era punk and post-SST/Dischord hardcore (even further scrambling the underground jet fighters by adding a distinct flavor of outsider metal and sexual ambiguity), changed all that. It was the moment there stopped being distinct mainstream and outsider contingents in American Caucasian music. Personally, I think when that happened we no longer needed MTV News. The Hipster Elder who gently (or not so gently) pointed you towards "good" music was no longer strictly necessary in the post-Nirvana era, and soon, internet immediacy would eliminate the need for weekly music news roundups.

None of that high-falutin' zeitgeist stuff is meant to obscure this: MTV Networks in the 1980s was a magical place to work. Imagine a high school full of amiable smartasses where no one had to go to gym. Imagine a place where you got paid to walk around all day with a smile on your face. Imagine entering a building and knowing you were walking into the lizard brain of mainstream culture and the mammalian brain of hipster knowledge. In 1990, I left MTV News to take over a much smaller music news department at VH-1, and I left there in 1992 to sign bands and help people make records at Atlantic Records. All told, I put in about seven years at MTV Networks, and I have not one single bad memory. Truly.

2021, *Rock and Roll Globe*

Aim for the Spaces, Not the Cars (an Acid Story)

I have taken LSD once in my life. It was such a brilliant, life-altering experience that, then and there, even at the relatively risk-seeking age of 23, I vowed never to do it again. It felt too beautiful and dangerous, and since the first time had gone so right, I figured why take the chance?

This is an account of that remarkable evening, and how it provided me with certain creative lessons that have valid applications, I think, for anyone thinking of making any kind of art, even if they would never dream of using hallucinogens.

The identities of the great friends who guided me on the trip have been concealed.

Let me tell you a story.

It was dawn on the 21st of May 1985. The evening before, I had met my great friend Patti at her apartment on far East 14th Street. She was a college radio deejay nonpareil who spread the gospel of Nancy Sinatra and the Cramps like a hip Constantine. Patti lived in an ash-colored tenement that was very typical of the time; you walked through an open door, past smashed mailboxes, into a tiled hallway the color of an un-restored old master painting. Patti lived up five flights of wide stairs, behind a heavily bolted door. Inside was a thrift store playhouse where the early and hearty heroes of indie rock were honored. Patti worshipped Alex Chilton and the Soft Boys, the Ray-beats and the Beach Boys, ESG and the Fall. Arto Lindsay and Pat Place, Jean-Michel Basquiat and Peter Buck knew her name and paid homage, much as I was doing this evening.

In 1985, New York was still one of the great cities. Despite some small foreshocks of the improvements that would later turn into a monsoon that rained money on Crapsville, great swaths of the City remained shattered, shuttered, sepia and crumbling. The West Side was still punctuated by Dresden-like brick piles, and the East Village was still a serious no-go zone past Avenue B. Soho was still full of artists and ripe, smart girls. The city was still patrolled by cinema-ready Checker cabs, and most everyone I knew slept on a mattress on the floor, along with two crates of records that hadn't yet been stolen by pissed-off girlfriends. Although the picturesque ruin of the Beame years was slowly giving way to a brighter future, there was enough of the Old Towne left to thrill.

Manhattan was just ending the era when it was the Kingdom of Outsiders.

We had come from Rye Neck and Great Neck, Calgary and Cambridge, Brooklyn and Brookline, Charlottesville and Chapel Hill, Portland and Palo Alto and Commack and Queens. Middle class or more, mostly, each of us the only children in our towns who dreamed of Lance Loud and Lou Reed, who practiced posing like *Low*-era Bowie and Warhol's Little Joe, the only ones in our grade who knew who Sondheim and Stuart Sutcliffe were.

You won't know all of those names, but each had beamed its way into our suburban winters and promised us that there was something beautiful, intense, literate, sensitive, artful, full of power chords and perfect highs just the other side of the Hudson (or the East River, for those who lived on the Island).

In our suburban bedrooms we blissed out on narrow beds sealed between headphones, shivering with joy when we heard *Horses*. In study halls we read *Creem* and *Trouser Press* and even *NME*, or Christopher Isherwood and Patrick Dennis and E.M. Foster, or maybe all of the above. We heard rumors about revolution in England and tried to imagine what it was like. We made friends with teenagers who dressed their heads rooster-red like Bowie or black-eyed underlined like Frank-N-Furter. Chubby and fey or theatrically thin and almost always supernaturally afraid of gym, we found allies in record stores thumbing through the Kinks section, and we smiled at broad-shouldered girls in Cheap Trick T-shirts. Huddled at home, the TV and all of its five channels gave us newscasts from the heart of the city and glimpses set to song of the Seville hotel and the Ritz thrift shop, the slim cast of *A Chorus Line* and the lite-brite black and white dream of the *Million Dollar Movie* credits.

On Saturdays and Sundays, those lucky enough to live within commuting distance of the '70s shabby Apple, that strange, smoky, hoarse burned-out carnival lightbulb, climbed on trains still smelling of hockey fans and the fathers we swore we'd never become. We'd start our City adventure under the white bright light of the Waverly, and hearts beating fast, spread like spiders across Village streets that made no sense and all the sense in the world, pointing out basements on Barrow Street and dormers on Bank Street where we would live one day. Sun setting, we 15-year-old peacocks slid through charmless Penn Station, clutching bootlegs and Beatle boots and maybe a *Penthouse* or two.

We all knew we belonged in the Kingdom of Outsiders.

And in 1975, 1976, 1977, 1978, 1979, 1980, 1981, 1982, 1983, we would make it there, on some pretext or another, maybe involving NYU or SVA or an internship or an older sister or a friend of a friend with a couch.

And before long, we made up stories that erased our suburban selves, and our Cuban heels were clicking on Soho cobblestones, finding art in shadows and glimpses of stairways and especially the pattern on the manhole cover. We walked and walked, walked past shattered East Broadway full of synagogues as wrecked as Warsaw, spotting Verlaine in French restaurant doorways. Six hours after sunset, we'd wind around green-copper colored Union Square (which only the dumb or courageous would cross after dark) to the narrow stairs of Max's, that brilliant dull-black box full of junkies and idols, or head south to great rock and roll cellars on West Broadway, or uptown all the way to 62nd Street to see panicked English children flown over just to play the shiny Hurrah, and the city was ours, and we were all kings in the Kingdom of Outsiders.

And this brings me back to Patti's beautifully cluttered apartment, in the spring of 1985. Last call for the Kingdom of Outsiders had already been proclaimed, but there were still a few pints left to throw down.

It was Patti's idea, planned well in advance, I suspect, to place a tiny pink tab of acid on my tongue. Patti and her roommate, an obscenely talented cult musician of some note, were going to guide me through my first trip. For the next eight hours, the roommate and Patti played me records, protected me, tolerated my obnoxious insights and my distortions of time and my matter-of-fact explanations that it might be time for me to die. I watched the walls melt, I saw dimensions compress and expand, I saw paintings of geese fly off the wall through the hole where the window used to be. I smiled gently from a deep hollow in the ancient green couch in the center of the living room as the past and future became entirely visible and compressed into a now that would fit into a matchbox. As the sky turned from gray to pink I started walking towards the window, certain that if I chose to walk off the ledge, it would be absolutely the right time to move onto the next plane, that all was right with the world of existence and mortality, which had merged into one idea called lifedeath.

But mostly I listened to music.

I recall that the musician/roommate and Patti played me three albums over and over; it is entirely possible that is not accurate, since when you trip you choose the reality that best suits your experience and only encode these in your memory. Those three records were *Pet Sounds* by the Beach Boys, *Sister Lovers* by Big Star and *I Often Dream of Trains* by Robyn Hitchcock.

While absorbing the music from within the multi-leveled cocoon of the hallucinogen, a condition which made the pauses in songs sound like God's breath, creating a time stoppage/slight backwards reverb effect that left you hovering above and within certain parts and magnified unmercifully the warmth and depth of the bass, I found myself thinking that music at this moment felt as I had always dreamed it would, as if it was all around me and inside of me, instead of just the target of the angled projection of a left and right speaker.

I discovered space that night, and I do not mean that in any psychedelic or mystical sense. I suddenly realized that music was open space and that the art was in tastefully, subtly or aggressively filling that space; but the space always came first and was always to be reckoned with and recalled, like the person in ancient Rome whose job it was to whisper in the emperor's ear that all glory was fleeting. With instruments and voice, you could paint within that space, and even the space itself could be painted. But the extraordinary prism of aural colors between sounds, no matter how sliver-thin or slab-wide those sounds might be, were to be respected at all costs.

I mean, think of the Ramones. Virtually a perfect band. And the Ramones are not defined by what they play; they're defined by what they chose not to play.

Following my chemically induced revelations, I immediately applied my newfound respect for space to my own music, and it led to my feeling that I now *owned* the sound I had been working on creating. There was something I heard in my head, and I couldn't find it in my music collection. I had found it, between my ears.

Which brings me to my main point, but not before I state, with absolute, resounding sincerity, Please Don't Do Psychedelics. They are dangerous fuckers, and although my experience was generally pleasant (except for the dwarves I "saw" on the L train — to this day, I do not know if they were really there or not), I also came perilously close to death, I really did. I was ready to walk out that window in Patti's apartment, I actually felt that it would be the totally safe and sane thing to do. I was staring out the window, saw that there was no difference between life and death and that death could be a perfectly pleasant place, and I think only Patti or her roommate's intervention saved me. So, instead of being an exercise in musical revelation, the evening could have easily ended up with me splat on the sidewalk on the south side of 14th Street between First and Second Avenue. I also feel that the extraordinarily delicate balances of one's brain chemistry and emotional state have to be so carefully aligned to avoid what one could call a "bad" trip. In fact, Patti, who was within three feet of me for virtually the entire experience, had a horrific trip at the very same moment I was having a "good" one. Now, that's the end of my Public Service Announcement, but I could not be more fucking serious about this. I never did psychedelics again, now that I knew how potent and dangerous they could be.

So, back to my point. That night, I did not invent the originality I was capable of, but I did recognize that it was there. I identified one of its primary ingredients and, to this day, I will proselytize about the importance of space. As my driving ed instructor once said to me,

"Aim for the spaces, not the cars," and this in turn led me to become aware of one of the most important things I can tell you:

The best reason to make a musical noise is because you're looking for *something* in your music collection and you just can't find it, so you have to make it yourself. You are looking for a song or an album. You can hear what you want in your head pretty clearly. You know the mood it is supposed to create, the way it sits in your heart, the way it causes your heels to lift and push your toes into the floor and your heels to lift again. You know the thoughts it will inspire and the work it will inspire you to do. Honestly, you can feel in your teeth the way the music will hit you, You crave that song in that area just below the sinuses that gets full of thrillsome, amphetaminized air when music hits you the right way and turns your mouth into something halfway between gritted teeth and a grin.

You are looking for something that will be intensely personal, and then you will want to share it with the world. You are looking for a song you will restart six or eight times before it's even 12 seconds old, because those first chords are *so* aurally outrageous, and you love the moment when silence turns into something stunning and hope-hearted. *You want that.* You want it, where is it?

Depending on your age, you are either scanning your iPod for the song, or flipping through your CDs, or putting on your 1.75 magnification reading glasses, purchased at Rite Aid, and reading the weathered spines, cracked with the sweetness of use and your youth, of vinyl albums.

You are looking for *something.*

But you can't find it. You just can't find it. No matter how hard you look, you can't find the precise thing you hear in your head. You hear something desperately powerful and beautiful and necessary in your head and you can't find it anywhere.

So, you realize you have to make it yourself.

This is the best reason to make music: because you hear something in your head and you can't find it anywhere. And that sound is so special and essential to you that you know you are going to have to make it yourself.

Conversely, why make music if someone is already doing it?

There are other good reasons to make music, and we can discuss many of these; but there's no better reason than needing to hear something and not being able to find it and therefore desiring to make it for yourself.

And anything is possible. Which is to say, anything you hear in your head can be produced.

Now, by no means am I saying that you won't succeed if you don't have this mindset or that you won't be famous unless you do. That's not the case at all. I just know that I have found no better way to sate the desire to fill my vibrating shins and hungry soul with music than to try to reproduce the sounds I hear in my head, and only in my head, and fill the desperate gaps in my music collection.

2012, *previously unpublished*

Part 3: Music (in Context)

I've always been deeply interested in writing about music within the context of our lives (that is, how it accompanied, balmed, inspired and informed all the different stages of life). Likewise, I consistently write about music and memory; music and the larger story of our culture and our republic; and a life spent listening to music and obsessed with music and utterly consumed by music…

…and what it all meant.

And while doing that, or attempting to do it, I've tried to say things that were, well, obvious to me, but may have been contrary to the accepted narrative. Other times, I've attempted to take the reader on a voyage to exciting barely charted lands, or to point out magical caverns within landscapes we thought we knew. That legitimately sounds mighty pretentious, but, honestly, it's the same thing I was doing when I was in 9th grade and had to tell the kids at my lunch table all about this guy who had been in Pink Floyd named Syd Barrett.

So, lunch table friends, some of the pieces in this section cover basic history or, rather, my attempts to shine a flashlight on exciting things I thought others might have missed (i.e., my deep dive on Phil Ochs, or a novel analysis of the birth pangs of punk rock); some of them question the oft-repeated myths and legends of so-called rock and roll history (like my takes on *Woodstock* and *Sandinista!*); some of it is just deep appreciation (my aching peans to R.E.M. or Sinatra); and some of these pieces are just fun (like my attempt to investigate the Grateful Dead).

How R.E.M. Changed Everything

At some point in the last 10 or 15 years, I began to realize that it wasn't just that a significant amount of my generational peers had an enormous affection for R.E.M.; we were, in fact, Generation R.E.M. (an idea I plan to describe in far, far greater detail in a full-length book in the future — but that's literally another story).

One of the first steps in recognizing how utterly vital R.E.M. was to so many of us is to recognize this peculiar concept: R.E.M. was the true pied piper of "us and them-ism" in the landscape of American alternative music culture. The more I looked at the road signs, the more they pointed to that reality.

R.E.M. were the American Sex Pistols.

Um. Okay.

Nostalgia and wishful thinking have caused us to forget that the Sex Pistols were, essentially, a failure in the United States at the time of their initial album release in October 1977. Likewise, the American punk movement in the mid/late-1970s, although it had many adherents and produced some extraordinary music, remained a cult. In the shadow of punk, the American music industry did not press reset; rather, it hit the snooze button.

It was a different story in Great Britain. In 1976 and '77, the Sex Pistols and their compatriots assembled many of the extant elements of outsider music and fashion under a single flag, changing the public face of music and style in one giant leap forward (or backwards, or sideways — in any event, it was a leap). We still feel the reverberations of this seismic event: every day, I see a haircut or jacket or pair of pants that has some root in the '77 shock or hear music touched by the strum and roar of the era.

But there was a delay in the United States. Well into the 1980s, the United States remained, essentially, on the same Farrah/Stevie/Blow-dry Patchouli Hayride it had been on since roughly 1970.

Ask anyone who was there: the early 1980s looked a great deal like the 1970s.

Prior to 1985 (a date I am assigning as the time when R.E.M.'s ubiquity as a Champion Outsider Band reached critical mass, *prior* to mainstreaming), alternative music culture in the United States was a diverse assortment of tribes and subcultures lacking any real or consistent visibility or power in the mainstream music industry. That is to say, despite flares of style and quirk, we were still in Henleyland.

First, let's go back to basics:

To understand rock and pop, you have to understand that it is the sound of America's disenfranchised made mainstream. But there is a powerful secondary element that defines our experience as listeners, consumers and lovers of rock and pop: pop and rock enable outsiders to find their tribe. It also provides a way for people — especially adolescents — to feel different, to feel some frisson of an identity, while still having a pack to travel in.

Now, take that idea and apply it to your own life as a listener, lover and consumer of rock and pop. Consider David Bowie. You discovered him, perhaps, when you were in 9th or 10th grade. Like many adolescents, you felt alone, unloved, never to be kissed; you considered your own body, this rage of pimples and continuous trash-fire of desires, a stranger, an enemy. All around you, people were saying that these were the best years of your life, but you knew this was a fetid lie. It frequently occurred to you that things would never get any better.

For you, maybe it wasn't Bowie. Maybe it was Laura Nyro, or Robert Smith, or Frank-N-Furter, or Dave Gahan, or even Jerry Garcia; but all of these people said the same thing: "Here, friend, is the key to the Kingdom of Outsiders. Welcome."

Teenage vulnerabilities stretching into adulthood: this is who we were in our twenties, and it is precisely this feeling that R.E.M. translated into sound in the 1980s. R.E.M. not only consolidated the college rock revolution that had been bubbling since the late 1970s, but also became its town crier, its totem, its flag and its flag carrier. They spoke for this giant and influential constituency who said, "We are different but user friendly; we are charismatic but full of the quirks of the bullied; we are the bullied, triumphant; we are the army of the charmed disenfranchised; we have taken every insult that has been shouted at us — Hey, faggot! Hey, Devo! Hey, punk rock! Hey, Blondie! — and turned it into pride."

Only the rarest band achieves this: only the rarest band achieves *us*.

Many artists become gods, but how many artists make *us* into gods, empower our flaws, encourage us to wear our vulnerabilities on the outside?

R.E.M.'s sense of charismatic quirk, their distillation of virtually all extant elements of college rock into one charmed package, set the template for much of guitar-based pop for the next 30 years, from Nirvana to Arcade Fire. If you were a guitar-based act that combined charisma with vulnerability, sex appeal with the downcast eyes of the once-bullied, you can trace your lineage back to R.E.M.

True, MTV shifted the industry and the marketing format of pop fundamentally, but it was R.E.M. that reset guitar pop's emotional core, something that MTV took little interest in. It was R.E.M. that hung up a sign saying, "Sensitive Souls, Freaks and Geeks, welcome here." They recognized that there was an outsider army, the heart of the college rock movement, who could be empowered.

Of course, in subsequent years guitar-based bands emerged (and prospered) that had little or no link to R.E.M.'s Vulnerable Revolution — for instance, the Sunset Strip Hair Metal movement almost intentionally contradicted it. However, the more metalish side of the grunge movement — namely Pearl Jam, Stone Temple Pilots, Alice in Chains, Collective Soul — were absolutely defined by their affection for and adoption of R.E.M.-esque traits. It is also arguable that contemporary country music very much takes off where R.E.M.'s arpeggiated mid-Atlantic/mid-South guitar pop ends, though credit for this branch in the musical tree probably ought to go Hootie & the Blowfish and Garth Brooks, both of whom knowingly took R.E.M.-isms into the country mainstream.

R.E.M. were the rock band of our time. They weren't necessarily the best band, or the one we loved most or longest, or even the best-selling, but they altered the landscape immensely. R.E.M. dragged the college rock era into the mass consciousness (where it would stay); they moved us out of the patchouli era and into a future where even the most helium-filled and stadium-filling, sky-reaching rock was sensitive and bookish.

2018, *REAL CLEAR LIFE*

Rock and Roll Welcomes Us to the Kingdom of Outsiders. Admission Is Free.

This is about U2, but not about U2. In fact, very little of it is actually about U2. The inspiration for this piece was a particularly rockist and slogan-filled appearance by U2 on Saturday Night Live. *But then the article became something else, something bigger, something broader — even something softer.*

Very recently, I saw some respectable men in their late fifties prancing around on TV. They were sitting shiva for rock and roll.

I generally give U2 the benefit of the doubt — they've worked hard, they energetically support decent causes and their musical heart is rooted in the post-punk so very, very dear to the briny, cranky and tough artichoke heart of my youth — but here they were on *Saturday Night Live*, shouting into bullhorns and cranking out mediocre versions of early-'90s KROQ grunge riffs and generally sounding like they were doing a hazy imitation of Stone Temple Pilots. Also, in 1998 the International Court at The Hague determined that the Mekons would be the very last band ever allowed to use the words "rock and roll" in the chorus of a song. Look it up.

U2 were posturing themselves as saviors of their genre, because this is what rich old white rockers do. In reality, they are actually saying, "It's already dead and we are the only survivors, so we better bring in some EDM producers, because, you know, that's what the kids like now, and my GOD, we wanna be relevant!" They also spit out a bunch of fuzzy and meaningless slogans (including some mumbling about "Refu-Jesus"), not one of which, I suspect, will lead to a productive dialogue between England and the European Union about how to handle the looming Ireland/Northern Ireland border crisis.

First of all, rock is most certainly not dead. Truly. I think that's an ugly myth created by people who are unable to distinguish *music* from the *music industry*. Music is fireworks, pearly supernovas in migraine fugue rainbow colors that turn a deep blue 10:00 p.m. sky the shade of summertime 4:44 a.m. purple; music pulls oohs and aaaahs unconsciously out of the most cynical; it massages old memories and provides mnemonics for new ones; it screams when it whispers and it whispers when it screams. And rock and roll is something intensely social and deeply personal; it is the sound of America's disenfranchised made electric, and it is the reason you got on that train that took you away from your low, leafy suburb and into the spires of the city; and in that city (and your city could just be a college town, a city is any place of escape and social refuge!) you found friends because of rock and roll: rock and roll made you welcome in the Kingdom of Outsiders. Deep down, a part of you never left that place.

The music industry as we knew it died. Dead. Gone. Buh-bye. But the music did not die. This is the profound mistake so many people make; they have commingled the artform and the economics that sold that artform. But the music industry is an ugly old fireworks shack on a two-lane blacktop on the sun-burnt wrong side of a South Carolina beach town, waiting to be blown over by some September storm, washed out to the marshes. Even if the shack is destroyed, there's still a Fourth of July.

I was exposed, again and again, to magical new music this year, music loaded with the spirit of invention, emotion, energy, rhythm and maximum minimalism that has defined rock and roll for 70 years. In fact, I'd say it was the best year for new music in decades. Yet *Rolling Stone* magazine, ignorant as pigs and arrogant as kings, tried to convince us that the old animal was on life support and being given daily heart massages by a couple of approved elders, like Dave Grohl and U2. It was literally impossible for creaky, farting, desperate old *Rolling Stone* to envision music existing without a music industry.

They forgot the promise made by Saint Ian Hunter that rock and roll's golden age will last as long as "the children feel the need to laugh and cry." True, that is corny as sweet shit, but it works: rock and roll is a feeling, a social network. It transcends business. It most certainly does not need Bono leaning over the gurney, going "Hand me the paddles! I am the only one who can save the patient!"

Say it again: the music business died, *not* the music. It's very, very possible that what may emerge is not a new commercial model but something that involves maximizing the power of ubiquity, plurality and availability. Think: If everyone can have something instantly and for free, then you have to figure out a way to make that work. Take that as a given, a starting point, and its very availability should be a sign post or map to empowerment.

I think rock and roll is so beautiful (and, by the way, I use the phrase "rock and roll" to encompass the sounds of all the sons and daughters of Storyville, from Gene Vincent to Biz Markie, the Collins Kids to Hawkwind, and so very many more), so soul reinforcing, so healthy, so necessary, that it *should be* given away. I mean, if music is to ever have any true power for activism, if it is to lead a revolution, if it is to achieve an energy that overwhelms its devaluation as an asset, it must conjure a way to be more powerful than its lack of economic value.

It can do this any number of ways: by truly meaning something; by being fearless in its advocacy; and by being so adamant in its outsider spirit that it becomes a necessary accessory of the essential tribalism of youth.

Necessity will be the mother of the new model, so make it freaking necessary. To stretch this concept to its natural conclusion, the Bible is usually given away for free, and that hasn't diminished the power of The Word.

It is possible to attempt to take advantage of the economic catastrophe that robbed the music industry of the usual way it had done business for 70 or 80 years. Start again. Steal this music, steal this revolution, steal this insane, empowering ability rock and roll has to inspire teenagers at exactly the moment they need to be inspired, when they socially and psychologically need to separate from the adults and create tribes with their peers.

Teenagers want to feel special, but not *that* special; they want to rebel but not be lonesome. I know of literally no better device that enables this than rock and roll. The absolute brilliant beauty of rock and roll is that it can allow a listener to feel special, different and set apart from the status quo while at the same time supplying a simple means by which they can find a peer group. I am someone special, but not so special that I don't want friends. Will you be special with me?

Remember how much junior high *sucked*? Remember how much you needed rock and roll? Remember how you wore *that* T-shirt to school, just *hoping* it would help you make a friend?

Teenagers fiercely need to find the beacons that bring us home, bring us to our tribes and guide us to the Kingdom of Outsiders. It is so difficult to do this these days — your parents like the same music you do, and even the most obscure cultural memes can be accessed with little or no effort, so how do you determine what's necessary? Therefore, the people who believe in rock and roll need to create something that *must* be heard, that is a necessary catalyst to *that moment*, just as childhood is breaking into the awful maze of puberty, when we most need to feel separate from the status quo — yet embraced by a tribe.

And we need it to be given away for free. We need rock and roll to be like the army or like a smudge of Banksy graffiti. It needs to be free, obnoxious and everywhere. It needs to offend and create tribes and be a call to arms and it needs to take advantage of the plurality of the current media and web environment.

Rock and roll gives teenagers *genuine* social power and the *illusion* of cultural power when they absolutely need it the most. This is the foremost irony of teenage life: we want to be different, yet we want some friends to be different with.

I never thought I'd miss MTV (and I am talking, very specifically, about the old MTV, which ran a steady stream of rock videos, each and every one inviting some kind of opinion or judgment). MTV's playlist was an easy target for derision. There were many times when it felt like an ugly weapon of the mainstream, encroaching on and insulting my more exotic punk rock, art rock and college rock tastes. But MTV deeply understood the equation I outlined above: here's some loud and/or sexy and/or strange stuff that's going to piss off your parents and draw enough lines in the sand to create the tribalism that is absolutely essential to adolescent life.

MTV (again, we are talking about 1980s MTV) understood that teenagers needed names they could chant and T-shirts they could wear around a campfire in order to create tribal identity. And I fear that this vital element is one of the things largely absent from today's pop culture: the clear-cut heroes and villains. Where are the totems we dance around, so that in a decade or two (or three), young people can feel the way we did when we *found* Bowie and Bowie *invented* us? I really want you to consider this: think of how the entire arc of your life was changed because of the way you once loved a pop star. Pimply faced and bursting with fuzz and hormones, you stood by their totem and found friends and lovers and direction. You found the table you sat at in the lunchroom by the west-facing window that looked out at the teacher's parking lot. You may have even found a college, and that open door you walked through on the floor of your dorm, that open door that *changed everything*, wasn't that, in some real way, shaped by a decision you made to align with a certain musical tribe?

Find heroes. Find Che, Allen Ginsberg, Elvis, William Grant Still, Patti Smith, Woody Guthrie, Samuel Delany and so many wild-eyed children of these United States and get it to the people who need it: teenagers looking for a way out of the status quo and into a tribe.

Remember: Every single time we wrote a band name on the back of a notebook, we were saying, *NOTICE ME. FIND ME.*

I address this to anyone who thinks rock and roll, or the spirit of rock, is dead. It's easier to find something if it's free. Now, go say something important, loud, offensive, passionate, something that has to be said or has to be heard; say something so good that you want to give it away.

2017, *REAL CLEAR LIFE*

Phil Ochs on A&M: Lost in America 1967–1970

I have often said that Phil Ochs is "the" artist of my life. No artist has stayed with me longer. I fell in his thrall when I was barely bar mitzvah age, and I have stayed fascinated, enchanted and obsessed with him ever since.

I have always favored the five albums Ochs made for A&M between 1967 and 1970; at some point, I recognized these had to be seen as a single coherent piece of work.

In the second half of the '60s, many artists attempted to make albums that addressed the state of America. These sought to combine the creative and technical ambitions of, say, *Pet Sounds* or *Sgt. Pepper's* while being conceptually fueled by the remarkable social and political tumult of the era and include *The American Metaphysical Circus* by the amazing Joe Byrd and the Field Hippies; *Kick Out the Jams* by the MC5; the Beach Boys' *SMiLE* (even if it wasn't released at the time, it is an extraordinary attempt to capture a musical and social era in transition); Jefferson Airplane's *Volunteers*; and Van Dyke Parks' *Song Cycle*. I'm sure there are many others we could add to that inventory.

But there's another major work that's almost always left off this list. In fact, it's not one record, but a series of albums that can be viewed as one coherent piece. Between 1967 and 1970, Phil Ochs recorded five albums for the A&M label. From the first in this series (*Pleasures of the Harbor*, 1967) to the final one (*Gunfight at Carnegie Hall*, recorded in 1970 but released in 1974), Ochs tells an astonishingly complete story: a deeply sensitive, articulate observer of America goes from youthful curiosity and optimism to despair, then denial and finally a vision of a new solution. These stages are accompanied by radically varying musical settings that underline the evolution, stasis and de-evolution of the composer.

Ochs moved to A&M after making three "folk" albums for Elektra between 1964 and '66. Although essential, these Elektra albums are not our concern here. Ochs' first two A&M albums, *Pleasures of the Harbor* and *Tape From California* (1968), tell the first stage of the story: a growing artist and hyper-aware American investigates his creative, social and geopolitical world with curiosity and optimism.

As he stepped away from pure acoustic folk, Ochs opted for a persuasive and rich Los Angeles sound (as opposed to the blustery, blue-snarl garage rock of Dylan, the amped-up jug band honk of the Lovin' Spoonful or the ecstatic Beatlisms of the Byrds). It's the sound of an optimistic and engaged artist discovering new territory and new colors for his paintbox.

Amidst some of Ochs' most superficial observational material, *Pleasures* features three extraordinary pieces. On "I've Had Her," the artist sees himself as he once was, at his glittering best and, recognizing there's nothing at the core, opts for suicide. It's strangely out of place on this collection, but makes sense when we see the A&M albums as one piece; It's a dark harbinger of the deeply despondent landscape on 1969's *Rehearsals for Retirement* and reveals that this theme of despair was always within him. The title cut, "Pleasures of the Harbor," is one of Ochs' most gorgeous songs, a beautiful evocation of a soul searching for a port. It would have sounded perfect on Scott Walker's *Scott* or *Scott 2* (both of which have textural and textual similarities to these first two A&M records). The album ends with Ochs' masterpiece, "Crucifixion." Against a musical setting (created by Joe Byrd) that is lush and minimal, electronic and organic, Ochs explains how the (first) Kennedy assassination was turned into media spectator sport and the source of gossip and *schadenfreude.*

Tape From California is witty, investigative, even optimistic. The singer is setting out to new shores musically, geographically and lyrically; he still thinks Vietnam can be resolved with adamancy and poetry, but there is foreboding of failure. "When in Rome" is the masterpiece here, a drop of darkness amidst Ochs' "lightest" record; in just over 13 minutes, it details the fear that there may be grave disappointment at the end of the '60s dream. Like "I've Had Her" on *Pleasures*, this foreshadowing underlines the peculiar and beautiful consistency of this five-album run.

The key album in the series is 1969's *Rehearsals for Retirement*. It reveals the second act of the drama: despair and disillusionment.

Rehearsals for Retirement was created in the shadow of the riots at the 1968 Democratic convention (Ochs was a participant), the Chicago 8 conspiracy trials (Ochs was called as a witness) and the election of the much-despised Richard Nixon. Every moment of the album is shaped and shaded by these events. This brilliant, affecting album, probably Ochs' best in any objective sense, is a snapshot of the precise moment this unconventional patriot has his heart broken. Virtually every song chronicles how the anger and optimism of the anti-war movement ended with broken bodies and cynicism; after a long and often achingly gorgeous catalog of hope turning into hopelessness (among other things, *Rehearsals for Retirement* is Ochs' most effectively poetic album), he ends the record with a couplet of dark resignation.

Even though he would live another seven years, *Rehearsals for Retirement* is the closest Ochs would ever come to writing a musical suicide note (excepting the extraordinary set of songs cataloguing his mental illness and depression he composed in the year and a half before his death, which exist only in primitive home recordings).

The third stage of the arc follows: retreat, denial and a desire, tinted with melancholy, to return to a time before all the disappointments were imaginable.

Greatest Hits is not a greatest hits album; the title isn't ironic, Ochs is alluding to the greatest hits of his *life*, the highlights of his nostalgic memory. After the disillusionment detailed on *Rehearsals for Retirement*, the defeated Ochs looks backwards to a time of presumed innocence before the battles were fought and lost; the very first line of the album is "I want a one-way ticket home," and virtually the entire collection describes a more innocent time, with occasional lapses into deeply moving self-pity where the singer mourns the cost of battle. He sings of Elvis, cars, James Dean, his own childhood and the grim remains of his fame. Indeed, "Chords of Fame" — one of the album's five country-rock numbers — is one of Ochs' greatest songs; it delineates the fall into dissolution and drunkenness of a singer much like himself (Ochs' recording of the song is disturbingly upbeat, which was corrected in superior covers by Melanie and Marianne Faithfull).

The fifth album in the arc is both the strangest and the most revealing. *Gunfight at Carnegie Hall*, a partial documentation of two live performances (in a single evening) at the legendary venue on March 27, 1970, displays a revisionism that offers hope for a new solution. Ostensibly a perverse and nearly career-killing exercise in (literally) putting on Elvis Presley's gold lamé suit and singing oldies, in reality Ochs is proposing a new kind of rock star who (in his own words) is half Elvis and half Che, a revolutionary who accesses the most primitive and feral spirits of rock to advocate and accomplish his means. Ochs is, of course, brilliantly and presciently anticipating punk rock, at least in its most idealized and politicized form.

I have virtually no doubt Ochs would have felt at home with punk rock, and early associations with both Jim Carroll and Patti Smith seem to underline this. (Curiously, Ochs appears to have deliberately edited/tweaked the album to give a more negative impression of the audience reaction and also to emphasize the oldies that were, in reality, only a relatively small part of the full set. The album includes only four of the 16 original songs he performed, yet it includes five of the seven covers. Most accounts of the two Carnegie Hall performances that were taped for the live album state that, in general, his performance was significantly better received than the album indicates.)

And thus ends Phil Ochs' contemporary recording career. He never attempted another full-length studio album after *Gunfight*, and he suicided in April 1976.

The rise and fall of Phil Ochs (and his descent into a strange kind of shabby madness that in many ways echoed the arc of his A&M albums) is detailed in many other places; but he left us with an extraordinary quintet of albums that say more about the state of our democracy at the end of the 1960s than the work of any other recording artist. Ochs' A&M output represents a complex, sometimes painful, continuous story that should be placed alongside the very greatest concept albums in American history. Recognition is long overdue.

2015, *THE NEW YORK OBSERVER*

Sinatra's Master Class and the Bleak Genius of *Watertown*

When a vocalist steps on stage, this is the least and the most we can expect of them: they should sing each song as if every word, every syllable, was a story coming straight from their heart to yours; they should sing each song as if it had never existed before that day, that moment. Each song should be an ecstatic conversation between artist and listener.

Frank Sinatra was almost 76 years old when I saw him at Nassau Coliseum on November 5th, 1991. On that evening, he sang as if every hiccup of the heart and every twist of fate in the songs he sang were occurring to him for the very first time. He sang as if his career, as if everything we would ever think about him, depended on what we would see (and see him feel) this evening. I had seen other artists perform like this — I have watched everyone from Axl Rose to Paul Weller play sets where they seemingly wanted to convince everyone watching that the seal of their heart had opened up at that very moment, only for them. But here was Sinatra, one of the most famous men of his century, a man with so little to prove that it seemed like a miracle that he was even standing in front of me performing as if there was nothing as important as the words he had to sing in that room on that night. That evening set a standard for every live performance I would ever see again.

Although I have enormous affection for Sinatra's recordings and a deep fascination with the shadow he cast against the backdrop of his time, on that evening in 1991 nothing else mattered but the miracle of emotion, intention and communication he displayed. It was a master class in the most important thing a musician should know:

whether you are the most famous artist on Earth performing in an arena or a teenager playing fifth on the bill at some DIY hardcore show in a crappy part of town, the majority of people watching you have never seen you before. You must play your set as if this is the one and only chance you will ever get to make the listener a fan for life. You must convince that listener that they should be a partner in your dream. You have one chance. You will very, very likely never have that chance again.

Sinatra played that night as if it was his one chance.

On Frank Sinatra's hundredth birthday, I also want to celebrate one of his most remarkable albums. *Watertown* (1970) is virtually the definition of "little-known concept album." It was one of Sinatra's poorest-sellers — possibly *the* poorest-selling Sinatra studio album — and, until very recently, had been long out of print. Considering that it contains no trademark Sinatra songs and is about as cheerful as watching a group of children in a cancer ward do a performance of *Requiem for a Dream, Watertown*'s obscurity probably isn't that surprising.

It made some sense that Sinatra would attempt a story-driven concept album, considering he had helped pioneer the thematic concept LP in the 1950s.

But on *Watertown* Sinatra did something truly risky: he told an entire album-length story from the point of view of a character who was most definitely not Frank Sinatra.

Even in his darkest moments (on, say, *In the Wee Small Hours)*, the listener is damn aware that Sinatra is still, well, Sinatra. The scotch in the glass that reflects his tears is still 18 years old, the Marantz audio system he had installed in his lonely hotel suite is still playing *Kind of Blue,* and in his right front pants pocket he still absentmindedly fingers a $500 chip from the Desert Inn. We know that, for all his mourning, the doorbell will shortly ring and Tura Satana will be standing there wearing a fox fur with nothing underneath, mumbling the words "Vic Mature sent me to cheer you up."

But on the extraordinary *Watertown,* Frank Sinatra plays the role of a middle-aged working stiff who lives, loves and loses far, far away from the Big City Lights, in a slightly on-its-heels heartland town. The concept of *Watertown* is relatively simple. A woman leaves. Kids are involved. Spoiler alert: There's no happy ending. To quote Wikipedia at its most effectively dry, "...tracks 1-5 tell the story of the main character's disbelief in his wife leaving ... tracks 6-10 tell of the main character's desperation."

And there you have it. Sitting somewhere between Lou Reed's *Berlin* and Bruce Springsteen's *Nebraska, Watertown* details an ordinary life split apart and the ordinary extraordinary pain of trying to go on. The mood of the protagonist (he sounds like Sinatra, but why is he worrying about getting promoted and making small talk with the old guy who waters his lawn?) fluctuates between desperation, disappointment, optimism, memories cloaked in morbid, bittersweet tones and resolution; mostly, he convinces us that he has lost his only chance at love, his only shot at holding his family together, the only bright spot in his dull existence. The deeply dramatic, slow-moving songs seem to belong in a world Scott Walker, Gavin Friday or even Elliot Smith should live in, not the brash glamor we associate with the Sinatra brand.

Watertown features one of Sinatra's greatest recordings, "Michael and Peter." In the song, Sinatra considers the two children of the now-split couple, and he details how each does and doesn't resemble their parents. He uses this as a starting point to describe how normal life goes on (and doesn't go on) without his paramour, while repeating an increasingly desperate couplet about how the children are growing. In mood and style, "Michael and Peter" reminds me of another of Sinatra's greatest moments — his recording of Rodger & Hammerstein's "Soliloquy" from *Carousel.*

Although *Watertown* is occasionally rousing, these moments are deliberate red herrings, reflecting the many swings in mood and circumstance of someone who has lost his one true love. Peculiarly, the current reissue omits the album's epilogue, "Lady Day," the only track where the protagonist steps outside his self-abnegation long enough to recognize that the one who left may have had dreams bigger than him and Watertown. Instead, the album now ends with the profoundly depressing "The Train," where the excited narrator, sounding truly upbeat for the first time in 35 minutes, waits at the station for his returning love, who never comes. At this point, we want to say to Sinatra, "I'll just leave you with this full bottle of Valium and a glass of Diet Dr. Pepper. I'm going to Friendly's. I'll make sure your sister takes good care of the kids."

(Some *Watertown* scholars have suggested that the album is about a spouse who has died. It's certainly possible — and that idea fits the album's sleepy melancholy — but I think it's more likely that the wife has just left for greener pastures.)

The album was produced by Bob Gaudio, the mastermind behind the Four Seasons, and composed by Gaudio and Jake Holmes (who is, perhaps, most famous for having written the song "Dazed and Confused" before Jimmy Page claimed to have). For the most part, Gaudio avoids the abstract indulgences of *The Genuine Imitation Life Gazette*, the remarkable concept album he had produced the year before for the Four Seasons. Whereas *Life Gazette* seems to be weighed down by its almost Goliathan pretensions (it sounds like Van Dyke Parks and Joe Byrd got together to record the Moody Blues' *Days of Future Passed* with Morton Feldman looking over their shoulders), *Watertown* is mostly taut and concise, offering the breadth and darkness of *Life Gazette* but without its nearly stupefying pretension.

If you listened to *Wee Small Hours* while you were in your twenties or thirties, you may have thought, "This is a great account of loss, but he shall love again." *Watertown*, on the other hand, delivers the devastatingly more realistic message that life, age and class may conspire that we will never again love or dream as we once did.

On the other hand, we will always have moments like November 5th, 1991: moments when an artist, regardless of age or the extraordinary silk-lined swaddling of profound fame and success, displays the ability to identify with a song or a lyric as if it was still a wound or a ribbon on their heart and communicate that feeling to an audience, as if it was their sacred duty. This is the amazing grace of live music: give me something tonight that will brand my memory, an evening where I believed both in your truth and the joy you took in imprinting that truth on a room full of strangers. I've seen Dylan do that, Patti Smith do it, Lux Interior and Joe Strummer do it, and on 11/5/91, it was my enormous great fortune to see Sinatra do it.

2015, *THE NEW YORK OBSERVER*

Tusk vs. *Sandinista!*

The nascence of this fun yet, uh, terribly serious piece was pretty straightforward. For 35 years (at the time of this writing), I'd been hearing people go on and on and on and on about what a monumentally wonderful album the Clash's Sandinista! *was, and, well … I had disagreed with that for 35 years (and every time I returned to* Sandinista! *my issues with the project were confirmed and underlined). For just as long, I'd been hearing about what an indulgent mess Fleetwood Mac's* Tusk *was, and I knew that wasn't true either.*

Both Sandinista! *and* Tusk *have come to symbolize the height of a certain kind of pre-Radiohead indulgence, so I thought, let's throw out the preconceptions, go deep and compare and contrast!*

The result was one of my more popular and shared pieces.

See, when you accept the accepted wisdom, you make an ass out of u and me. Or something like that. We have ears and hearts and minds and our own bloody history with music, right? So, let's bring that afresh into every experience and smash the myths.

Deep in the heart of every rock musician, from the most credible to the most commercial, there lies someone whining, "*Je suis un artiste!* If only the world knew what a deep, tortured soul I am, and how exotic and eclectic my record collection is!"

The more practical of these musicians merely pepper their catalog with maudlin and heartfelt ballads. Let's call this the Bon Jovi method: "Perhaps you will forgive that 'Slippery When Wet' stuff if I sing another song that is the musical equivalent of the page in the yearbook dedicated to that 11th grader who died." Other artists make severe left or right turns and produce albums dripping with uncharacteristic drama and musical complication; here I direct you to *Music From 'The Elder'* by KISS, a histrionic, orchestra-laden and incomprehensible concept album from 1981 that very nearly ended KISS's career. (It's actually a pretty good record, by the way, and features three songs co-written by Lou Reed and members of the band.)

Pop/rock history is absolutely strewn with these artifacts, from *Pet Sounds* to Bad Religion's *Into the Unknown* (a fascinating pop/prog exercise from 1983 so offensive to the group's fans that it was excised from their catalog). In between these extremes, there's Springsteen's bold and courageous *Nebraska,* McCartney's remarkable Firemen albums, Neil Young's fascinating genre exercises (like *Trans, Everybody's Rockin'* and *Arc)*, the Beastie Boys' game-changing *Paul's Boutique* and, of course, the great daddy of all of these sorts of records, Reed's *Metal Machine Music.* There are also entire careers that are built on thwarting expectations, e.g., Scott Walker, Beck, Bowie and Prince.

In the fall of 1979, Fleetwood Mac, a wildly popular and influential band at the peak of their visibility and commercial prowess, released a much-anticipated double album that was interpreted by fans and media as radical, even experimental. Almost exactly a year later, the Clash, a wildly popular and influential band at the peak of their visibility and credibility, released a much-anticipated triple album that was interpreted by fans and media as radical, even experimental.

Fleetwood Mac's *Tusk* is lean, effective and almost completely without waste or filler. It showcases a great band at their prime. Alternately precise and luxurious, *Tusk* is one of the most underrated albums of the era.

It is the anti-*Sandinista!*

Sandinista! is a sprawling mess, resembling some kind of well-meaning dish that combines far too many undercooked and overthought ingredients ("I'm not sure yet if I'm making a soup, a stew or a salad, but maybe we should we throw some cardamom and fenugreek in there!"). *Sandinista!* is like a perfect storm of mistakes, and it's one of the most confounding and overrated albums of all time.

Respectfully, I "get" what the Clash were going for on *Sandinista!*: they wanted to present a travelogue of the sound of the disenfranchised classes of Jamaica, London and New York City. But it appears that no one was running the show or making sure takes were satisfactory; seemingly, nobody cared if overdubs made any sense or if the mixes were coherent; it certainly sounds like no one was insisting that a song be fully composed before the tape was rolling.

For 36 years, *Sandinista!* has been defined not by its content but by the way it has been interpreted by an audience desperately eager to see genius where there was only confusion.

Sandinista! is a prime — perhaps *the* prime — example of what happens when a well-known artist does something so contrarian and obscure that it gets mistaken for greatness; let's call this The Radiohead Effect. "This is so effed up, it *must* be good!" says the listener, who may also be the type of person who has spent far too much of his or her life listening to live recordings of "Dark Star," owns a copy of Elvis Costello's *The Juliet Letters* and thinks liking Primus makes them really, really weird, *maaan*. Listen, pally, you want weird *and* good? Sit down with all four CDs of Tony Conrad's *Early Minimalism Volume One* and *then* talk to me about your uncle who taught you all about Captain Beefheart and Talking Heads.

The standard line about *Sandinista!* is that there's an album worth of good stuff here. Well, that's not quite true. There may, indeed, be an album's worth of good *material*, but barely an EP's worth of good *recordings*.

Only a year earlier, the Clash had released one of the greatest albums ever made. On *London Calling*, the Clash also deviated from expectations; they crafted a near-perfect double album that accessed influences from all over the world, from all over their heart, from all over the 20th century. *London Calling* is an album about the conflicting public and private faces of the West, referencing the music that had touched the Clash and made them the band they had become, from Woody Guthrie to Mott the Hoople to Jacob Miller to Lonnie Donegan.

The big difference, as far as I can tell, is that on *London Calling,* someone was in charge (specifically producer Guy Stevens), and the Clash circa 1979 were a band seeking a form of perfection; the band that made *Sandinista!* were, I believe, deliberately seeking a scattershot account of the 88 different types of music in their heads.

However, I don't think they anticipated the desultory effect an undisciplined writing, recording and mixing process would have on the finished product.

I'll point out some specifics. In no particular order: "Junco Partner" is one of the more coherent recordings on the collection, but why didn't someone ask violinist Tymon Dogg to tune up? It's precisely this sort of problem — *stop the tape and tune the freaking violin* — that consistently plagues *Sandinista!* "Rebel Waltz" is painfully close to being a great song, but it's about four passes away from a decent mix. Again, a track like this — which, if it had been more thoughtfully arranged and mixed, would have fit in well on *London Calling* — underlines why *Sandinista!* is such a troublesome album. "The Sound of the Sinners" also could have been a helluva song if it had been produced or mixed by someone who wasn't really, really high; and there's *almost* something to "Ivan Meets G.I. Joe," except, well, it's dumb, and they made the standard stoner mistake of not being able to distinguish between the sound effects and the music (the video game sounds are mixed as high as anything else in the track).

Let's keep going! "Look Here," like many of the album's worst tracks, is an idea, not a song — "We'll try to do a jazzy, swingy, kind of thing, um, I mean, let's not spend too much time on it, and, uh, I have one melody line I can repeat a lot, and if it doesn't sound quite right, we can just overdub some more stuff on it, and I think it will be, like, jazzy!" "Up in Heaven" is a solid riff and a fairly decent verse and … nothing else. Nada. No one bothered to write anything more. "Something About England" is a good song, but it sounds like it was mixed by someone who just drank a lot of Benadryl and Baileys and chases shiny objects without any sense whatsoever of an "overall" coherent mix — "Oh, that's a cool guitar part! Let's turn that up! Wow, I like the sound of that piano, let's put that fader up for a while!"

And on and on.

Sandinista! is mortally flawed on every level, except for one: it's not pretentious, and its fascination with various urban music styles is sincere. In this sense — the way in which it is genuine, and simultaneously under-and-overthought — *Sandinista!* is reminiscent of Bob Dylan's *Self Portrait*. But Dylan did something pretty brilliant on *Self*

Portrait: he kept things small, and the performances and arrangements are on the minimalist side, as opposed to *Sandinista!*'s universal tendency to throw more and more crap into the gumbo.

Now, let's extract a pretty solid EP from the album's entire 144 (!) minutes:

"Magnificent 7" is a pioneering song with real style and swagger, effectively recorded; "The Call Up" is dynamic and strange, with a compelling lyric; and "Hitsville UK," although drenched in the weed-friendly reverb haze that surrounds virtually all of *Sandinista!*'s non-mixes, is a very solid song, even if it smells a bit like a second-rate Jam composition. *Sandinista!* does have three unapologetically great tracks — "Somebody Got Murdered," "Police on My Back" and "Lose This Skin" (though "The Call Up" comes preciously close) — but I suspect it is no accident that two of them were not written by the Clash. "Police on My Back" is a first-rate cover of an even better recording by the vastly underrated Equals, a terrific and pioneering mod/bluebeat band from the 1960s led by Eddy Grant; "Lose This Skin" was written (and sung) by violinist Tymon Dogg.

There's more: The thing that makes *Sandinista!* not just a curious, well-meaning face-plant but also a true catastrophe are the dub tracks. The half-dozen-plus dub tracks on the album are sorry and confused examples of the genre. Generally, dub is the act of taking away elements, and affecting those that remain, to create a psychotronic, mesmerizing, hypnowoofer effect. The dub tracks here have more to do with "Revolution No. 9" or a bad sophomore year music concrète project. Whereas I can concede that most of *Sandinista!* is well-intended, the dub tracks are just a disaster, a sign of what a misdirected and ill-conceived mess this whole thing is.

Now … *Tusk.*

I'll be honest. You can't even compare these two albums. From hushed, flickering ballads to constricted, tightly wound pop built out of the closely arranged Legos of genius, *Tusk* is a masterpiece, or very goddamn close to one. It must be one of the best — and most absolutely rewarding and consistent — double studio albums ever made, and it has dated exceedingly well. To rediscover *Tusk* (or to investigate it for the first time!) is like stumbling upon a lost masterpiece by the Go-Betweens, XTC, Nick Lowe, Kimberly Rew, the dBs or any other artists from the early 1980s who were trying to create a highly conceptualized yet non-indulgent uber-pop resonant with emotion and depth.

On *Tusk,* Fleetwood Mac distill the very best of their past (the uncluttered intensity of the Peter Green era, the gorgeous, sad restraint of the Danny Kirwan years and the harmony-laden FM glow of *Rumours* and *Fleetwood Mac*) into one package and present it in a detailed, fastidious fashion; every sighing and soaring note and iridescent guitar is placed with nearly mathematical intent. The result is an album that easily equals the best credible pop of the era.

Contrary to the hype that usually accompanies *Tusk*, this isn't just Lindsey Buckingham's album; in fact, if you remove his tracks, you're still left with a terrific record. Christine McVie's exquisite "Brown Eyes" is a cool, shimmering, dusk-purple spray of hooded-eyed sadness; the bass-chord driven "Never Make Me Cry" is such a great example of late-night low-volume electric melancholy that it is reminiscent of Mazzy Star or Malcolm Burn-era Chris Whitley (and despite Lindsey's more deliberate efforts, it might be the most successfully arty track on the album).

As for Buckingham's much noted achievements on *Tusk*, they are artful and meticulous, and — like the work of Mitch Easter-era R.E.M. — endlessly fascinating, with new production quirks and onionskin-like overdubs revealing themselves on every new listen. When you combine Buckingham's precisely tweaked pop gifts with McVie and Nick's luxurious, poignant sigh-pop, and *then* paint the whole megillah in the intimate tones that *Tusk* is bravely produced in, the result is rare magic. I think the album most comparable to *Tusk* is the Beach Boys' *Smiley Smile*, which also balanced Brunelleschi-like brilliance with Gropius-like simplicity, creating a pastoral yet ecstatic album. (Two architects mentioned in one sentence! I knew those NYU classes in urban design would pay off!)

I can't say enough about *Tusk,* but it's really stunning how this emotional yet disciplined album, so richly composed and edited and mixed to masterpiece-like effect, is virtually the opposite of *Sandinista!* Let's put it this way: *Sandinista!* absolutely insists you call it brilliant, because if you refuse to, you'll see what a true piece of crap it is. At some point in 11th grade, some friend of yours — possibly someone you wanted to hook up with — showed you one of their poems. It was pretentious nonsense full of typos and combined the worst aspects of Kahlil Gibran, Richard Brautigan and Kurt Vonnegut. But you had so very, very much invested in your friendship with this person that not only did you say you liked it, you actually convinced yourself that you did, that it was brilliant. Generationally, we had so much invested in believing the Clash were The Only Band That Matters (especially after the Everest-like triumph of *London Calling)* and so much invested in believing that they were *our* Beatles, *our* Stones that we not only tolerated the babbling, incomplete and indecipherable nonsense that was *Sandinista!,* we actually convinced ourselves that it was as good as the band thought it was when they were really high and recording it.

I shall end this anecdotally. Two anecdotes, actually.

One day in 1981, in my role as teenage journalist and correspondent for the UK music weekly *Sounds*, I found myself talking to Christine McVie. I told her I had heard that the Clash wanted to make sure that their new triple album, *Sandinista!,* would sell in stores for a lower price than Fleetwood Mac's *Tusk.* McVie arched an eyebrow and said, "Ah … the Clash … I believe that's one of those bands Lindsey likes."

One day in 1981, in my role as an NYU student who made virtually daily pilgrimages to a record store on St. Marks Place called Sounds, I ran into Joe Strummer. He was walking on the north side of Eighth Street between University and Broadway. He was holding a small brown paper bag full of cherries. Being a strident but generally amiable 18-year-old asshole, I felt compelled to tell him all the things I didn't like about his latest album, *Sandinista!* I also told him how very much I liked the just-released album from his pre-Clash band, the 101ers.

Strummer listened politely, never losing eye contact. When he saw that I was done, he smiled and said, "Want a cherry?"

2016, *THE NEW YORK OBSERVER*

What Was the First Punk Rock Record?

A lot of people write about punk rock. A lot, a lot.

A lot.

I've always been a little stunned by the degree people get it, well, wrong, and get it wrong again and again and again. And that's not just a subjective opinion.

For something that was — and is — such a significant chapter in the story of recent and current Western music, fashion and culture, it always seemed to me that actual, genuine, deep and accurate scholarship about punk rock is profoundly, sorely lacking. Again and again, people just repeat the same myths about punk rock. It's like they write about punk rock without actually doing the work or connecting any dots.

This piece was a small effort to try to set the record straight about one important aspect of the punk rock story in a (presumably) legitimately analytical way. I had read a lot of fucking nonsense about what was the "first" punk rock record; I wanted to actually reason that crucial question out. I decided the way to determine, truly, what was the first punk rock record was to find the hand that lit the firecracker.

Oh, the date of the original publication of this piece is significant: it was the 40th anniversary of 1976, so a lot of people were waving around a lot of ridiculous ideas about the origin of punk rock.

This year, we're going to hear a fair amount of noise about 2016 being the 40th anniversary of punk. A lot of it will be bullshit, and no doubt there will be a plethora of quotes from Dave Grohl. There's also an HBO series that will celebrate the birth pangs of the genre, filled with extras whose haircuts do not remotely resemble anything actually from the era (*Vinyl* even features crowd surfing, a phenomenon that did not emerge for at least another half a decade).

Regardless, punk rock is a goddamn fascinating and important subject that deserves the kind of joyous but critical examination that it's almost never received.

There's a large body of literature regarding the "first" rock and roll song. You can also find a lot of writing about the "first" rap song. But I don't think I've ever seen an even marginally thoughtful piece about the first punk rock song. Most journalists just wave around the first Ramones records, throw in a line or two about the Stooges and the Dolls, and Bob's your uncle.

So, what was the first modern punk rock record? I'm going to take a stab at examining this question as academically as possible.

First of all, let's define our terms. What's punk? Let's put it this way: we all know what punk rock sounds like, and it doesn't sound like "Little Johnny Jewel" or Pezband. True, in the mid-1970s, there was a flourishing of exciting and progressive music that sought to repudiate the indulgences and fripperies of the existing rock landscape; but to accurately address our question, we must separate artists who emerged during the punk era from artists who actually played punk rock. Prior to 1976, artists like Patti Smith and the Residents were making music of almost brutal innovation, but they weren't making modern punk rock. Likewise, acts like Blondie and Television played fresh, engaging, contrarian music that fueled and defined the style and spirit of the punk era, but they didn't play punk rock. (A comparable thing was happening in the UK, where, prior to 1976, bands like Ducks Deluxe and Brinsley Schwarz were clearly swimming against the tide, but they weren't wading in the rivers of punk rock.) You could make a good argument that the beginning of the punk era dates to events that happened in 1972 and '73 in New York City at Club 82, the Mercer Arts Center or CBGB/Hilly's on the Bowery, but these dates won't tell you anything about the first appearance on vinyl of modern punk rock.

Also, in our search for the first modern punk rock record, it's disingenuous to find it in the work of the amazing precursors who recorded in the 1960s and early '70s, like the Velvet Underground,

Sonics, Stooges, Monks and Troggs (not to mention Bo Diddley, Roy Orbison, Johnny Burnette and a pile of other rockabilly primitives). Certainly, these artists made music that was aesthetically and structurally similar to the punk rock that emerged in the mid-1970s; but I am specifically searching for releases that set off a firecracker with immediate impact, and not the elders who lit a match in the darkness.

Towards that end, I am only considering the work of artists who *didn't* release records or have active performing careers in the 1960s or early 1970s and were relatively new when they released the relevant material. This admittedly subjective criteria eliminates *Raw Power* by Iggy and the Stooges, which, in many ways, could be labeled the first modern punk record; but I think the lineage of the Stooges (who had been together for nearly a decade by 1976) places them firmly in the proto-punk category, even if *Raw Power* is a distinctively forward-looking record. The same is true of the original Modern Lovers who, in simplifying the Velvets' template, landed on a sound that was virtually identical to the punk rock that followed half a decade later. If I changed the rules of this search a bit I'd probably name the first Modern Lovers LP as the first true punk rock record.

Finally, not one word below is meant to diminish the extraordinary music and titanic legacy of the Ramones and the Saints, who are without a doubt the Ur-bands of the modern punk rock movement. Although neither group released vinyl until 1976, there is definitive evidence that the Ramones were playing modern punk rock in 1974, and the Saints by the end of 1973; but what I want to do here is delineate the first vinyl release(s) of modern punk.

Traditionally, three records are cited: the first Ramones record (April 1976), the "New Rose" 45 by the Damned (October '76) and the Saints' debut album, *(I'm) Stranded* (September '76). Each of these sounds as fresh today as it did 40 years ago, and each is amongst the greatest records ever made; but none was the first "modern" punk rock record.

So, what are our candidates? I've targeted six records, all but one released prior to 1976. Each could stake a legitimate claim to being the first modern punk rock record.

- "After Eight" by Neu! (from *Neu! 75*, released early 1975)
- "Two Tub Man" by the Dictators (from *The Dictators Go Girl Crazy*, March 1975)
- "Sick on You" by the Hollywood Brats (from *Grown Up Wrong*, recorded 1973, released 1975)
- Eddie and the Hot Rods, *Live at the Marquee* EP (July 1976)
- "She Does It Right" by Dr. Feelgood (from *Down by the Jetty*, January 1975)
- "You Really Got Me," a 45 by the Hammersmith Gorillas (September 1974)

Without any doubt, Neu!'s "After Eight" sounds like a modern punk record. Over thundering, unrelenting drums (think of Rat Scabies imitating Mo Tucker), a savage rhythm guitar spits out a more-or-less continuous three-chord blast, while someone howls like, well, a howler monkey doing an imitation of (the yet to be anointed) Johnny Rotten. We also know that John Lydon, Wire, the Buzzcocks and a pile of other first-gen punk artists were very aware of this track, and therefore there is a genuine connection between the innovative sound of "After Eight" and some of the most prominent early punk acts. However, the fact that this song appears on Neu!'s third album (they had been recording and releasing remarkable and groundbreaking music since 1971) may fiddle a bit with the criteria I've set to answer our question.

Though it could easily be mistaken for a Tubes-esque clod-rock pastiche, there's a striking immediacy, arrogance and aural rage that makes "Two Tub Man" by the Dictators sound like an honest-to-goodness punk rock song. Around the time of the New York band's debut, there were a number of excellent new bands working in a post-Who/post-SAHB/post-Free riff-rock genre that had certain things in common with punk, but was clearly not punk (e.g., Cheap Trick, early AC/DC, even KISS). *Go Girl Crazy* has some scent of that, but on "Two Tub Man" it most definitely sounds like the Dictators have stumbled onto something different, and they knew it. Likewise, the version of "California Sun" on *Go Girl Crazy* dispenses with any niceties and just throws the sunny bitch against the wall and screams at it until it hands over its lunch money; it too, sounds like a punk song, not a proto-punk song.

Although a sloppier version of the Dolls seems highly improbable, that's a good way to describe the magical and mysterious Hollywood Brats. A London-based band with some Norwegian members, the Brats dispensed with the more "difficult" old-school R&B and blues influences of the Dolls; instead, they made a messy copy of the Dolls' most basic and primitive elements. The result is, well, punk rock. Their sole album — recorded in '73 but not released until '75 — is full of ridiculous delights, but (for the sake of this piece) it is most notable for a track called "Sick on You."

A churning, chunky, snotty and primitive blast of arrogance and disgust, howled virtually amelodically and featuring a noisy, buzzing guitar that threatens to burst out of the sides of the vinyl, it is utterly and unmistakably a modern punk rock song (and virtually indistinguishable from the '77-era artists who favored the trashy edge of punk, like the Lurkers, Slaughter and the Dogs and the vastly underrated Boys, who covered "Sick on You," in a version less unhinged than the original). I almost certainly would anoint "Sick on You" as the first modern punk rock record, except for one important fact: its visibility at the time of initial release was relatively small.

Unlike, say, the Feelgoods, Neu! or even the Dictators, I don't necessarily see a direct line between this amazing song and the fires of '76. However, curiously, the Hollywood Brats significantly shaped an entirely different movement: the Brats were a major influence on Hanoi Rocks — at times, the music of the two bands is almost indistinguishable. And since Hanoi Rocks had a fundamental effect on the Los Angeles hair-glam movement — Hanoi Rocks are to hair-glam what the Ramones were to punk — the peculiar legacy of the Brats lived on in a very real and significant way.

On the surface, Eddie and the Hot Rods' *Live at the Marquee* EP should be a standard pub rock sweat'n'amphetamine boogie record, but there's something different about it; they've added speed, slop and overdriven distortion to the pub rock formula, with an emphasis on a bruising rhythm guitar and four-beats to the bar kick drum. In doing so, they've made something that is indisputably a punk record. Although it's the only post-'75 release on this list, it must be cited because of its significant influence on both the musicians and the audience who defined punk rock in 1976.

Whereas there was a certain southwestern laissez-faire to most of the British pub rock bands (the Hot Rods excepted), Dr. Feelgood took a different road entirely: if you visualize the early Stones and (especially) the Pretty Things as a coiled metal spring, the Feelgoods wound that spring virtually to the point of snapping; simultaneously, they removed all traces of late '60s/early '70s whiskey flab from the roadhouse band sound. The Feelgoods bit down on covers and compatible originals with unprecedented speed, economy and an almost desperate desire to get from A to Z as quickly as possible. "She Does It Right" is a dentist-drill burst of ultra-streamlined R&B, and although it has a foot in Hamburg Beatles, it also has a bigger foot in the imminent punk explosion.

Now, what makes the Feelgoods (and *Down by the Jetty*) not just hyperactive but transcendent is the work of guitarist Wilko Johnson. Instead of playing old-school boogie rock with the shortnin' bread slur of Keith Richards or Johnny Thunders, Johnson played with a manic, constantly strumming trebly chop that in its own way is as reductionist as the work of Johnny Ramone or Neu! "She Does it Right," recorded at the end of 1974 and released early in '75, exemplifies the best of the Feelgoods' pioneering sound: a three-chord blurt of mad R&B that careens downhill faster than a fat kid in a shopping cart, and it sounds like someone's teeth chattering while they pee on an electric outlet.

It is especially noteworthy because of its influence: in the first years of British punk, there were essentially only two guitar styles on display — the Ronson/Ralphs/Thunders grwoooooar to be heard in, say, the Sex Pistols or Generation X and Wilko Johnson's electroshock shiver-me-treble, which was faithfully reproduced by the Jam, the Damned, the Vibrators and the Stranglers. (The Clash, uniquely, mixed both: Strummer did Wilko, Jones did Ronno.) Another artist who borrowed hugely from Wilko Johnson was Elvis Costello; he not only replicated Johnson's guitar sound, he borrowed his onstage persona and physical gestures as well.

Speaking of pub bands, there's a relatively little-known oddity from way back in 1974 that sounds and feels like a blast from the future. The Hammersmith Gorillas looked like Blue Cheer dressed as Slade, and for the most part they sounded like Canned Heat on speed playing glitter. But on "You Really Got Me," a 45 they released in 1974, the Gorillas turned the Kinks classic into a hoarse, joyless, feral plod akin to early Motörhead. This sounded nothing like a glitter record and nothing like smiley-faced Britbeat bop (maybe it sounded vaguely like a Slade demo if Slade had switched instruments, turned off one channel of the mix, and let the janitor sing); mostly, it sounded like a punk rock record in a way virtually nothing else released in 1974 does.

This is a very serious contender for first modern punk 45, though its moderate obscurity — and the fact that it doesn't seem to have lit any fires in the way, say, "She Does It Right" did — likely mutes any potential claim it might have to being the first modern punk record. Though, man, does it *sound* like a punk record.

So, where does that leave us?

Although the Hollywood Brats and the Hammersmith Gorillas both made legitimately modern punk records prior to 1976, if one single record could be said to have been punk rock's patient zero, it was "She Does It Right" by Dr. Feelgood. The release of this tightly wound spring of frills-free over-stimulated R&B almost certainly marks the point where existing pub rock, glitter, glam and garage vapors coalesced into the spark of punk rock, and there's a direct line from the appearance of this song to the fires of '76 and '77.

However, we note this: The Feelgoods, who proudly waved the flag of high-energy, sweat an' ale R&B (as championed by the Pretty Things, the early Stones, the Sonics, even the first feral releases of the Kinks and Them), almost certainly would neither have aspired to be a punk band nor identified themselves as such; in fact, in the fierce and charging albums they released for the rest of the 1970s, chock full of R&B covers, they adamantly declared an identity in marked contrast to the first-generation punk acts, virtually all of whom were eager to distance themselves from the influence of black American music and the blues that had been a constant undertone in Britrock up until the punk era. (Noted exceptions — and there were precious few of them — were the Jam and the Clash, though the Clash more regularly sourced Jamaican music.)

I don't think this necessarily changes my basic conclusion — I still believe that more than any 45 prior to "Anarchy in the UK," "New

Rose" or "I'm Stranded," "She Does It Right" was the fuse that lit the Britpunk firecracker in 1976. But it does provide an interesting aside, and perhaps a very slight boost in status for the more purely feral and less American R&B-obliged pub acts like Eddie and the Hot Rods, the Hammersmith Gorillas or even Strummer's 101ers.

2016, *THE NEW YORK OBSERVER*

July 1959, plus or minus 9.75 seconds: When Eddie Cochran Invented the Modern

This is a story about Eddie Cochran.

It is also a story about That Trinity Moment. That crack in progress after which nothing can ever be the same. Those moments when the peeled, scalded eyeball of God fills the sky, summoned by Oppenheimer to save a million and condemn a billion. Those moments when the future is forever changed.

These are Trinity Moments.

I have long loved to search and collate these moments where a remarkable scene change occurs in pop: your Autobahns and Overkills, Hallogallos and Birmingham Bounces, Bo Diddley and You Really Got Me and so forth. But those, of course, are all lies; nothing emerges in and of itself; no dust, no DNA, no atom, no synth throb nor guitar tic nor absence of guitar tic, emerges out of thin air. All form is empty of a separate self. "There is no thingness, no whole without parts, that persists independently from all other things," writes Barry Kerzin, a physician and monk. To put it another way, we do not have "Surfin' Bird" by the Trashmen without "The Bird's the Word" and "Papa-Oom-Mow-Mow" by the Rivingtons. Papa-Oom-Mane-Padme-Hum-Mow-Mow. The apple was always eaten, even when it was a seed; the eaten-ness was inherent to it.

So, Trinity is dependent arising, Trinity always existed, it was present (yet not yet revealed) when Oppenheimer was taunted on the playground, it was present when he burned his first bug with his second magnifying glass, at that moment a sky filled with an unholy fake sun; it just hadn't manifested yet.

I think I have found the moment modern rock and roll — distinct from hillbilly/rockabilly/vaudeville-as-hillbilly/vaudeville-via-shave-an'-a-haircut — was born. I have found the moment when the slap-back snare and combo-jazz lurch of Sam Phillips, Wynonie Harris and the rumble rail-beat of New Orleans became the straight-arrow autobahn jet-age needle gun V1 sputnik chemtrail beat that we associate with, basically, all modern rock, whether it's played by Motörhead or the MC5, the Stones or Stereolab, Manic Street Preachers or the Monks.

And that moment happens about nine and three-quarters seconds into "Somethin' Else" by Eddie Cochran.

After the initial riff (that riff that sounds like a car engine sputtering and spitting and hollering and saying 'L'IL DAVE DAVIES, ARE YOU LISTENING?') and the two bars of stop an' start (which pretty much predict one of the Who's prime musical signatures, that ACCENT/pause/ACCENT/*flourish*), at NINE AND THREE-QUARTERS OF A SECOND INTO THE SONG, the verse on "Somethin' Else" kicks in with drummer Gino Riggio smashing down on the beat like it's London '44 and the snare, the kick and the crash cymbal is a ten-month-old baby he's trying to throw under the bed when he hears the whistle of one of Werner Von Braun's buzzbombs (y'know? That's EXACTLY what it sounds like). But it's it's not just that Riggio slams down on the one beat like he's an ingenue leaping off the Empire State and demolishing a 1947 Chevrolet Fleetmaster (her name was Evelyn McHale, by the way); it's what he does after that really makes this recording *Nude Descending a Staircase.* In support of Cochran's lustful pleas, Riggio heads off down the stretch of ol' 66 from Santa Monica to San Berdoo veering a little too close to the center stripe, not even slowing down to take a nip from the pint bottle of Old Smuggler Scotch rattling against his right pocket, with a very slight puffa-puff in-an'-out which he picked up from hearing the freights run about a third of a mile behind his house when he was a kid back in Glendale (his first-ever memory was lying in a crib just as the sun was rising, a thin, light blue baby blanket tucked under his chin, and the room was full of the pink light of just pre-dawn, and off in the distance he heard the pale staccato of the comb-whistle of the freights, and I guess that stuck with him, right?). But 'cept for that homage to the rail rhythm (it's a wee little "push" on the third beat that you're way familiar with if you're a fan of Slade or Neu!), Riggio's in-your-face kick and crash and snare just sails forward, determined and a little thick, like an arrow on a humid day. As utterly brilliant as Eddie is (and man is he brilliant, if he hadn't died when he was just 21 years young, I am TELLING you the Beatles wouldn't have been necessary), "Somethin' Else" really just HANGS off of the framework and suspension of Riggio's MODERN drums, the first modern rock drums. And there is a direct line from what happens starting at nine and three-quarters seconds of "Somethin' Else" to what the Sonics did, what the Trashmen did, what the Ramones did, what Pixies and Generation X did, even what the early Fabs did, and on and on to everyone who treated rock as its own mad animal, wholly distinct from hillbilly/R&B/electrified vaudeville. It's the moment rock becomes a DISTINCT creature, literally the MOMENT that modern rock begins, July 1959 plus or minus nine and three-quarters seconds.

Now, contrast Riggio's mad-act on "Somethin' Else" (his drumming feels like the time you accidentally got kicked in the teeth on the monkey bars when you were eight, seriously straight in the teeth, the lips were completely missed, just a freaking 3rd grader's Keds straight to the incisors, you still can taste the blood, rubber and gravel) with the drumming of the legendary Earl Palmer, inarguably one of the greatest of all time, on Cochran's "C'mon Everybody." (Man, that was a bus plunge of a sentence.) Palmer — who pretty much literally put the "roll" in rock and roll and somehow was able to translate the classic, rumbling, tumbling, gigantic New Orleans parade beat into the spine of small-combo rock and roll — sits back and BREATHES with the riff on "C'mon Everybody." Palmer refuses to allow Eddie to just square it with the proto-Who/Kinks riff the song is built around. Instead, Palmer's spacious, almost stoned drumming forces it to swing. But there's no such finesse on "Somethin' Else." Riggio just leaves the gate and figures, what the heck, it's a short race and I'll just go all out, Eddie can just hang on.

(From an article about the Boulder Station casino in the January 10, 2000 issue of the *Las Vegas Sun*: "Gino Riggio, 63, is the 'senior ambassador' for Boulder Station. Among his many duties is to help organize the events. Riggio can even be found dancing with the members when he isn't busy doing something else." Curiously, although the article does mention that Riggio drummed with Cochran and Trini Lopez, I suspect that "something else" pun was completely coincidental. Riggio passed in 2020 at age 83, outliving Cochran by 60 years.)

Whatever Riggio is doing on "Somethin' Else" — and I don't know the why, I just know the effect — it *feels* like modern rock and roll is born at that exact moment. Now, I'm not claiming what Riggio and Cochran did was *better* than the past — and honestly, it doesn't get better than "Bo Diddley" (the song that connects West Africa, the satanic plantations and the sooty urban tenement steps with Alan Freed and Heilung), nor does it get any freaking better than the ghostly, captured fog of Elvis's slow version of "Blue Moon" (one of the greatest goddamn recordings of all time, it sounds like Elvis is imagining the first and last breath of his stillborn twin and somehow thinking, "What would that sound like if it was a song?") — it's just that the modern rock we all grew up on, in all its beauty and horror, begins at THAT moment.

I mean, there are other reasons to consider Eddie Cochran the father of modern rock. Cochran may be the first rocker to consistently make electric small combo music that did not have transparently clear roots in hillbilly, R&B or electric vaudeville. Although some of his work does have tendrils in those forms, his most famous work represents something new: it opens the door to the fat, flat riffing and non-swinging, interstate rhythms of modern rock. It is a step into the profoundly modern, sort of like the Seagram Building. Contrast this with Buddy Holly, who by and large whelped up hepped-up vaudeville with a pale Diddley beat and a little Jimmy Rodgers/Hardrock Gunter snarl; most of Holly's songs placed in a different setting could have been sung by Jolson, Dick Haymes or ol' Ukulele Ike (harsh, yeah, but I mean that). He was a fairly straight-ahead B+ level Madison Avenue songwriter who applied an effective, lightweight if primitive Texas swing and hiccup to what he did.

Honestly, if Holly had lived, I believe he would NOT have investigated new corners and dynamics in rock (as some have said); he would have mainstreamed, he would have become Bobby Darin or Slim Whitman or Marty Robbins. No one could mistake "Somethin'

Else" for one of those well-constructed Buddy Holly songs. Chuck Berry, of course he's revolutionary (and his stuff has dated extraordinarily well, better, I would argue, than the stuff it inspired, but that's a different story), but that's because he took Louis Jordan and crunched it into small electric combo rock; sure, the building blocks and context were different, but the architecture belonged to the (near) past.

And Elvis, well, he's Oppenheimer-as-hillbilly, he filled the sky with the power of a thousand suns, but, like, he's still fairly rooted in the hillbilly thing, he just happens to inject it with that messiah charisma that comes around once a century or so (a grotesque simplification, I know, and as an Elvis worshipper I feel bad about that; I merely want to stress that the King worked generally in neo-hillbilly and electric vaudeville forms).

But Cochran is different. He does not write vaudeville songs, and his most extreme work anticipates a future based on clobberhead riffing and dumbangel rhythms with little or NO connection to R&B or hillbilly; I mean, Cochran's work leads directly to the Kinks, the Sonics, the Trashmen, the Troggs, the Who and beyond as none of those other early rockers do. The other rock pioneers pointed the way to an attitude, a volume, a style, even a combo format; but Cochran actually did it, he actually made modern rock.

2022, *THE ROCK AND ROLL GLOBE*

Sha Na Na Was the Most Important Band at *Woodstock* (and I'm Not F*cking Kidding)

I pick on Woodstock *a lot, and for good reason. In this piece, I try to explain why.*

Woodstock is a place where we dump our cultural trash, a frequently employed punctuation mark that is often misused, like the apostrophe and the ellipsis.

Like those other gigantic landmarks from the summer of '69 (the three M's: the Moon Landing, the Manson Murders and the Miracle Mets) we pull *Woodstock* out of the Tupperware every now and then because we think it tells us something *très importante* about who we were, or who we became. I understand why we do this with the Mets and the Moon: for those of us who were very young at the time (I was seven), those events gave us a warped and healthy/unhealthy faith in science and miracles at precisely the time we were surrendering our belief in dinosaurs and Santa Claus. But that Manson thing was a false flag. *Look, hippies are killers, too! So, let's ignore that we are sending all those kids to die in Southeast Asia!* (The same week as the Tate–LaBianca murders, 225 young Americans died in Vietnam. But those horrifying, unnecessary deaths are not nearly as sexy or Tarantino-riffic as the savage huzzahs of the Manson crew.)

Woodstock's ultimate "meaning" is also likely a false flag. First and foremost, I think people were amazed that you could put half a million young people in a muddy field for a few days and they didn't end up dead or killing each other. It's like when you must go to the emergency room and you're out of the house for ten hours and you come home and the dog is still alive, and you're like, *oh shit, it can do that*?

Our amazement about that fact helps us overlook the reality that with the possible exception of a landmark performance by Hendrix, we do not really chatter about *Woodstock* because of the music (like we do when we watch concert films of the *Newport Festivals* or *Monterey Pop*). Instead, we cite *Woodstock* because of this crap idea of *meaning*. We go gobble-gobble about a *vibe*. When I consider *Woodstock* '69, here's what I see: an experience whose myth and significance comes merely from the fact that it existed without undue collapse and that it accomplished existing, and not via any greater depth or consequence. Here's what I don't see: anyone taking the opportunity to engage half a million young people to actually take meaningful political action.

Once again, music was a false flag.

Rather than being a highlight of the 1960s, *Woodstock* was a forecast of the dullard-ism of the 1970s. This is largely because, in the United States at that exact time, rock and roll, like the Alex Keatonesque mammon-seeking rebellious child of hippie parents, was turning its back on everything that had made it brilliant, liberating, hot and hysterical. It was abandoning boogie, space and simplicity; it was convinced it was ever-so *superior* to the rhythm and spirit of plantations, Storyville whoreshacks, Louis Jordan Fish Fry chants, coal-fogged Appalachian hollows and the Juba Diddy Wah'isms of Diddley.

The Woodstock Nation ultimately stood for inaction and complacency. The rather safe idea of Peace & Love was even less threatening to Nixonland than George McGovern (now, fucking George Wallace, that's who Nixon was *really* afraid of). It is absolutely essential that we understand that Peace & Love and the vapors of *Woodstock* did not bring down Richard Nixon: some clumsy burglars, a bizarrely ethical Attorney General and an unnaturally honest Presidential lawyer did.

At *Woodstock*, smirking Arlo Guthrie gleefully reminded the masses that they were far more interested in planes carrying in drugs than planes carrying in caskets. I can find no song that sums up the emptiness of *Woodstock* better than Guthrie's set-opening "Coming Into Los Angeles." The *Woodstock* attendees welcomed, with weakened open arms, all those mewling bands that just wanted them to get high and sit in the mud until the Eagles formed.

We cite the *Woodstock* ideal because we somehow think it poses some solution to our current state of affairs. It doesn't. Figuratively, with our chatter about the *Cats* trailer and Area Freaking 51, we continue to sing along to "Coming Into Los Angeles." [*At the time this was written, in 2019, my GOD everyone was going on and on and on about the* Cats *trailer.*]

Of course, there was some wonderful music at *Woodstock*. I'm not overlooking that. There was Hendrix (who mainstreamed the frenzy and slug-riffing of pre-Fabs Northwest punk rock better than any other artist, even the Raiders); a Feelgoods-anticipating ramalama from Ten Years After; the lazier but still gratifying Bayou boogie of Creedence and Canned Heat; bruising, charismatic and accomplished bursts of multiculturalism from Sly and Santana; the proto-stoner rock snarl of Mountain; and a lesser display by the greatest live band of all time, the Who (Keith Moon gives a particularly sludgy, sleepy, behind the beat performance). But *what did* Woodstock *actually achieve*? It created the myth of peace and love at precisely the time that Nixon was arriving to bring his sordid, creepy flop-sweats into America; it did nothing to prevent Kent State or Attica; and it certainly encouraged the Eagles. It was Sominex and a peace sign when we needed amphetamines and the finger.

However, it also reveals this very powerful idea.

In physics, the observer effect is the theory that the mere observation of a phenomenon inevitably changes that phenomenon. This is a fascinating quirk of quantum physics that compels us to question the very fabric of reality. The observer effect also reveals that Sha Na Na were very likely the most important act at *Woodstock*.

Sha Na Na looked like two things at once, depending on what slit in the lab you saw them through. Circa August 1969, Sha Na Na was likely perceived as some sort of corny, comic relief, a flashback to an Eisenhower past when people were not enlightened enough to sway to Ravi Shankar or appreciate the Dead's lysergic, heretical desecration of bluegrass. Certainly, the cutaways in the *Woodstock* film during Sha Na Na's performance tell us precisely how the producers and filmmakers wanted their presumably with-it audience to perceive the group. We see shot after shot of slack-jawed, sneering, smug long-haired audience members. They clearly want you to virtually *hear* these future America and Eagles fans thinking, "Oh, we are so much *above* this greaser nonsense of our childhood."

Fuck you.

But the fact is, undeniably, when Sha Na Na hit the stage at *Woodstock* '69, we are seeing the future. It's like some Greaser TARDIS from 1977 has landed a mile or so north of Bethel, New York shortly after seven in the morning on Monday, August 18th, 1969, and dropped the future onto the farmland, amidst the sleepy longhairs. To quote something Sha Na Na *sneer* out on their 1973 live album, *The Golden Age of Rock 'n' Roll,* "We's got just one thing to say to you fuckin' hippies ... rock and roll is here to stay."

It's integral here to address the fact that you likely associate Sha Na Na with their family-friendly early-evening variety show, which ran from 1977 to 1981. By that time, Sha Na Na were peddling nostalgia in the wake of moronic, catastrophically inaccurate *Happy Days*-ism; but at *Woodstock* '69 (and for about the next half decade), Sha Na Na were peddling revolution, a toothy, careening, hyper-speed alternative to the slow drools and acoustic patchouli of the Bread brigade (heck, they were doing something only a few steps away from what Mott the Hoople or the Dolls were doing, plus a pile of UK acts I will mention shortly; we also note that Mott recorded a song called "The Golden Age of Rock 'n' Roll" two years after Sha Na Na's album of the same name). If you are over 55, perhaps you recall how you would spin through the radio in the pre-punk days, and after hearing "Year of the Fucking Cat" or England Dan & John Ford Fucking Coley you would come across the oldies station (WCBS 101.1 in New York!) and Little Richard, the Marcels or Dion & the Belmonts would sound like manna from heaven.

But back to *Woodstock*. (As it happens, *Woodstock* was one of Sha Na Na's very first gigs; the band began, fascinatingly, as a spin-off of a Columbia University a cappella group. The name of the band comes from a repeated refrain in the Silhouettes' 1957 hit, "Get a Job.") We meet the band with an acrobatic, double-time dash through Danny & the Juniors' "At the Hop." Sha Na Na race through the song in about 90 seconds, taking it nearly a full minute faster than the original. This introduction to the group can be seen as roughly simpatico with the MC5's (contemporary) set-launching "Rambling Rose." The MC5 analogy may not be as silly as it sounds: a live clip of Sha Na Na's opening number at the Fillmore East in September 1970 — a bruising, sloppy, amphetaminized tear through the instrumental "Walk Don't Run" — appears to indicate that at times (at least some of) the band may have been consciously modeling themselves after the MC5.

We also note what Sha Na Na were wearing at *Woodstock*. At the time it may have appeared silly to all those shirtless, mud-caked attendees, but this is a fact: Sha Na Na undoubtedly look far less ridiculous than almost anyone else at Woodstock. The three men in front are clad, sloppily, in unadorned, understated gold lamé; they could probably slip into a less well-groomed Roxy Music. The rest of the large band wear standard greaser casual, that is, white and black T-shirts and tight jeans. In fact, two members, with their black jeans, black T-shirts, black leather jackets and puffed-up D.A.'s, are dead ringers for one of the coolest looking guys in rock history, Pete Farndon of the Pretenders. All in all, Sha Na Na at *Woodstock* look pretty much like two-thirds of the bands that you'd see on any given night at Max's or CBGB's in 1977 or '78. They also do not look like a fucking joke — they look like guys who work at the gas station but had also seen a couple of Warhol movies, had confused feelings about Joe Dallesandro and are now intent on getting in hippies' faces and telling them the truth.

Sha Na Na are ripe for serious reconsideration, not just as a shortcut between wasted *Woodstock* and speed-swallowing punk, but also as an important influence on the high-energy, backwards/forwards looking British acts of the 1970s who tenderized the public for punk's rotten meat.

In England, where Sha Na Na were taken a bit more seriously, they were an absolutely fundamental influence in what came to be known as the Rock'n'Roll Revival movement. The Rock'n'Roll Revival movement made a significant impact on the charts (and the media) in the UK in the years before punk. Roy Wood's Wizzard, Showaddywaddy (who sounded very much like Sha Na Na-via-Joe Meek), Shakin' Stevens, even Gary Glitter, Mud, Slade and the Bay City Rollers can all be seen as direct descendants of Sha Na Na. Perhaps most interestingly, in their gold lamé jackets, D.A.'s and hyper-rhythms, we can clearly see Sha Na Na in the image and sound of early Roxy Music, who I have a strong feeling were fans. (To my knowledge, no one has asked any Roxy member if they were aware of Sha Na Na, which, to my mind, is an unfortunate oversight; likewise, the physical/fashion similarity between ca. '75 Roxy Music and contemporary Showaddywaddy is striking, to say the least.)

Also significantly, in the churn, howl and wallop of black-jeaned Sha Na Na we see a direct connection to the immediate forefathers of punk, the oldies-obsessed high-energy pub bands. Specifically, I am talking about the gob-smackingly phenomenal Dr. Feelgood, Eddie and the Hot Rods and Joe Strummer's 101ers. (It's important to note that pub rock really meant two fairly different things: quirky, country/Laurel Canyon-flavored Americana filtered through a Cockney bias as played by, say, Brinsley Schwarz, Bees Make Honey or Kilburn and the High Roads; and high-energy R&B, as played by the Feelgoods, Count Bishops, Eddie & the Hot Rods, Ducks Deluxe and the 101ers.) For instance, when we hear the Hot Rods blast through — and I mean fucking steamroll — a series of covers on the live tracks of 1976's *Teenage Depression* album (U.S. edition), we are just hearing them treat '60s garage rock the way Sha Na Na treated '50s greaseball. Likewise, on Dr. Feelgood's *Down by the Jetty* (released in June of 1975), the Feelgoods tightened and streamlined the glitter excesses of the Rock'n'Roll Revival movement and released something that is, essentially, the very early Stones or Pretty Things tempered with the rhythmic simplicity and urgency of punk. *Down by the Jetty* is the exact mid-point (artistically) between Sha Na Na and the Ramones. Arguably, the more greaser-obsessed 101ers (who were essentially a more simplistic and roots-rocky clone of the Feelgoods) were even closer to the image and ideal of Sha Na Na.

I would also strongly suspect that there is a direct connection between Sha Na Na and Phil Ochs' gold-lamé-clad oldies set at his legendary March 1970 Carnegie Hall show. I mean, there has to be: in August of 1969, Sha Na Na dressed in gold lamé and played oldies in front of a skeptical audience searching for *meaning, maaaan;* just seven months later, Ochs did exactly the same thing at Carnegie Hall.

Perhaps the biggest surprise when we take a dive back and re-examine Sha Na Na is that they made one really goddam good studio album featuring (mostly) original songs. Who knew? In 1972 (after the initial flash of attention for their high-energy, gum-snapping revivalism, yet prior to their resignation to kid-friendly nostalgia-slinging) Sha Na Na released *The Night Is Still Young,* which features a handful of covers against a backdrop of truly first rate songs that sound, very goddamn much, like Dean Friedman, Steve Goodman and Mike Nesmith forming a supergroup to make an imitation Bonzo Dog Band album. Listen, I'm going to type that again, because I want it to sink in: the half dozen originals on Sha Na Na's third album, 1972's *The Night Is Still Young,* sounds like Dean Friedman, Steve Goodman and Mike Nesmith forming a supergroup to make an imitation Bonzo Dog Band album.

The Night Is Still Young has the cool, creamy FM-flavor of the Beach Boys' *Holland* (which it bears some spiritual relationship to, for reasons that would I would need another 2,800 words to explain; suffice to say that it is often overlooked that the Beach Boys, at their root, were very much a doo-wop group, an element that resurfaces around the time of *Holland* and the lesser *Carl and the Passions*). In addition, *The Night Is Still Young* contains (likely) the only anti-Nixon doo-wop song ever recorded, Richard Joffe's "Vote"; a rather wonderful straight-up imitation of Mike Nesmith's country-pop, Scott Simon's "Oh Lonesome Boy"; and a totally bizarre, totally Bonzoid ballad, "Glasses," that ponders how blurry people's vision must have been in the 14th century, and maybe they "were more tuned into sound." Now, this delightful oddity, which some hipster band MUST cover, was written by BOWZER, i.e. Jon Bauman. So, put that in your Marlboro pack and roll it up your sleeve.

Honestly, I see pre-variety show Sha Na Na as an absolutely essential cog in the shaping of the course of rock and pop in the 1970s. I think it is undeniable that Wizzard, Showaddywaddy, the Rollers and Gary Glitter emerged directly out of their shadow, and very likely that Roxy Music did, too. I also think Sha Na Na's spirit — mixing the beautifully basic and the blue-moon ludicrous with a New Yawk City pizza-folding spit an' drawl — probably made KISS possible and found echoes in the '50s-via-Dead-via Doors-isms of Blue Öyster Cult.

So, take Sha Na Na seriously. And that process begins at *Woodstock.*

2019, *ROCK AND ROLL GLOBE*

Young Marble Giants Explode a Graceful Bomb Over Manhattan

There are certain moments when you see or hear something and nothing after is ever the same. You are changed. And not just slightly. It is not merely that a new pathway is revealed, but an entire new country. You hear or see an artist and they don't just elate you but hand you a passport and a ticket to a country that you never heard of, but where you will fall in love and be altered, forever.

What I thought was possible in music changed forever on the evening of November 21, 1980. That was the night I saw Young Marble Giants perform at Hurrah, a venue just west and north of Columbus Circle in Manhattan. It was the first of their two nights at Hurrah, and I was fortunate enough to attend both.

I had already fallen for the clicking, chiming, wet/dry grace of their album, *Colossal Youth,* which seemed to take the tickety-tock and open landscapes of the remarkable new post-punk and set it within childsong, within a shoebox diorama. But live, the sound and presence of Young Marble Giants exploded; yes, that's the word. And what was wonderful on record became a miracle onstage. What was fresh to the ear when heard on vinyl became an entire clear, immediate and crisp art form revealed. Watching and hearing it, to be wrapped in it, we felt like cavemen seeing the second act of *La Bohème,* or *Nude Descending a Staircase,* or the floating, impossible, majestic grid of the George Washington Bridge for the first time. That's how it felt, yes.

Three unassuming people stepped onstage that night. Then the room exploded with grace, a furious and confident kind of tranquility, and a maximum minimalism so perfect it makes me think of

Avebury Henge in the snow or the first Ramones album. And when they stepped off the stage, the world had changed. Honestly: I had no choice but to recast my world, the musical future-iceberg I had only until then seen the top of, with the tools, skills and new way of seeing that Young Marble Giants had taught me.

Who did I go to Hurrah with that night? Was it Evan, was it Dorian, was it either of the two Jims? Did I interview them for WNYU, as we interviewed virtually every other newish UK band that landed in New York City? When I waited for the A train at Columbus Circle to take me back downtown (back then, the vast, echoing subway station had the charmless chill and permanently off-smell of a football stadium restroom), was I alone or was I with friends? All this has vanished, you see, because memory is mercury, and when it is not mercury, it is a liar. We may not realize it, but we need not imagine what an alternate universe is like. We already live with one, within one, adjacent to one, every single minute of every day of our lives.

This alternate universe is the place of lost memory. It is the land where things have actually happened, but they have vanished from virtually all ability we have to recall these events. These are things that occurred, that existed as surely as anything else in our life existed, but any trace of memory of them has vanished. This lost memory is truly an alternative universe. I know this, because Leonard Nimoy told it to me in a dream, which was set in two pasts and one present.

But we feel the impact crater of the lost world of memory, this alternate universe, even if we cannot summon the dimensions or the contours of the meteorite.

Until that night at Hurrah, I did not know that punk rock or post-punk, this simple, electric music full of slants and shocks that had changed my life over the past few years, could also be truly quiet, fierce but hushed. I did not know that it could simmer, whisper, yet also explode. Until then, I had always assumed punk and post-punk were coupled to volume, to maximalism; I had assumed it not only colored outside the lines but filled the whole page. But on that night, I discovered maximum minimalism, the ability of music to occupy a very, very small space in the world of volume, but a giant space in the world of electric imagination, intensity and heart.

A whole new world was revealed to me. This was a world where hushed, intense, electric, starlit whispers could absolutely knock you on your ass, could scream and shock with meaning and power. Until that moment, I had always assumed that on one hand there was loud music (played with electric guitars and fronted by sneering anti-heroes) and quiet(er) music, played by earnest men and women standing behind acoustic guitars.

Until that moment, until that night at Hurrah, I had not conceived of the idea that something quiet could be so electric, so massive and could invade and occupy my brain and cause me to clench my fists and scream the way the Stooges, Buzzcocks, Damned or Gang of Four could. Young Marble Giants, on record but especially on stage, were vulnerable but solid. The name of the band, and their album *Colossal Youth,* seemed absolutely perfect, because it felt like we were standing in the shadows of a great, ageless stele, a sweet, gigantic, blue-lit golem. And this golem was so deeply electric that it roared, even as it was small (tiny, in fact). And to DISCOVER the ability of something that was so contained and so simple to fill a room, fill and inspire your soul, change your world, was something that still creates awe in me today, as it did on that night 40 years ago.

In theory it was austere, but it was, in fact, gigantic. In their clicks, twangs, chirps, ticks, chimes and sing-song sigh songs, Young Marble Giants seemed to be doing the very best thing a musician can do: inventing something entirely new out of a fever dream of Shadows and Suicide and Soft Machine and the sound of news bulletins and elevators. It was the amazing, impactful ghost-music of the glowing gray light we saw in the quarter-moment between when the TV commercial ends and the show begins.

Most of all, that night we saw three artists (Moxham, Moxham and Statton) creating music for the best possible reason: because they were desperate to hear something, couldn't find it anywhere in their record collection, so they had to make it themselves. Seriously, there is no better reason to create: to invent out of the heart's need, out of joy, not pretension.

The crowd at Hurrah was stunned, silent. Someone whispering or clinking a beer bottle could be easily heard over the music (which truly had the depth and heft of the Who *Live at Leeds*, even if it had only had the weight of shy but deep words of love spoken in the rain);

but I don't recall any sounds like that. I genuinely don't think they were any (if I may presume what memory can't access) because the nearly packed room remained in respectful awe as we watched this miracle, this silent bomb, explode in front of us.

I know there were others who had tried to work in the arena of quiet bombs, and I would soon discover them. But until I saw Young Marble Giants, it seemed that no one else had found a way to make quiet punk rock. No one else had been able to take the simplicity, the inner-city tension, the chugging maxi-minimalism of punk, with all its industry and angst, and bring it to the campfire, to the darkened bedroom lit only by the escaped light of the hallway or the city, to the crib-world at dawn with the sound of the highway far away and then near. Until I saw Young Marble Giants, no one had been able to take punk to the dreamworld of the hush underneath the blankets, where we create dreams in which we invent sounds like this, like this searing, shocking, giant yet almost silent *Colossal Youth*.

Forty years later, I understand nuances and wit I would not have understood when I was a child (and if you don't think that age 18 is childhood, you must be 18). The blend of Shadows twang, British television ident music, the nodding, steady rhythm of krautrock, the melodies with roots deep in the valleys and the mines — back then I intuited this but could not label it. Mostly, on that night 40 years ago (or was it two nights?), I was just stunned, shocked, stripped and dipped in dawn's gold and dusk's pink by this neutron nude bomb, which sounded like little velvet fists crushing coal into diamonds.

Personally, I was never the same. I began to seek out music, new and archival, that echoed that maximum minimalism, that dream noise, that intensity that was simultaneously a whisper and a scream. The neutron nude bomb I experienced that night in November 1980, when I was baptized with a handful of punk rock rose petals, recast my entire taste. And I found it.

I found it in (the second and third albums by) PiL, in *Pet Sounds* and the song "Surf's Up" by the Beach Boys, in *Faith* by the Cure, in Charles Ives and in Moondog, in the hushed but insane repetition of Neu!, even in the intensity of the more verdant moments of *Murmur, Reckoning* and *Fables of the Reconstruction*.

My entire taste in music was recast by that single night; so much so, in fact, that four years later I went about creating my own quiet bomb of a band, Hugo Largo.

Everything I thought I knew about art and music was altered that night at Hurrah. No moment in my musical life, not even the amazing revelation when I discovered the Beatles, Beach Boys or Neu!, ever equaled the impact of that moment. At the end of their second night — November 22, 1980 — Alison Statton calmly announced from the stage that this was the band's final gig. There was a collective moment of inhaled breath — we had no reason to think that the vital, shocking, confident, original, vibrant group in front of us had reached the end of its run — and then the audience reacted with the loudest noise, the most intense roar of applause and approval, I have ever heard in a small space.

With all those years — honestly, a lifetime — between then and now, I find myself thankful to have never seen the band again. There is a great purity to the event, to the arc between artist onstage, the reaction in my mind and how it changed my life. The moment was perfect, complete; it needed no additional layers of occurrence, no matter how wonderful they might be. I had been changed.

2020, *ROCK AND ROLL GLOBE*

Bob Dylan 2018: Painting a New Masterpiece Every Night

We are here because of the heat of a dream.

The dream is rock and roll, which we first encountered in the pages of a magazine or as a rumor seeping out of an older sibling's closed bedroom door. Then we found that the waking truth was better than any dream. The truth was the heat we found in the moment: the strange, hot spirits that danced in the sweet smoke of a hockey arena, in the fuzz and text emanating from under the blue lights of some old vaudeville theater with sticky floors and a greasy fly-paper colored old chandelier in a crumbling part of town. Maybe we even found the dream in a paneled, shagged basement, in front of a cheap amplifier, behind a battered drum kit, in the chords of a Kinks song, the only song we all knew. This is where memories were made, when we fell in love with a tangle of worlds and a beat that could be traced to the rhythm of the railway or the holler of some old brakeman on a clear channel radio station.

This heat is still within us. It is slow-fading smoke. It conjures genies in black jeans and red-haired fairies and Cuban-heeled demons whose eyes are clear but whose edges dissolve, because memory is smoke. But it remains. It defies the instantly frozen time of a cellphone photo or social media post.

The fire that made the smoke is the real thing. It is the Clash and it is the Fall, and it is Joe Ely, even Jello Biafra or Cowboy Mouth, all the artists and snarling acrobats who leapt for the sky and landed in Sun Studios. And it is what I felt when I saw Bob Dylan and his band perform on November 18, at Symphony Hall in Springfield, Massachusetts.

Bob Dylan in 2018 demands that you be in the moment. If you go with him, you will experience 120 minutes as intense and rewarding as any Dylan trip you ever went on as a teenager, when you first discovered the magic of his eternal poetry and his American exceptionalism. He will defy your instinct to consign him to memory, and he will create new memories. He will put you at the edge of your seat, stick feathers and pins into the edges of your heart.

What if a great artist painted a masterpiece every night, one that could not be found in any museum, any bookstore or on the internet?

Bob Dylan is painting masterpieces every night. These exist for two hours or so and then vanish, evidenced only by the sparkling warmth and buzz in the memories of those who were in the hall (and a steady stream of roaring, echoing, hushed and harsh audience tapes, which, in some strange and beautiful way, reflect the character of the shows themselves).

Just as we have studied, intently and sometimes ludicrously, his past work, we must recognize that Dylan's current live performances, these rolling, rollicking, elegiac, swooning, swinging, snarling evenings, are as important as an album. They are a stage of development unto themselves. They represent the artist saying to his audience, just as I gave you *Blonde on Blonde* and *Blood on the Tracks* and *Desire* and *New Morning* and on and on, now I give you this; and I ask you to share with me this moment in time, which is as important, intense and intensive as any album I gave you.

I strongly believe that Dylan '18 is creating a body of work, an entire stage of his development that only exists on the concert stage, and for the concert stage. It is brilliant, graceful, complete, engaging and demands that we use memory as others use their cellphone camera or stereo. Bob Dylan's medium is memory — his and ours — and his current work is an affirmation of Bob Dylan's voyage, what he has witnessed, what he has dreamed, what he has aspired to, what he admires.

The intentionality of the performance, of the whole Never Ending Tour, is also revealed in the strict prohibition against photography or cell phone videos/pictures during the performance (this is enforced, too; spotters are stationed throughout the hall, and anyone raising a phone to eye-level will quickly be told to put the phone away). This allows for absolutely singular magic. It insists on the energy of our presence and the archaic engine of attention. And we are rewarded with the glow of in-the-moment joy. Unlike so very many shows, it exists for *us,* and for the artist, and not as a platform for boasting photos to be posted in social media.

Dylan's performance becomes both moment and memory. We experience something exquisite when we abandon the expectation of a future fake "moment" artificially frozen by technology. See, a picture is not a memory. It is a simulacrum of memory.

Every night Dylan actively battles the Paul Shafferizing of the Music of Our Lives; he refuses to dishonor his genius by xeroxing it. Instead, he lifts these famous texts out of their frames and re-examines them every night, relives them every night, gives them new life every night. Dylan isn't just playing the music of our life; in these unfamiliar, startling arrangements of this familiar material, he is also playing the music of *his* life. Bob Dylan and His Band are one-third greaser rock, one-third Frenchman Street New Orleans rumble and roll and one-third greasy, loose-elbow Texas swing. Nightly, he is restaging his treasured memories, revisiting his favorite places: the southwestern Roadhouse, the blue, loud streets of New Orleans and the VA halls and roller rinks he played as a teenager, when he stood behind cheap cigarette-burned upright pianos and pounded out dry and wet hump prom rock for flattops and acne-scarred moon-faced greasers under the low, blue skies of Minnesota's flatlands.

In fact, it is literally impossible to watch and hear Dylan '18 — he spends most of the set standing, legs apart and slightly bent, behind a piano, playing a rollicking New Orleans/Memphis style of boogie-woogie piano — and not imagine teenage Dylan, before he became a Guthrie acolyte, playing rock and roll in a teen dance band. I think this is the most evident clue to understanding Dylan '18: he has returned to his true roots, before he invented himself. Yet he somehow accesses his own future, gathering all the music he was to write, all the music he was to discover, all the avenues and lanes and cities and hills he will live in and learn from.

There is this, too: Dylan and his band (Dylan on piano, Charlie Sexton on guitar, Tony Garnier on bass, George Receli on drums and Donnie Herron on pedal steel, lap steel, electric mandolin, banjo and violin) are one of the greatest rock and roll bands I have ever seen. Period. In terms of finding the marrow of rock and roll and somehow cracking the bone and exposing it to stage lights, in my personal experience only the Fall, Motörhead and very early Sonic Youth have left me so alive in the moment yet also aware of rock and roll's smoky past. That is not to say that Dylan '18 leaves no room for varying textures. Notably, "Like a Rolling Stone" is performed with a plaintive, almost Lanois-like touch, which is utterly *right*: to perform "Like a Rolling Stone" with the arrogant, judgmental snarl of youth would be a lie; it makes much, much more sense recast as a more sympathetic, forgiving memory.

But back to the band. Charlie Sexton, fleet and inventive, changes styles and cultures literally from bar to bar, tossing off insane, hyper-jazz changes, post-punk/pre-Beatles melodic leads and ripping blues and raunch-hand lines, all without ever making a grimace or stopping for applause. If you want to see someone make a lot of faces and let you *know* how versatile they are, go see an expert hack like G. E. Smith or Waddy Wachtel. But if you just want to see one of the best electric guitarists in the land inhale everything sweet, spicy and elegant about American music and exhale it effortlessly, see Charlie Sexton.

Amazingly, Sexton is only the third most spectacular player in the group, and that's because Dylan has one of the greatest rhythm sections in the history of rock. I have almost no hesitation in saying that George Receli is the best drummer I have seen in at least a decade. He is a robust, adept and joyfully New Orleans-style player, using the kit as an expressive gateway to centuries of rhythm. He relies almost exclusively on the skins, not the cymbals, simultaneously playing light and atomic; he is always rumbling and rolling, moving steadily like a freight train, hovering mysteriously like a pelican and working his way around the songs like a late-night detective who listens to a lot of WWOZ and surf music. It's almost like watching Keith Moon if he had been trained on Rampart Street.

Bassist Tony Garnier keeps an eye and an ear on every member of the band, and he *feels* like the bandleader. He plays over, under, on top of and around Receli, Sexton, Herron and Dylan, but he especially takes out a thick, greasy laundry marker and underlines Sexton's quick melodic pops, while at the same time bold-typing every one of Receli's tom hits. If Receli is the primary author of the agile New Orleans rumble that defines the band, Garnier makes sure there's always paper in the printer to tell the story.

You may buy the ticket because it has Dylan's name on it; you will leave having seen one of the greatest bands you will ever see.

As for Dylan himself, for the most part he stands behind the piano, attentive and happy, with the wide-legged stance of the roadhouse bandleader. On a few occasions, he emerges to approve of his band or relish the surroundings. On these forays — like a boss making a tour of his place of work — he walks with the slow but steady stiff-legged gait of the aging Charles Foster Kane, proud and powerful. On one (and only one) occasion, he leaves the piano to stand behind a microphone to sing; while doing so, not only does he sway like a proud old rocker, he also holds the mic stand aloft and twirls it — a deliberate, odd, almost flowery gesture that would seem to be unique to this tour. The last time I saw Dylan — about 15 months ago — he stepped out from behind the piano to sing about half a dozen songs, and when he did, he cut a completely different physical form. Then, he took a wide-legged stance, somewhere between a classic 1930s crooner and a long-distance runner awaiting the starter's pistol, and he cradled the mic like a baby he was cooing to sleep. But this time, he rocks with the mic, fondles and spins the mic stand, and sways like an old dancer remembering the serpentine moves of his prom night. It's a curious example of how he is continually rewriting his performance story.

His face has changed, too, in the last year. His chin, an essential part of that famous profile, has collapsed into his neck; the sly almond eyes and slash of a half-smile we know from 1008 pictures seem to be folding into the aging face. However, the hair remains a defiant puff of history, a burning bush that he carries with him as if to say, *I remain who you know from the posters, let this light me, even as I allow the rest of my face and body to age, just like you.*

Most significantly, it is clear he is in control of his voice, and any "deterioration" or grunt or growl that some may note is, I believe, deliberate affectation. Generally, I think Dylan '18 sounds like a cross between the gasping, gravelly Dylan you hear on his very earliest demos (listen to the very first recordings of "Talkin' New York") and the crooning, high-lonesome Dylan that was revealed between 1967 and 1972. Any doubt that he knows exactly what he is doing is set aside when he effortlessly jumps an octave, or slips into a sweet, high range, conjuring the spirit of Jimmie Rodgers, Slim Whitman, Pete Seeger or Hank Williams. His radically transformed arrangements are not contrarian, but deeply honest; he understands, as the Buddha said, that you cannot put your hand in the same river twice: each time you touch the skin of the water, it has moved on, it is a new river. It feels as if he is inside his material, not just imitating it.

Which is to say, again: Dylan knows exactly what he is doing.

The Never Ending Tour may be one of Dylan's most important and honest works. It links the threads — thorny, wooly, silky, sunset pink, winter-night violet and Route 66 sun-bleached white — that have been accumulating since Dylan first made music, imagined music, dreamed music. It is all there onstage, in the worn and hot fingers of Sexton, Receli, Garnier and Herron, in his ancient, wise and vulnerable voice, in the parade rumble of the beat. In 2018, Bob Dylan hangs the smoke-stained crepe of forgotten proms, VA halls and snow-ringed ballrooms unto his own delicate and legendary texts and gives us the gift of in-the-moment magic.

2018, *INSIDEHOOK*

Barbra Streisand and Bob Dylan Go Very Deep on an Extraordinary and Beautiful Duet

I truly believe what I wrote in this passionate, vaguely unhinged piece: neither our ears nor our creative minds ever exist in isolation. As Thich Nhat Hanh wrote, "All phenomena, including us, are the products of infinite causes and conditions. There is nothing that is separate or independent. Everything in the universe is present in a single flower (and in us) except one thing — a separate self." And this very, very much applies to the music we make and the music we hear, all of which are just extensions of the extraordinary, near-infinite legacy and trail of our causes and conditions.

"The Very Thought of You," the gorgeous and deeply moving duet Bob Dylan and Barbra Streisand perform on Barbra's all-duet album *The Secret of Life: Partners Volume Two*, is striking. "Striking" is not a word I use casually. The performance strikes the heart because it is truly a spray of beauty, exotic and familiar, a great surprise that comes as no surprise (please trust these words, this song will lash you deep); and it strikes through the heart of the listener's world and their grandparents' world, too; and it strikes through the history of these two monumental artists and their lost times. "The Very Thought of You" is the sound of two gifted and solemn artists playing "Taps" for *Der Arbeiter Ring*. I believe this, truly, and that is the foundation of this song, which is so beautiful it breaks my heart.

(*Der Arbeiter Ring* is the Yiddish name for The Workers Circle, formerly The Workmen's Circle, which was established in 1900 as a mutual aid society to assist America's Yiddish-speaking immigrants.

Throughout the 20th century, *Der Arbeiter Ring* was deeply involved in the social, political and cultural life of America's Jews, especially those in the working classes, and those fighting for fair wages and equality in the workplace. Perhaps this is a presumption, but since The Workmen's Circle was an integral aspect of Jewish life in America in the first half of the 20th century, I think it's fair to assume that the parents and grandparents of Streisand and Dylan would have been familiar with the organization.)

Every song you hear, every song someone creates, is about something much, much bigger. This is not necessarily intentional; it's instinctual. Every time you listen to a song, every time a song is made, it contains the entire social, historical and genetic experience of the creator and the listener. An artist may think 180 minutes went into writing a song; a listener might presume 4:44 seconds went into listening to it. That's wrong. A thousand years created this encounter. The experience of the listener and the creator — both are creative, engaged acts by the way, even when you listen on the most casual or ambient level — is within us and around us every second.

A song heard, a song composed, a song performed, regardless of the lyrical or melodic content, is actually about your father's time in the ROTC, or your grandmother's fight with the butcher in Midwood, Brooklyn twenty years before you were born; it is about a teacher's strike in New York City in 1968, a train missed in Poland in 1936, a cold caught in a Dollar General store in 1993 (and that's just the 20th century). Neither songs nor your ears are virgins; they are extensions of your mind, your experience, your DNA and every single thing that made you.

So: I sing Kaddish for a lost world. And yes, this is a record review, too, stand by after Channel 2 signs off, bombs bursting in air, here is the late news after *The Late Show*. I have only to gently scratch my medial temporal lobe and I find the time when there was such a thing as *Late Shows* and sad sign-offs until our broadcasting day resumes; and this time also breathes within Streisand and within Dylan and within so many of us, yes? It is the lost forever we only know as the ago. We won't call it "gone," we only call it "ago"; that makes us feel better.

And I am also New York City, a palimpsest, a place on Earth and a palimpsest, and my people are a palimpsest, the world rewrites its resentments again and again on our backs and our chests.

On "The Very Thought of You," this powerful, enchanting, sealskin of a track, Streisand and Dylan duet with a grace and luxury that is gorgeous and weighted, iridescent and timeless but far, far from ageless. Every breath, every phrase, is a mirror, a mandala, time itself. But mostly: Dylan and Streisand are singing Kaddish, for a way of life, a way of listening, a way of working with the gravel and seeds of the present and believing in the fruit of the future, a way of opening the gates to the trinity moments in music. "The Very Thought of You" is a Kaddish, yes, a Kaddish for a different kind of Jew who believed in socialism; who believed in The Workmen's Circle; who had been spat on enough in Lemberg markets and high school hallways to know that art was the armory of fury's fingers and that a song sung is the sword of the disenfranchised.

This is key: When Streisand and Dylan were born, only 11 months apart, there were still people alive who had fought in the Civil War. Hundreds of them, in fact. They had names like Pleasant Riggs Crump (who had witnessed Lee's surrender at Appomattox Court House) and James Albert Hard (who had fought at Antietam, Chancellorsville and the first battle of Bull Run). Yes. They walked the Earth when Dylan and Streisand were born. So, when we listen to Streisand and Dylan, we know this: right now there are people alive who were alive at the same time as veterans of the Civil War. We live and listen alongside those who breathed the same air as those who fought alongside the half a million who died in the original war of American secession.

When Streisand and Dylan made their NYC debuts, just nine months apart (both in the red-lit cellars of Greenwich Village, filled with sloe-eyed turtlenecked women and sideburned young men), seltzer was still delivered; Bleecker Street still burst with the flower-bloom morning fire smell of new bread; New Yorkers still referred to the subways as the IRT, BMT and IND (and they cost 15 cents); and no man had yet pierced chaste and mysterious space (though, true, a handsome Soviet with one eyebrow nearly wholly missing would orbit the Earth just one day after Dylan's NYC debut. Isn't this an interesting convergence of history and its cadets and comedians?).

When Dylan debuted in the city that became His City, 15 weeks into JFK's presidency, no man had been in space, not ever in history (at least not for another 24 hours). Yet this one last night, this one last cool humid haze of a wet spring night, would pass before a human violated the sacred virginity of the Karman line, intact since we crawled from the sea. Oh, and he sings, exactly one year almost to the day, before the New York Mets would breathe the Rheingold spiked air of the Polo Grounds for the first time. And he still sings, loaded with all this, I guarantee you, every gram of this history recalled and forgotten and felt and ignored, and it shows on "The Very Thought of You."

And on this night when Dylan sang for the first time in NYC, the Beatles were in the second week of their residency at the Top Ten Club in Hamburg and the Empress Zita was in happy exile in Switzerland (but more of Zita soon). *The Adventures of Ozzie and Harriet* was still on in prime time; the Berlin Wall had not yet been built. Imagine that. That was their world, Barbra and Bob's world, the news they read while waiting to take the stage in the wine-smelling barrows below 14th Street. Oh, and again, seltzer was delivered, in foggy blue/green bottles in ancient wooden crates.

And we consider this world, their world, growing from Ashkenazi roots that pervaded every aspect of their dreams and art, and always would; and ours, too: even if our mind does not remember, our body most certainly does. Not a day goes by when our cells don't recall shofar and Oppenheimer, the two complimentary terminals of the battery, the temple walls falling and the promise that the temple walls would fall again, this is Titus and Trinity, this destruction is our alpha and omega, ha.

And this is still a record review. There are many, many artists, some extraordinary, some merely ordinary, who have tried to say "something" about America. But this song, just the existence of this song, "The Very Thought of You," says it all. We are a palimpsest, we Americans, though we forget it quickly in a *Real Housewives* haze; we touch the air touched by those who touched the air who touched the air; I am a ship out of Lviv via Liverpool, who are you? We have made artists and heroes out of fools, how are our grandchildren to know who the real artists are? How are they to know that the sons and daughters of the Pale of Settlement were once kind and passionate socialists and the epitome of compassion?

And the song itself — it says a lot, even if we just limit the discussion to, well, music. (But that's impossible.) Streisand and Dylan's version of "The Very Thought of You," a lovely, bruised and hopeful standard first recorded in 1934, is exquisite. It aches but also smiles, it is understated yet gigantic, persuasive yet nearly hushed. Dylan delivers a vocal that is one of his best in years; it is sweet, sincere and cool, full of all the history and heart that I am banging on about. It is full of years and taste and tears. It is an exquisite coda to the heart treasure that was *Rough and Rowdy Ways*; it is the emphatic footnote to that album's pressured gentleness and grace. "The Very Thought of You" also underlines the fact that Dylan's much-overlooked, even mocked America songbook era was some of his most extraordinary work because, like so much of Dylan's best for 60 years, it reached, it reached and ached and aspired, it challenged, it felt, oh, most of all, it felt, it reached for stars and imaginary ballrooms and the old skating halls where he first saw the stars, and it was honest, and it asked to make time with your heart because first and foremost it made time with his. (Note to you, friend who tolerates this crazy wisdom and is still here: Dylan's third and final American songbook album, 2017's *Triplicate*, is one of his essential works.)

I intentionally did not listen to the rest of the Streisand album because her duet with Dylan is so utterly complete in and of itself. It is a palimpsest (that damn word again), an echo of unimaginably crowded train rides across the scarred lands of central Europe; the inexpressible relief of a passport stamped and ferry rides to Brooklyn and even more train rides to Minnesota; it is kishka and herring at grandma's table; it is a child, pale and clutching a first primer for Hebrew school, walking past a former slave on the street and dreaming of man in space to pass the time while the rabbi drilled aleph bet gimel, aleph bet gimel, aleph bet gimel; it is a parent who told you about Eugene Debs or Henry Wallace or Meyer London, a Jewish member of the Socialist Party elected to Congress from NYC's 12th district, a hundred years before Mamdani or Ocasio-Cortez; it is a Kaddish, a lovely, lovely, sad, lovely overwhelmingly powerful Kaddish, and Barbra Streisand and Bob Dylan are singing Kaddish, though they would not call it that, but they certainly know this. They know this because they are both grandchildren of men and women born in empires that no longer exist (like so many of us are); his grandparents born under Nicholas II, weak and cruel, hers under stately and ever-so-slightly more tolerant Franz Ferdinand. These are the great glacial gorges of history, only just past our fingertips; after all, the last Hapsburg Empress, the final Empress of Austria and Queen of Hungary, the lovely Zita, only died the same year the Pixies released "Here Comes My Man" and the B-52s put out "Love Shack" (this is a fact); Zita of Bourbon-Parma, crowned Empress five days after Christmas 1916, yet still breathing when Barbra made *Yentl* and Bob made *Oh Mercy*. Oh my. History is a great comic and it is the devil, because it convinces us it is only what is standing in front of us. Only the devil can convince us that the pogrom and the Auto-da-Fé somehow went away just because we have an iPhone.

And I say: Aleph, Bet, Gimel, Alpha and Omega, Tin Roof Rusted and Zita, the empress of Austria and Queen of Hungary, still alive when Bob and Barbra were no longer young and I was on MTV, and she ruled under the slogan *Austriae est imperare orbi universo*, AEIOU, AEIOU, Aleph Bet Gimel, Alpha and Omega, *Yis'ga'dal v'yis'kadash sh'may ra'bbo*, and Bob and Barbra, your voices, your presence in the world, remind me to sing Kaddish for The Workmen's Circle, *Der Arbeiter Ring*, and even I remember the seltzer bottles, delivered to our door, sitting at our suburban table, while I dreamed of Desire, while I parsed the story of Isis.

2025, *ROCK AND ROLL GLOBE*

Taylor Swift Understands the Little Girls, and Nothing Else Matters: Some Reflections on *The Eras Tour* Film

Note to musicians, aspiring or extant: putting a teenager's thoughts into a song and creating something that they want to put into a yearbook quote or a text to their paramour is a major motherfucking step to having a hit record. This is one of the things we celebrate in the piece below.

Taylor Swift, in many ways, did the impossible. I believe she is the first artist since the Beatles to be as big as the Beatles, an achievement long thought unattainable. Just as remarkably, she has created a generation of music fans, and that is effing huge. Whether you are a fan of Swift or not, her achievements — the bond with her fans and the degree to which she has created a legion of people utterly engaged by music and album culture — are extraordinary.

This was another "quick" piece: it was written in minutes, very shortly after returning from taking a 12-year-old niece to The Eras Tour *film.*

This is a rare and extraordinary gift:

The ability to set the deepest and most everyday thoughts and feelings of teenagers to music.

All the rest is lagniappe. Really. That gift is awesome, truly, and nothing else matters.

Taylor Swift has that gift. And when you are in the presence of someone who has that gift — the ability to lift a lightbulb over a young person's head, and make them go, "That is what I feel! I wish I could have said that!" — nothing else matters. Again: Nothing else matters.

This skill, this capacity to tell young people the very thoughts that are in their expanding, assaulted minds and their continually rebirthing, swollen hearts, and to be able to do it with power and simplicity and without the obstruction of artful intentions or pretensions — oh, this is rare and amazing.

It is not merely the ability to tell teenagers the words they wish they could hear; many have done this, that is just called a love song, or a song of desire. Done well, that's magical, but I am talking about something far more beautiful, rare and awesome: the ability to look into the lives and minds of young Americans and create pop music that, universally, makes them go, "Hey, those are *my* thoughts, but I couldn't have said it so well." To be in the presence of an artist who can achieve this utterly defies criticism and defies, denies and obstructs all cynicism.

Most pop songs just talk at you. Generally, pop musicians tell you what they want (think of the proliferation of the phrase "I want" in pop songs, or some variation of it), or they quack at you what *they* think you should want or what *they* think you should feel. Honestly, the primary function of most pop music is as a mnemonic — "Oh, this is the song I think of when I remember..." and so on. Pop music is so busy acting as a bookmark — or is so wrapped up in its own presumed ability to dictate your feelings — that it usually fails to legitimately empathize.

But Taylor Swift has the ability to hold a mirror to the hearts and minds of her listeners; they see her in that mirror, mouthing the words they are thinking but can't articulate, the notes and texts they so desperately wish they could write. Seriously, if you want to conjure Taylor Swift, imagine a girl in 9th or 10th grade looking into the mirror but seeing Taylor Swift's lips moving. When a pop star appears to be able to read your mind and give language to the scribbles in the crowded margins of your notebook and your brain, when they can give words to the thoughts, fears, hopes and heartbreaks that you are having at that actual moment, that is stunning and rare. Imagine a musician appearing to be your friend at the time in your life when you need a friend the most. That's Taylor Swift.

Of course, I recognize (and celebrate) that Ms. Swift's audience reaches far, far beyond the teen/tween demographic: her message of empowerment and self-awareness has power and meaning for every human of any age, race, class or sexual identity. But maybe you recall how a certain artist — or maybe it was a book or a film — reached you at precisely the time when you most needed to be reached, a time in your life when you felt unheard or unseen in that way you can only feel when you are a teenager. This sense of someone connecting with you during this time, affirming the sense that there is power, joy and commonality in what you are feeling or experiencing, and that there is someone to share the extraordinary terror and mystery of adolescence with. That is so important, even lifesaving. You never, ever need that "something" in your life more than you need it when you're a teenager, and I want to honor Taylor Swift's ability to make this connection so universally and on such a large scale.

True, we could analyze smaller or larger points of the artist or *The Eras Tour* film (for instance, the nearly oxymoronic difficulty of documenting a show designed to be best experienced in the last row of a stadium; or the simple fact that at least half of Ms. Swift's songs are musically — though not lyrically — based on easily cited, extant material; or her clear debt, as a performer and songwriter, to earlier artists). But this sort of analysis is utterly picayune, unnecessary, childish, whining. It is nonsense, and it is dwarfed by this reality: it's not that the little girls understand (though that's certainly true), it's that Taylor Swift understands the little girls. And the little boys, and their older sisters and brothers, and parents, too. Taylor Swift writes and sings the best yearbook quotes of all time, again and again, and sets them to adept, catchy, sugary, bright and bittersweet pop music.

Nothing else matters.

There is a time in our life when nothing matters more than the perfect yearbook quote, finding someone else's words that say exactly what you're thinking and feeling.

Taylor Swift lives in that place, forever.

2023, *ROCK AND ROLL GLOBE*

NOTE: The Eras Tour *film is the loudest thing I've ever heard, with the exception of what I experienced during the three years I performed with the Glenn Branca Ensemble. I'm not joking. I strongly suggest bringing something to muffle the sound or protect your ears.*

Bruce Springsteen: Overrated but Still a King

Again and again, I am confronted with my sieve-like memory. Revisiting these pieces has been a fascinating and exciting experience, like meeting a treasured friend you hadn't thought of since high school or finding an old book you thought you had lost. Other times, it's like running into a beautiful woman you have no memory of having gone on a date with.

Which is all to say I honestly have zero idea what inspired me to write this appreciation of Bruce Springsteen, where I tried to resolve my innate (and acquired) crankiness, snobbishness and cynicism with an awareness of what a vital and gigantic figure he is. I do recall (as I allude to in the piece) that for some reason — now entirely lost in the crusted, back-of-the-fridge baking soda box of time — I sat down to write something negative about the Great Man … but the process of unpacking the thoughts led me on a very different path.

He honored the old gods: the stomping garage gnashers of the 1960s, the Vitalis'd, tremolo-voiced cool cats of the 1950s, the earnest red folkies and peaceniks who sang of lung cases, picket lines and soup kitchens. And in his hosanna, honk and holler, he even summoned the spirit of the hardscrabble Chitlin' Circuit kings, the acrobats and tearjerkers and boogiemen who split the atom of rock and roll.

No star, never, no great public figure, ever, had a better heart or was more sincere.

With every hoarse breath he tried to remind us of the power of rock and roll; with each muscled pump of his Telecaster he sought to share with us this amazing gift that made suffering electric, which was built out of the pain of the cotton field yet relieved the pain of the suburban bedroom.

With every fiber of his G.I. Joe body (so similar in shape to the jobber wrestlers who usually sweated under these same arena lights), he tried to turn the enormodomes he was doomed/blessed to perform in into face-peeling medicine shows where he preached the horny gospel of the one, only and true rock and roll cure.

He came of age in an era of lessened expectations, an era where louche, Learjet'd bronzed fools lazed on stages larger than houses, in arenas as populous as small cities. To many, he was their only connection to the wild, acrobatic, hollering heart of rock and roll. To these people, he might as well have created it; no one else provided them with this kind of honest, muscular, spontaneous and engaging experience. In the land of the mall and miracle mile, his screaming, shaking, swearing congregation often mistook him for the only resident of the kingdom of the authentic — when he was merely an ambassador.

When he emerged, a sylvan, wool-hatted Dylan singing tripping, sweet and elastic poetry about carnies and bus stations and dead cities and adult children dreaming of a way out, he was surrounded by the fake, fey, lazy and decadent; this made him seem hyper-real, hyper-authentic. And when, three albums in, he loaded his character-rich James Dean-via-Needle Park stories into a Spectorian cathedral, he claimed what was rightfully his: he would be the golden rocker in the cold, copper-colored age of the Cream of Eagles, he would be dirty/pretty Vince Everett/Terry Malloy/Hamburg John in the time of Styxian folly.

It was heresy to say the truth: that he was "a" real thing, not "the" real thing.

It was an understandable mistake; if you spent your concert money in high school staring at light shows and crumbling walls, distant, swaying Stevies or narcoleptic Jerrys, it was certainly startling to see A Man Alive in the dead zone of 1970s arena rock.

When I saw him for the first time, a generation or more ago, I distinctly remember thinking, of course he's godly to these faithful: he's the only frontman they've ever seen who looks grateful to be there, who acts as if he is excited and energized by the rare gift of being able to stand and stagger and stomp and swagger and run laps on stage. They have never ever seen anything remotely like him.

My god, I thought, squinting through the smoke, these people have never seen Lux Interior flop and howl and shake fists and ass at an audience; they've never seen Jello Biafra prowl and charge around a stage like he was outrunning the devil; they've never seen Alan Vega shriek like a loveless cat caught in a car door and demand the spotlight as no one else ever has; they've never seen H.R. do a backflip and strangle a microphone while doing an unholy frug; they've never seen Joe Strummer, his eyes screwed tight, his thrash-hand slashing across the guitar strings, his legs pumping intensely, summon exactly the same barroom gods this arena giant is summoning. This man, who I am watching from seats so far away he is barely a pinky-nail tall, he is only one of the many geniuses, rare but not extinct, who catch rock and roll in the teeth of his heart and shakes it until its neck is broken.

I am fortunate to have known and seen so many who had the same blood type as him, who drank from the same well of folk and garage and beat and blue and possessed the same desire to gift their audience with the body and the blood of rock and roll. He is not the greatest. He is one of them. Let us speak their names and honor them, these Elvis Dylan men, these Eddie Cochran Allen Ginsberg men, these Wynonie Harris Hunter Thompson men, these Sonic Raiders and Woody Ryders, these men who swing and shout and sing beautiful truths about the rosy, rising roads, hallelujah pinkorange sunsets and dark sacred nights of America.

Joe Ely, Joe Strummer, the deep and witty New Orleans balladeer Paul Sanchez and the one of whom we are speaking; these are four faces of the same sage. Ely, Strummer and Sanchez (to name only three) did not have a stadium setting that turned their smoky magic into TNT; but I assure you they had, and have, the same spirit in their hearts, in their strumming hands, in their tight-but-loose jaws and perfect-worn jeans, in the boots that tramp stage after stage after stage after stage, in the songs, graceful and adamant, that tell of lovers and losers and mourning and mornings in motels and midnights in taverns.

And I am loath to say what I came to say, because I honor him and his true joy so much: he is the most overrated artist of all time.

This is not because he isn't great, because he *is* great; it is because he is not the greatest, and the world so wants him to be! He emerged in an era of lessened expectations, when the barroom bleat of his band sounded extreme, when his honest and urgent athleticism and sincerity seemed so rare as to be unique. And I honor him, I pay tribute to him, by saying that he is overrated: a talent so true and tough and lasting deserves to be returned to the earth, deserves to be seen through the same beery, road-weary kaleidoscope as the music he keeps alive.

Seeing him as a god, or rather, as *the* God of rock and roll does a disservice not only to his real, amazing skills and sincerity, it also masks the many glories of the performers who came before him and after him and also shared his rock and roll heart and his hell-stomping boot heels. I sense he would be delighted to come down from the clouds and stand alongside the songwriters who also captured a blood-and-sepia snapshot of the discarded, shabby world and the hearts that beat therein: so, we honor Chris Bailey, and John Prine, and Phil Ochs, and Kinky Friedman, and Stompin' Tom Connors, and Ramblin' Jack Elliott, and Fred Neil, and Billy Joe Shaver, and all the others who also had the breath of the road-hearts in their lungs and soul.

He is better than a king. He is the resident of the rock and roll lands. Long live the man who is better than a king, and all of those who share his old heart.

I confess: I came to bury him. I had grown tired of the accounts of the endless shows (these seemingly equated quantity with quality), but mostly I knew that believing in the infallibility and supremacy of any one artist — be it martyred Lennon, shattered and betrayed Elvis or the Jersey Colossus — was misleading. This kind of deification not only betrayed the vulnerable geniuses who have moved and affected us, it also somehow cast a shadow on all the others who had not been so weightily anointed. Each and every one of rock and roll's sages and geniuses achieved this status precisely because of his or her infallibility; so, we must love the fallibility and reject the idol worship. Gods, by definition, are permanent, so we must remember that there is no dance, no sway, no rock, no roll, without impermanence.

But then I remembered the light in the eyes of my dearest friends when they recalled how he had changed their lives. Bob Giordano, to whom he was the inspiration to go beyond expectations, to find a city, a cinema screen, a life of imagination and action; Mark Bryan, who was presumptuous enough to look him in the eye and tell him that he had achieved fame and fortune playing guitar only because of him (him, not "Him") and who received the warmest, sweetest hug from the man in return; Mary Susan Herczog, who became inventive, hysterical, excited and articulately inarticulate just at the sound of his name.

So, burying him was impossible. And I hope that by providing perspective, by suggesting that he is not the only one, but only one of many who revived rock and roll's heart, transplanted it in their own body and preached the awful, strange and beautiful truth, I honor him and everyone who has loved him.

2016, *THE NEW YORK OBSERVER*

Uncle Schrödinger's Band (or How I Learned to Stop Worrying and ~~Love~~ ~~Like~~ Listen to the Grateful Dead)

At some point in my life, I realized that I had never actually really listened to the Grateful Dead in any substantive way. In 2015, I decided to do something about that and write about the experience. To quote Neil Innes, "I have suffered for my art. Now it's your turn."

As you age, you go through a natural process of expanding your musical tastes and loosening the grip on long-held musical prejudices. For longer than I would care to confess, I've hated the Grateful Dead. What they superficially embodied made them an ultra-convenient whipping boy for someone wrapped up in a cultural point of view shaped by punk rock, drone music and minimalist art rock.

But I hadn't actually listened to the Grateful Dead.

I'd *heard* them, of course, but I had never intentionally sat through an entire song, much less a whole album. I only knew them as the chalk-outline of a socio-culture phenomenon, and I had only the vaguest idea of the music, impressions gathered from scraps heard in college dorm hallways and on archaic FM stations.

Clearly, it was wrong to hate a band without actually having listened to them in any depth. So, I figured I'd give the Dead a shot.

But where to start? The Dead's catalog is comically huge. I mean, you can buy a 73-disc (!) set (*Europe '72: The Complete Recordings*), and all I have to say about *that* is that it really ought to include a 74th disc, Hawkwind's *Space Ritual*, just to provide contrast.

I asked for recommendations but got such vastly different opinions that they effectively cancelled each other out. So, I just dove in and started following leads. I would find a composition or performance that intrigued me and then listen to multiple versions of that same song. I repeated this process again and again, occasionally stopping to clear my palate by listening to Blue Öyster Cult, the Beach Boys and Goatwhore.

Here's what I found:

Like faith in the resurrection or the Buddhist belief in the transmigration of souls, being a fan of the Grateful Dead requires certain prior assumptions and an allegiance to ideas that transcend elements of logic and common sense. In other words, to be a Grateful Dead fan, first and foremost you have to believe you are a Grateful Dead fan.

Let's call in Schrödinger's Cat. I am not going to attempt an in-depth explanation of this famous paradox. For the purpose of this screed, let's boil it down to this: the observation of the experiment itself affects the outcome. I also considered citing the Double Slit Experiment, except that there are no umlauts in the Double Slit Experiment, which automatically makes it less interesting.

Where were we?

Ah, the observation of the experiment itself affects the outcome.

My voyage to the Land of the Dead made me conclude that loving the Grateful Dead is like ridin' that train to Hogwarts — you must *believe* that the track exists in order to climb aboard. The recordings — both studio and live — seemed woefully anti-climactic and full of flaws that might deter a non-committed listener (dear god, did they *ever* do a vocal rehearsal, or a second take of a vocal?). *This* is what all the fuss was about? But with the Grateful Dead, the fan — *not just the listener, but the fan* — closes a loop that the band and their recordings leave very, very much open.

Nonetheless, there was enough evidence in the grooves to reveal what others could find engaging and exhilarating. The Grateful Dead are a sleepy but persuasive trawl through a large pile of American musical memes. At their best, they chime, ring, sigh and have an urgent sadness and deep originality. At their best *and* worst, the Dead sound like Doc Watson swallowing eight Benadryl and trying to play Steely Dan songs while backed by (an off-night) Galactic, with a little of the garage band down the hall leaking through and throwing an occasional "Farmer John" in the mix. At all times, their performances balance precariously on a rickety lanai built out of the laziest, milk-water pale New Orleans rhythms, and often that lanai is so flimsy that it seems to be held up only by hope and wishes.

Throughout, the listener roots for the band to not fall nor fail. In this way, he or she becomes one with the band, and that's a big part of the picture. The Dead's stock in trade is dangerous changes in tempo, key and mood; because it seems like these broken-legged spiders can't possibly pull off such acrobatics, when one of these dramatic scene changes *is* successfully executed, there is a great release of tension. I also appreciate that odd little hiccup in their timing that so accurately reproduces the spatial displacement caused by weed; it's likely no other band has encoded that so effectively and so regularly into their sound.

As I stumbled from album to album and live take to live take I found a few songs (such as "Terrapin Station," "Uncle John's Band" and "Franklin's Tower") especially engaging. But I still wondered how a novice, and one not the least bit interested in drinking the Kool-Aid, could "get" this phenomenon and empathize with the blissful self-hypnosis of the Dead Fan.

And then, *Eureka!*, I found it.

On a CD titled *Grayfolded: Transitive Axis*, the almost vituperatively innovative John Oswald took more than a hundred different live performances of the song "Dark Star" and remixed, rearranged and reimagined the tracks into a masterful and magical hour of starlight, tension, acid-dabbed sugar dust, metallic fairy jazz and planetarium-dome ambient malfunctioning laser-ray death/hope. This strange and beautiful record allowed me, I think, to hear the Dead the way their fans hear them.

What's next for me? Say, the hated Phish?

Oh lord, no. As my father once told me, "No one who owns a mandolin should, under any circumstances, be permitted to listen to an Ornette Coleman record while on drugs."

2015, *THE NEW YORK OBSERVER*

NOTE: *In the ten years since I wrote this piece, I have recognized that I had approached the Dead all wrong: you can't actually "listen to" or* *reckon with the Grateful Dead on a song-to-song basis, as I attempted to; nor can you judge them by anything remotely resembling conventional performance or recording standards. They defy being thought of or understood as a band that "records songs." You have to take it all in and relax with the idea that the Dead play sets, not songs. Honestly, it requires the same sort of light-but-intent attention, patience and abandonment of the rapid satisfaction-and-release of "pop" expectations that listening to classical music requires.*

I've become a fan. Not an acolyte — I'll reserve that kind of attention for the Greatest of Space Rock Bands, Hawkwind — but a genuine fan. I just had to forget what I thought I knew about what "bands" were "supposed" to do.

Weezer's "Africa" Is the Most Repugnant Pop Recording of All Time

As of April 2018, I didn't really have any problem with Weezer. However, a month later, they released a cover of the Toto workhorse "Africa." This caused me to type.

Weezer have released the worst record of all time. Their cover of Toto's "Africa" is not merely bad, but malevolent, malignant, actually evil. It takes your memories and your relationship with music and turns it into a cancer; then it crawls inside the feculent death swamp it has created and *laughs* at you.

This is a record that thinks it is smarter than you. This is a record that *hates* you.

Weezer's "Africa" is the most patronizing record ever made; it pretends to be ear candy, *ohhhhhhIlikethat*, but it is actually laughing at you, cruelly. *You are dumb sheep,* its creators say. Every single time you enter the word "Africa" into Spotify or YouTube it laughs at you some more, with the mad drooling cackle of a syphilitic overprivileged aging fratboy.

The horror that is "Africa" was made inevitable by multiple factors. These include the era of super-ubiquitous music streaming, which enabled both instant market testing and immediate satisfaction; the inability of our nihilistic and complacent era to distinguish memory from nostalgia and tribute from irony; and the replacement of creativity and originality with the crowd-pleasing Cup-o'-Tears of the TV talent competitions.

Weezer's "Africa" is the worst record ever made. And that's saying *a lot* — after all, just click on your touchpad and you can summon conceptually and creatively loathsome music like ELP's "Karn Evil 9," anything by Oingo Boingo, the bizarre Nazi-propaganda jazz of Charlie and His Orchestra and Bret Michael's cover of "Sweet Home Alabama."

But Weezer's "Africa" is the worst, not only because it literally *hates* the people who like it, but also because it has bad intentions: Weezer's "Africa" is the record that wants to kill rock and roll because it wants to ridicule you for ever having believed in it in the first place. Weezer's "Africa" is literally a parody of music, a cruel burlesque that mocks you for being touched or moved by music.

Now, I never felt much one way or another about Weezer, apart from the fact that they had a damn good churning guitar sound that took a Mick Ralphs/Johnny Ramone kind of wallpaper slobber and made it into something machine-like and hypnotic. Hats off to the awful f*ckers for that. Oh, and sometimes they sounded like the Undertones if the Undertones had decided to get down on their knees and fellate MTV for years and years (that's not necessarily a bad thing, not at all). And I am guessing they took their name from a lesser-known *Our Gang* character, and that's a good one, too. But there was always a moldy thrift store stink of irony about Weezer; and irony is to art what kryptonite is to Superman.

Irony kills art. Nothing can be moving, meaningful, joy-inducing or tear-wrenching if irony is involved, because anything that is ironic positions itself as superior to standard human emotion, superior to anything that can touch you.

"Africa" is pop music's ruffle-hair moment, where it dies, babbling, in its own waste. (I am referring to that incident when Jimmy Fallon, that distasteful, smirking human sow who giggles like a terrified eunuch five nights a week when most of America is watching Netflix, turned Donald Trump into your awkward uncle, totally negating meaningful dialogue for the sake of a "shareworthy" moment.) Weezer's "Africa," too, reduces the entire rock era to a joke, a joke Simon Cowell and all those awful Jennerdashians would approve of, because it is stylish and ironic and accomplished.

Was your rock and roll a joke? *Was it?*

Or was rock and roll where you first tasted rebellion, identity, joy, lust and companionship? Was rock and roll something that allowed you to separate from your parents yet find your tribe? Did rock and roll provide you with strange and charismatic gods, like Bowie, Prince, Nico, Joe Strummer or Stevie Nicks?

Weezer are screwing with you, mightily, on any number of levels, all of which basically add up to them announcing, "We are smarter than you." They want to make it all a joke because in the New Streaming Reality, they want to prove that Nothing = Something. They *know* they have made something of *no value*, and they *knew* it would be a hit. Is this not the definition of soul-eroding cynicism? Certainly, there have been other musical genres (and significant hit records) created purely to exchange emptiness for mammon — the more opportunistic end(s) of disco and bubblegum, not to mention the lesser precincts of 1980s hair metal spring to mind — but virtually no one else has tried to sell cynical vapidity as a statement in and of itself to satisfy the interests of both hipsters and the artists' accountants (for the sake of my sanity, I am avoiding discussing the entire career and raison d'être of Redd Kross).

By the way, Toto's reciprocal cover, "Hashpipe," isn't nearly as repellant, because as horrifying as it is, it is sincere. There is not a touch of irony to it. In Toto's archaic worldview, the style in which they perform "Hashpipe" — let us describe it as Skunk Baxter jamming with Nightranger, or G.E. Smith covering Journey's "Love Will Find You" — is, well, what makes sense to them. I do not like what they do — their "Hashpipe" is unlistenable, sub-Asia garbage — but Toto come to it honorably.

Weezer's "Africa," however, is a disgusting record, a record that literally mocks the meaning and power of rock and roll by reducing it to a saggy, sick and unfunny in-joke. Why does this matter? Why does one song get me so angry?

Because rock and roll matters. *That's* why.

Rock and roll is the sound of America's disenfranchised made electric. From the Juba beat of antebellum Tuckahoe Plantation to the modified Appalachian howls of Jimmie Rodgers and Hank Williams to the sex-calls of Louis Jordan and Elvis to the rhymes of Run–DMC and *all* the manifold descendants of *all* these pioneers, American music is the creation of those forgotten by the American dream:

truck-driving sons of Parchman convicts, the urban and rural poor, the immigrant Jews, Italians and Irish … *all* the people who had nothing and built America. They built American song, too, American pop, American rock and roll. No other art form was born of more suffering and brought us more pleasure.

I will not be silent while Weezer piss on this legacy for their own amusement.

Rock and roll, which filled every stage of your life with joy, distraction, companionship, poetry and energy, whose sages and fools put your feelings into words and your happiness and frustration into a beat, is a common language of the heart. It tells a story we all share. It should never treat your ability to find a friend in a song as a joke. Weezer, by digesting your memories and shitting out a sneer, want to take away the only thing you own that is entirely yours: your ability to interpret and experience your own memories and feelings in a completely distinct way. 2018, *INSIDEHOOK*

Hanoi Rocks Changed Everything

When asked what were the greatest live performances I ever saw, I mean the ones that left an imprint on my mind, soul and future as if I had stared at the sun, I generally list these: a Heartbreakers (Johnny Thunders' Heartbreakers, that is) show from the autumn of 1979; any of the four Bob Dylan shows I saw between 2017 and 2019; a handful of Fall shows between 1980 and 1983; a Cramps set at the Peppermint Lounge in 1984; Stiff Little Fingers at Trax in 1980; the three Clash shows I saw at the Palladium in February and September of 1979; any of the 30 or so sets I saw the Feelies play in 1987 and 1988 (Hugo Largo, a band I was in, supported the Feelies throughout much of '87, so there were a lot of opportunities); R.E.M. at the Peppermint Lounge in November of 1982; and the Young Marble Giants show (November 1980) I wrote about in this section. Now, that selection betrays my age and biases and reveals the prime gig-going years of my life; I happily admit it is a limited survey and make no claims to my experiences and opinions on this subject being definitive. It is a deeply personal list.

But when someone says, "Tim, what was THE best? What if you HAD to name just one?" I always have the same answer: Hanoi Rocks at Danceteria in 1983.

I allude to that show in the piece below (an early, longer draft of a piece that appeared in the LA Weekly*), but I really wanted to address the following: in the Slightly Secret History of Rock and Roll, Hanoi Rocks is an extremely important band and doesn't always get its due.*

We love rock and roll, therefore we live in the ecstatic shadows of the most outrageous and beautiful moments our eyes and ears have witnessed. We welcome a neon fugue migraine that enables us to re-call when we beheld the windmill that knows all, the E minor chord that touched the gown of God, the tom-roll at the beginning and end of time. We have measured out our days in memories of bent-knee leaps off of monitors, the sullen crouches of gaunt bassists and the narrow fingers of singers scratching at the smoke-fogged air of old burlesque theaters.

If you saw Hanoi Rocks in 1983 or 1984, you witnessed a certain kind of god. There it was, live onstage: the ultimate pink pop cartoon and the greatest gut-grabbing rock and roll dream, everything you had ever wanted the boogying electric rooster to be, in all its supreme and silly erotic terror!

Guns n' Roses' upcoming shows at the Staples Center and the fabulous Forum remind us that this slutty old leviathan owes almost its entire existence to one single artist. Heck, in the mid- and late-1980s, you couldn't throw a drink ticket in the 213 or 818 area code without hitting a band created in the image of Hanoi Rocks. The whole platinum, spiky and rouged middle of the decade looked like them: from the singers with the serpentine hips to the skipping, swirling guitar players wearing attitudinal hats to the too-cool, vested rhythm guitarists, it all had its roots in Hanoi Rocks.

And it wasn't just the look. It was the sound, too. Uniquely, Hanoi Rocks found a way to wrap a punk rock frame around the fleetest, fastest and most fist-pounding splices of Aerosmith, Thin Lizzy, Alice Cooper and the James Gang. True, they most obviously resembled the New York Dolls, but Hanoi Rocks almost completely discarded the Dolls' R&B aspect while retaining the sleazy, rolling, doo-wopabilly 1/4/5 churn.

Let's do a bit of biographical housekeeping. Hanoi Rocks formed in Helsinki, Finland in 1980, releasing their first album in 1981. In 1982 they moved to London, where the hugely influential British music press, mired in the gloom of post-punk and the earnest grimaces and greasy hair of the British north's Heavy Metal movement, quickly and enthusiastically embraced these loud cowboy peacocks like they were the Fruit Stripe Clash. A few more albums followed, and the band arrived in the United States in 1983 and, well, changed everything.

As you may know, the story has an unhappy ending. In December 1984, Hanoi Rocks drummer Razzle was killed in a car accident in the Hollywood Hills, resulting in a vehicular manslaughter conviction for Motley Crüe's Vince Neil. The devastated band threw in the towel barely six months later.

But I am not interested in that sad part of the story. What matters is that they arrived on our stages in 1983. There's life before you saw Hanoi Rocks and life after.

Onstage (and I first saw them at NYC's Danceteria in March 1984), Hanoi Rocks was a dervish blur of mascara, leopard skin, leather, scarves and suit jackets, announcing with every kick and spin and leer and leap that the circus was back in town. Singer Michael Monroe sashayed like Tommy Tune imitating Iggy imitating Jagger. He was narrow and breathtakingly beautiful, all elbows and knees, a halo of white-hot hair and a laser-cut jawline you could use as a yardstick; he pounced and hopped around the stage like an over-painted marionette, hanging from heating pipes and draping the mic cord around his neck, not as if it was a noose but like a dandy's ascot.

Many singers had glowed with confidence and charisma; it was what was around Monroe that made Hanoi Rocks immortal. Guitarist and co-leader Andy McCoy was clearly impacted by Johnny Thunders (though more in his physical mien then his actual playing): he snarled like Thunders, he did Thunders trademark half windmills (imagine snatching a bug off the top strings of the guitar and then throwing it up towards the lights), he mimed Thunders' slumped stance and then spun like a top, and he was clad in Thunderish suits of glowing game show-host colors. Bassist Sami Yaffa was a wide-stanced punk rock cowboy, the Alvin Gibbs/Pete Way/Paul Simonon manqué we all see in our head when we *think* rock and roll bassist. Rhythm guitarist Nasty Suicide also did the cool cat punkabilly thing, with a soupçon of Nikki Sudden thrown in. Put Nasty and Sami together, by the way, and you have a near-exact premonition of Izzy Stradlin's onstage persona, just a few years in the future.

You can't underestimate Razzle's contribution to the band.

Instead of the over-loud, over-reverbed snare and ludicrously over-played crash cymbals that personify most hard rock drummers, Razzle favored a rumbling low-end tom-heavy approach that owed a great deal to Jerry Nolan, Tommy Ramone and Rat Scabies (vastly different drummers, but all linked by the fact that they created a tumbling parade thump and not the brutal, un-musical "lookit-me mommy lookit-me-mommy I'm the only one in the band!" cymbal wash and double-kick coronary of many "traditional" hard rock drummers). In other words, Razzle was a thoroughly punk rock drummer, and a goddamn good one, in a hard rock band. When you coupled this with bassist Yaffa — who, again, favored rumble over the spotlight — you had a resolutely punk rhythm section in a heavy glam band. Now, that's kind of revolutionary, especially when you consider how frequently this same model was applied to other hard rock bands — both of the Sunset Strip and Seattle varieties — over the next decade.

(By the way, although the greatness of Hanoi Rocks is not necessarily evident on record — though there are bits and pieces here and there — it is evident on video. I direct you to *All Those Wasted Years*, shot live at the Marquee in 1983: it's pretty much *all* there.)

Towards the very end of Hanoi Rocks' sets (at least the ones I saw), there was a great revelation: the Stooges' "1970," only not the Stooges' version — Hanoi Rocks' rendition was very clearly based on the Damned's cover of "1970" (which appears on the Damned's debut album; if you need rock-solid evidence, compare Razzle's drum rolls to those of Rat Scabies). At that moment, even to my 21-year-old mind, it became crystal clear: Hanoi Rocks were trying to rebuild glam metal from a tradition (almost) purely rooted in the Dolls and British punk. The next generation of pop metal would come out of the ashes of '77, not '72.

Hanoi Rocks was essentially a punk rock band, tweaking the style and the marketing just enough to angle it towards a more mainstream metal audience.

This was a vastly radical thing to do. Consider that the (very) prevalent mood in Anglo/European metal at the time was the New Wave of British Heavy Metal movement (Iron Maiden, Samson, Def Leppard, Tygers of Pan Tang, Raven, Saxon, etcetera). NWOBHM shared punk's affection for indie labels and tearing down the lofty bullshit of pompous mainstream music, but the serpentine riffs, Tolkienesque imagery and Crimson-like time signatures of these acts clearly had nothing to do with punk. Hanoi Rocks were a million miles away from all that. (Motörhead would appear to be the exception to this, but that's not quite true: Motörhead's amphetaroar had its roots in old school rock and roll and the ballistic landscapes of Hawkwind, not in punk.)

True, circa 1983 in the U.S., there was definitely a metal/punk crossover beginning to bubble: in Los Angeles, Saint Vitus and DC3 were laying the groundwork for the slabby, sloppy stoner metal of the future (a flag soon to be waved more effectively by the Melvins and Fu Manchu, amongst many others), and other American acts were blending the influence of bands like Discharge and the Misfits with the harder edge of '70s bands like Budgie, Hawkwind and Blue Cheer. But the movement Hanoi Rocks both represented and anticipated was something else entirely: they played a form of punk rock that was in many ways inseparable from the chunk-pop of, say, the U.K. Subs, Generation X, Slaughter and the Dogs or the Boys, but they dressed it in the fabulously sexy swagger of hard rock.

This remarkable crossover, not a conscious selling of punk to metalheads or metal to punks but a natural absorption of the most lean and dramatic aspects of the two tribes, was Hanoi Rocks' gift to the world.

And an entire era in music was created in its image.

2017, *LA WEEKLY*

Are Heilung Papa Oom Mow Mow in the 10th Century?

Can I swallow dirt and the aurora borealis at the same time? Can I chant Pee Pee Mow Mow in both a whisper and a scream while feeling the chill and the spike of the rocks of the Black Sand Beach? Eureka! we shout, in a language we have not spoken since the time before we had language: Heilung have found the missing link between Black Metal and ASMR (Autonomous Sensory Meridian Response: a phenomenon where specific sounds or sights trigger a tingling, relaxing and pleasurable sensation), in the process making one of the greatest art rock albums of recent memory.

Somewhere between Bo Diddley, Penderecki's "Threnody for the Victims of Hiroshima" and *Dark Side of the Moon* you might find Heilung's majestic and amazing new album, *Drif*. A mix of the exotic, ambient, intimate, gigantic, ageless and immediate, it is likely the most adamant, artistic and complete statement of the neo primitive/dark folk/neo-Viking movement and perhaps the first fully great album to emerge from this enthralling genre. *Drif*, the third studio album from these North European makers of "amplified history," is full of magical dirt that stirs the soul-stirred mind and the mindless soul. *Drif*, a creature of starlight and studio night, is easily one of the year's best releases.

Now let's talk about the Beatles. (Yes, it's relevant.) The Beatles made sense in an era where we believed in our future, when we honestly thought that the quirkiness and newness of electric, studio-affected pop was a totem of social and political progress in and of itself. To many of us, the mere existence of the Beatles was a sign that we were on the right track; or if we went a little askew, the existence of awe-inspiring pop was a sign that things could be fixed. Electric, eccentric pop was the flag of our freedoms. Again and again, we mistook artistic, technical and even social progress for an indicator of consistent (and we thought irreversible) political evolution; that is to say, neither Marcel Duchamp, the Beatles, *Woodstock*, indoor plumbing, the iPhone nor even Dr. King somehow prevented us from arriving at this terrifying, if inevitable, moment in American history.

Why? Weren't we paying attention? We have been trained by the post-war entertainment industrial complex to consider variety of distraction the same as freedom, to consider it a means to happiness in and of itself. We believed in pop, we studied pop, we grew up in the shadow of pop's inventions, and we believed this was the frame of freedom, not merely a small aspect of the picture inside the frame. How many times have you run for City Council? Have you become involved in elections for the State Assembly, whose decisions impact so very much of the way you live, love and vote? How many times have you seen Cheap Trick? And we thought, didn't we, that seeing Cheap Trick SAID something IMPORTANT about who we were, and who we were in the world.

We mistook the froth of history for history. The Beatles' world — which is to say, Beatlism — was a world where we thought the quirky creativity and sugary inventions of the Beatles somehow insured brotherhood, largely because we lived in a world where such marvelous things could exist. The Beatles existed; how bad could things be? The Beatles were a charm against destruction employed by a generation that presumed charms were enough. We stand at the precipice of fascism in America. And you know what? Neither *Woodstock*, the Beatles, clever Todd Rundgren nor the grinning ubiquity of Dave Grohl prevented us from reaching this moment. In fact, it is arguable that these circuses actively distracted us from meaningful action and misled us into confusing freedom of leisure choice with actual freedom, the kind of freedom that guards, insures and enables freedom of belief, worship and love.

When the absolutely emptiness of pop gets me down, I sometimes remember those sage words of the Marcels — "Papa Oom Mow Mow Papa Oom Mow Mow" — and I recall that the greatest thing rock music can give us is a big fat Post-it Note reminding us of pop's absolute and necessary connection to our ancestral DNA. Rock is the sound of 30 centuries of the world's disenfranchised made electric. And I love music that reminds me of this! While building pyramid and plantation, while slaving in the coal mines of West Virginia or the satanic mills of the northern England, we made rhythm, we hummed lullabies, we rocked babies to sleep, we sang in unison to break rocks; and this became rock and roll, the sound that rocked peat-roofed homes, grass covered huts, the mildewed green poplar of slave shacks. We have been thumping and humming for ten thousand years or more. "When Jephthah came to Mizpeh unto his house, and behold, his daughter came out to meet him with timbrels and with dances." (Judges 11:34) And almost without doubt, Jephthah's daughter sang Papa Oom Mow Mow or Hoy Hoy Hoy or something very like it … and I am quite goddamn sure Jephthah's daughter would totally get *Drif*.

Drif is a different kind of vaudeville, rooted deep in the exploration and exploitation of the primitive unconscious and the magical sensation of sound and effect (the primitive unconscious is to Heilung what rockabilly was to the Cramps). Prior to *Drif*, Heilung dealt largely with spectacle, though they made a bloody terrific job of it. In 2020, I described Heilung as "KISS if they had been created by *Game of Thrones* fans; they are *Stomp* plus *The Blue Man Group* multiplied by *Wicker Man* divided by *Midsommar* … they are the nightmare you once had about Santa Claus going off his meds, slaughtering his reindeer and ho-ho-ho'ing in your living room while dangling Blixen's severed, flaming antlers and listening to Gary Glitter's 'Rock and Roll Part 2' played at 16 rpm."

Now, all of that remains more or less true on *Drif*, but the difference between it and Heilung's two prior studio albums (there is a live album in there, too, one that virtually reproduces their first studio record) is the difference between, say, Pink Floyd's *Piper at the Gates of Dawn* and *Ummagumma*. Heilung have found grace and hushed magic in the spectacle and legend they were built upon; on *Drif* they lead with that grace. They lead with the dust and sounds and seeds and stars implied by the millennia of noise and fury they source and no longer with just the fury and fire and stomp (though that's here, too).

Drif finds Heilung less volcanic and feral and more adept at sourcing the dewy howls and whispers of the forest and the mysteries of starlight, showcasing the subtlety, beauty and misty magic inherent in their exploration of primitive forms. They achieve this without sacrificing any of their mission of chants, stomps, thumps and conjuring of lost rites. *Drif* is sometimes evocative of Floyd and Sigur Rós (and again and again I think of Alvin Lucier, if Lucier was a Viking wandering through a world of high-end studio equipment and, uh, fire); it's a hard album not to fall under the spell of. Whether you are a fan of Fairport Convention or Impaled Nazarene, Kate Bush or Dimmu Borgir, Clancy Brothers or Cradle of Filth, Górecki or Sleep, or you will find something here, I promise.

Frequently, *Drif* is virtually ASMR-like in its dramatic and profoundly effective use of ambience, distance, proximity, whispers, chimes, drones, nearly subconscious chants and dustings of noise that dissolve into rhythms and melody, creating an extraordinary effect of intimacy and enormity (an excellent subtitle for *Drif* would be *Intimacy and Enormity*). Other times, an almost football-chant unity and intensity emerge out of the dawn fog. It's one hell of an album.

Maybe *Drif* answers the question, "What would happen if Brian Eno produced a New Orleans Second Line Parade while explaining ASMR to the Goths sacking Rome inside of Planetarium?" Oh yeah. In a destabilized world, I welcome this extraordinary blend of artistic adventurism, exotic, hypnotic, mesmeric ambience and a shameless, effective and even sometimes subtle appeal to our ancestral DNA or lullabies and work songs.

It is dark in America. All our original sins, all our celebrations of publicity and power over public service, have come home to roost. The older I become, the more I am simultaneously troubled by the destabilization of our world yet calmed by the certainty of passing time doing its job on me; I find myself turning to music of tallow, grace and age, music that reflects a world of candlelit night, etherless daylight, fire, utility, brilliance, invention, dreams of the cradle made obvious or elaborate: Górecki's *Symphony of Sorrowful Songs*, Wagner's *Parsifal*, Stuart Dempster's *Underground Overlays From the Cistern Chapel*, Immersion's *Nanocluster Vol. I*, anything by Moondog or Billy Childish, La Monte Young's *The Second Dream of the High-Tension Line Stepdown Transformer* — all works where the primitive and the inventive collaborate on the playing field of the imagination. I can't really say it was Heilung's intention with *Drif* to create something so deep, but I do think they meant to create something just as eternal: the dreams of the crib in the age of stone.

2022, *ROCK AND ROLL GLOBE*

Buddy Bolden Discovers the 20th Century: Zero Hour at Rhythm Trinity

Cornet player Charles Joseph "Buddy" Bolden (1877–1931) is generally regarded as one of the primary creators of the musical style known as jazz. He is a central figure — perhaps the *central figure — in the transformation of 19th century dance music into the unique form known as New Orleans Jazz, which integrated European dance music, American folk, pop and ragtime and West African rhythms in an unprecedented way. The more famous names who came in his wake — Louis Armstrong, King Oliver, Jelly Roll Morton — all pointed to him as the mad scientist who made their joyous, rollicking wail possible. He is a figure as mysterious as The Man in the Iron Mask, but possibly as influential as any musician who lived in the 20th century.*

Very little is known about Bolden; in 1907, at age 30, he was committed to the Louisiana State Insane Asylum, and remained behind its walls for the rest of his life. There is no known recording of his music. This story muses on the moment he discovered the Beat Century, the instant he joined the traditions of very distinct cultures and made everything we ever called rock and roll possible.

For Nik Cohn, Justin Joffe and, most of all, Louis Maistro.

It is a wet and warm late winter night, eight weeks into the new century.

The old church hall, rotten with a season-defying damp, is bursting with the smell of cheap pear schnapps, sweet gage smoke, bitter cigarettes made from cheap Turkish tobacco, the greasy resin-odor of lamp oil and the next-to-cheapest violet-scented perfumes.

Brassy, brawny, sobbing, screaming, thumping, sighing, shrieking ancient and modern music fills the room, ten centuries of noise condensed into a caress and a fist.

It comes, improbably, from the small string and brass band on stage. With every other measure and every eighth beat, the bandleader leans 12 degrees forward with his eyes open, then ten degrees backwards with his eyes closed. He throws a sinewy, sexy snake into the mechanical lope of ragtime, reaching across an ocean full of slave ships to grab the Juba beat of West Africa. It's the same rapturous, mesmeric rhythm his parents and grandparents danced to every Sunday in Congo Square, not eight blocks from where he is standing right now. He wraps the loping, jerking, heart thump under, over and around the familiar melodies of the new world and the old.

Some say he can see the future, when his gaze disappears into milk, when his music sounds so new that it sounds old and defies time, when it sounds so profane that it is sacred. Sometimes he thinks he can see the future, especially when he blows so hard into his horn that everything disappears in his vision except a bright white-pink sun in his head with a black-yellow hole in the middle, and he closes his eyes and turns them up to his brain, where he sees a forest of deep-orange trees against a blood red sky.

When this happens, it is all he can do not to disappear under those treetops, those brain trees, and sometimes he does disappear. He's not sure where he goes when time hiccups like that. He feels himself slipping; he holds onto his horn. He awakens holding the same note he was holding a measure earlier — or was it four measures — or eleven measures? At those moments, it's as if the note never started, never ended, as if the note was always there.

On this night, when the old church floor was back underneath his shoes, he took a breath, let the mouthpiece rest against his chest, let the clarinet wail and weep, and he remembered exactly where he was when the twin Saints of Gabriel and Eshu visited him, together, and gave him the vision.

It had been a few years earlier, the third to last spring of the old century. 1897.

He had woken up late in the morning, a sun-bright kitten of a migraine beginning to scratch at the back of his eyes and threatening to turn into a big ass feral street cat, dragging its fur through horse shit and tangling itself up in laundry lines and electrical wires before ripping at his nerves and tearing his vision to pieces. Often, a little gage helped with these matters.

He headed off to the barber shop at St. Claude and Piety to hook himself up.

He felt better as soon as he walked into the storefront. He always did. He loved the smell of the liniments, the oils, the powders and the soaps; he loved the swells and ebbs of the chatter and the occasional crack of a laugh that sounded like a wave scattering on the rocks. The tick and clink of the scissors sounded like birds making music. Before long, he realized he was standing in the center of the white-washed room, half smiling and saying nothing. His stillness began to attract attention. He had become lost, as he so often did, in trying to pick up the melodies and the rhythms of all the different elements and noises of the room. He had become spellbound by continual changes in the sounds as they were reflected by the mirror, altered by the phasing churn of the ceiling fan, amended every now and again by the door to the street opening, which modified how each sound related to every other one.

Then a flash of sunlight on a mirror bounced into his left eye as sure and sudden as an arrow, blinding him and bringing back the cat claws of the migraine. He remembered why he was there.

He bought the gage from Mister Nobody Special, who swept up the place and made sure the back room was always filled with iced beer and catfish, and he left without saying another word.

He crossed over to Desire and walked south to the river, maybe eight blocks. The streets were almost entirely treeless, and it felt like the bleached white sun was out to get him. The pain seemed to pinch the back of his nose and march down the back of his eyes and light matches under his cheekbones. To distract himself he hummed tunes to the rhythm of his footsteps, some of the songs his band played, "The El Capitan March" and some basic quadrilles. That helped a little, but with each step the phrase, "I am death, I am death, I am death," began to replace the melodies.

There was a little patch of green on the levee just to the left of the Congress Street Wharf. He could lie down there for a while, invisible except to the gulls. As he got near the river, he passed some girls playing Pom-Pom Pull Away. He thought their shrieking would just about kill him. He crossed over Chartres and climbed up the short, steep levee, took off his jacket and carefully folded it into a square that would cradle his head. He unbuttoned his vest and lowered himself to the earth.

Lying back, he closed his eyes and lit the roll-up. He inhaled once, lightly, then another time, deeply. He tasted purple, like a sugar eggplant, maybe with a little vinegar on it. The smoke tickled the top back of his throat, and he saw the eggplant. Then the eggplant dissolved into a place where vision and time meshed and stirred together, where the senses intermingled. He could taste what he was thinking, and he could hear what he was seeing. He could pick out the silhouette of reality, but all the borders were gone. He loved this place. He sometimes thought he would just go there to live one day.

With his eyes closed, he saw a flaming wagon wheel against an anvil-colored sky, like he always did when he had these headaches. When he squeezed his eyes, he could also see a field of 88 or so naked branches.

As he smoked, the winter trees of his migraine dissolved into a violet night sky, and on the tip of his tongue he tasted sweet magnolia. He could feel Satan loosen his grip on the back of his eyes and the devil's fingers unclench their hold on his sinuses. Then, with his eyes still shut, he saw a rose-color on the horizon. He watched Venus and Jupiter rise over the lavender horizon of his closed eyes. He focused on Jupiter, ice blue and effortlessly cool, and he watched Venus turn from red to orange to the pale color of a tongue. The wagon wheel thinned, and opened so it wasn't a complete circle, and he no longer held hands with death, he no longer tasted iron and blood.

He was almost half better when the whip-snap of a child's shriek shot a cheap, jagged penny nail right between the bridge of his nose and the inner edge of his closed left eye.

First, he could think of nothing but the pain. Then he felt hatred.

It was a pile of girls, maybe the same ones who had irritated him earlier. Couldn't have been more than three or four of them. Probably just three. They were about 30 or 40 yards away, but the moist New Orleans air was causing the sound to do that weird trick it did sometimes: it would be as loud as if it was coming from right at his feet, then it would vanish, then it would be back again, regardless of the distance. He talked to people about that strange effect all the time. Someone would come up to him in Backatown and say, man, I heard you playing last night, all the way from Algiers! Another time, some old wag on Rampart swore to him she could hear him from across the Lake. It was as if noise could just pack itself up into a cloud and fall like the rain.

The girls were Patting Juba. Some of the boys in the band who were from Mississippi called it Hambone. Pretty much the same thing.

And he took the last long draw from the gage, the gage that made the fiery rings and the white-hot brain trees go away, and it caused the sound of the girl patting Juba to sit over his soul just right. All the squeaky highs of the sound disappeared (and also made the lows sound like they were coming from inside your chest) like there were mittens, or kittens, or corn cakes over his ears. The noise the girls made when they were chanting and clapping was filtered perfectly, leaving just the rhythm.

He kept that last draw in his lungs a long time. The rhythm climbed in there with the smoke, and from inside his chest he heard wumpf-de-whump-de-whamp-hungh-huh-bom-bomp, wumpf-de-whump-de-whamp-hungh-huh-bom-bomp.

The rhythm climbed his throat and missed his teeth and set up house on top of his tongue and below the bottom of his mouth, wumpf-de-whump-de-whamp-hungh-huh-bom-bomp. It pulled apart his lips until he was smiling, and then like a thief in the night it settled in his taffy brain and worked its way around the brain tree meat, wumpf-de-whump-de-whamp-hungh-huh-bom-bomp. And as he exhaled, the rhythm slowed down and pulled apart and seemed like old millstones set far apart, casting giant shadows. So, he sat in the shadows and stood in the shadows and danced in the shadows, and then danced on the millstones, and behind closed eyes he watched a sunset that was orange underneath and pink on top and full of beams beyond color, like the Hallelujah clouds of a New Orleans sunset. He celebrated by singing along to the skeleton of the Juba beat that the girls had left in his head.

And for 18 minutes, he sang in his mind all the old songs, the old quadrilles and schottisches, and each and every one he set to the hippy hippy shake and sigh of the Juba in his head; and he hummed the newer songs his band played, the two-steps and waltzes, and he set them all to the sassy, hump-beat of the Juba.

Suddenly, he was ecstatic. He had heard the future, the beat surrender, the poontang anthems and the spo-dee-o-dee shrieks, all the dinner bells and the rattlesnake tails and the bricks that would build the Kaiserkellers and the chimneys made out of human skulls, the kling klang that knew no modesty, no beginning, world without end, gage, gage, gate, gate, paragate, parasamgate.

He knew he was no longer hearing music for dancing, but music for fucking, because the beat in his head, a-hunh-a-hunh-guh-hung, he-he-whuu-whaa, man, that was the rhythm of fucking, that was the rhythm of a woman's hips under yours, that was the telegraph of a woman's rose under your tongue, ha! And when you slid-slid-slid that beat, the Juba beat of his mother and her mother and her grandfather and his great-great grandmother, under any song, any old song, it did magic things to your song, it turned your song into sexbeat.

It was zero hour at rhythm trinity.

Soon enough (he could see it out of the side of his still-closed eyes), in those lightning flashes when he could see a slit and a slash of the future, the whole next century opened in front of his smoked out, sexbeat mind. Welcome to Madame Curie's new century! Lying there, lit by the rosy sunset of his migraine, he saw the crack of Wynonie's smile and the sassy grin of Louis Jordan and even the stomping glower of Bo Diddley. He saw a century of sway and swing and rolling wind balanced on King Oliver and lonesome Emmett Miller, he saw it all even if he could not name what he saw.

He had found the sad and high crossroad where the clenched songs of Europe and the swaying heartbeat of America's unwilling immigrants met and made sexbeat. As he lay on that levee staring at the back of his eyelids, he invented the future: Appalachia hollow and Gambian thatched hearth and English parlor and Scottish tavern all sealed together by the loose bride of Juba.

He had made the sound of suffering the sound of pop.

2017, *THE NEW YORK OBSERVER*

Part 4: I Have Complicated Feelings About the Beatles

I have complicated feelings about the Beatles.

None of these feelings deny their brilliance, their utterly unprecedented influence or their extraordinary, ageless, endlessly engaging body of work.

Mostly, I am interested in questioning divinity, especially when it comes to pop music.

I have often felt that many of us, in searching for endlessly diverting giants bigger than us who taught us how to relate to the world around us, went from firetrucks to dinosaurs to Beatles. Consider your life, and your life with the Beatles: I bet you fell for the Beatles right around the time you stopped believing in Santa, yes? But you still needed something in your life, something demonstrably larger than you, something full of myth and mystery yet with plenty of accessible history, in that same way you once stood in awe at the foot of firetrucks or under the whale at the Museum of Natural History.

Yet so very many of us never outgrew the Beatles. The Beatles are the childhood fantasy prince or the plush bunny we kept with us. And it's hard for us to be critical about that childhood bunny, isn't it?

I feel that the ubiquity of the Beatles may have done our pop culture more harm than good; more specifically, the impact they had (through absolutely no fault of their own, and I want to underline that) on the natural and fascinating evolution of American rock and pop was catastrophic. As significantly, I feel that Beatlism changed the whole nature of American music's engagement with social activism (when your gods have no skin in the game, it changes everything). I also believe — and again, this is something the Beatles themselves were in no way responsible for — that their almost universal deification by generations of casual and intensive music fans, music media and every facet of the music business has created an industry of Beatle hagiography which has discouraged any real or serious analysis or criticism of their music and their social and cultural impact; likewise, these persistent fumes of hagiography have left some peculiar holes in their story.

Some of the articles in this section address these things. Others are just, well, a little obnoxious.

I am especially proud of the rare interview with the late Chas Newby (who briefly played with the Beatles in late-1960/early-1961 and was offered — and turned down — the bass slot vacated by Stuart Sutcliffe) and the piece where I offer what I believe is some compelling circumstantial evidence regarding the "real" reason Pete Best was fired from the band in mid-1962.

And hanging over all of this, I suppose, is the peculiar irony that, regardless of the holes I may be appearing to prick in the indefatigable surface of the Leviathan Bunny Beatles, their golem-like presence demands that they're the only artist in this collection who merit their very own section (but that's only because I've omitted all those pieces I have written over the years about Hawkwind).

How England Made the Beatles

Part of the weight of the Beatles legend, especially in the United States, is that they emerged out of nowhere; that a dozen or so weeks after John F. Kennedy was slain, they materialized, in defiance of any sort of cultural biogenesis, on our shores to heal us and lead us into a new era.

But that wasn't true.

I have long believed that, at least to a certain extent, not only did the Beatles make the times, but the times made the Beatles. I have tried to explain that here.

There is so very much that is beautiful about the Beatles. Not just their monumental music, but also their impact on our lives as listeners, voyagers, friends of the world they created. I find that the Beatles bring such pleasure, and are such a constant in our journey of cultural discovery, that they not only defy analysis, they defy thought. They are so much a part of us that every bar of their music is like hearing our mother's heartbeat. They are not just a pop group, but also the diary, full of spice and color, for each day in each stage of our lives.

True, in the past I have written critically of the Beatles. I was not necessarily critical of their music, only the impact of their ubiquity. But any criticism is just spit in the ocean and ignores the magic we feel in the presence of both the Beatles music and the idea of Beatles.

For many of us — for most of us — the Beatles were the gateway drug not only to rock music, but also to a whole lifestyle that held guitars, smiled down from posters, smiled up from the well-thumbed horizons of record store racks.

55 years ago this week, the Beatles made their first appearance on *The Ed Sullivan Show*. That Sunday evening, they split our nation's cultural life into a definitive before and after.

When we watch the shiny monochrome clips of the Sullivan show appearance on February 9, 1964, we see a raw, flailing, stomping, grinning rock and roll band, plinking, snarling, thrashing and thumping with a kind of fervor that still seems revolutionary, virile and feral. After all, the Beatles are only 24 months removed from the saloons of Hamburg, and it shows. We also cannot help but note a few small, strange things: Paul's bass does not cut through the mix at all; John's vocals are mixed far too low; a great deal of the high-end frequency of the tiny, square mix is eaten up by Ringo's ride cymbal; George is so very on top of his game that his Hank Marvin/Chet Atkins leads seem more powerful than they did on any Beatles record up until that time; and on and on.

But this sort of hindsight, these observations that are both under the microscope and through the wrong end of the telescope, do not matter at all. We are not interested in the affect of Beatles, but the effect of Beatles.

The Beatles are the most deified act in the history of pop, yet this deification generally omits one vital factor:

Causes and Conditions.

It is easy to believe that whatever the Beatles are, they always have been. It is easy to believe that they were the atom that always waited to be smashed, the ether that always awaited being split by the blue fizz of radio, the Earth that would inevitably be lassoed by the immediacy and constancy of the internet.

But that is not true. Causes and conditions, kiddies, causes and conditions. On this anniversary, I would like to take a moment to celebrate these causes and conditions.

Anniversaries, after all, tell us very little. And traditional rock histories tell us even less. Traditional rock histories tend to focus on heroes, villains and easily described battles and victories. But rock and pop history, like "real" history, is not remotely simple. The roots of great trees are vastly important, yet very often hidden completely under the ground. The Beatles, with their "sudden" emergence on *The Ed Sullivan Show* on February 9, 1964, presented America with the illusion of a Virgin Birth.

Nothing could be further from the truth.

Despite the ubiquity of the Beatles, very few Americans have an understanding of the unique social and cultural causes and conditions that made both their phenomenon and their artistry possible. Without certain seismic developments on the English sociocultural landscape in the 1950s and early 1960s it is very unlikely that Beatlemania would ever have taken place, or any of the Beatles' epochal music would have ever been heard.

I have chosen six important factors — far from a comprehensive survey. Curiously, I am omitting any elements that are "just" about music. For instance, I will not discuss the profound, fundamental influence of the Shadows, the Everlys or Buddy Holly; nor am I addressing how the Beatles were, without a doubt, an aftershock of the skiffle movement. I am also not going to touch on the singular, nearly endless luck (well, not luck, but cause and effect!) the Beatles encountered at every turn: what if Mona Best had never started the Casbah Club, where the Beatles essentially came together? What If Joe Meek had signed them instead of turning them down — today, would they be as relatively obscure as the Outlaws or the Tornados? What If Ron Richards, who produced the band's initial sessions for EMI, had remained at the helm? Would he have allowed the Beatles to experiment in the studio and discover the future, as George Martin did? What if Vee-Jay Records had not fallen apart and held on to the band, would they have never achieved the visibility Capitol Records could provide? And on and on and on…

But the non-musical factors I lightly touch on below are just as important. They help explain that the Beatles were very, very much the product of a time and place. England made the Beatles, even more than the Beatles made England. In no particular order:

Imagine England in 1950, just a dozen years before Beatlemania.

It is 1950. The English lower and middle classes know their place. Less than a decade prior to the emergence of the Beatles, it was inconceivable that an artist (in any genre) from the north of England could attain massive mainstream respect and commercial success throughout the country. It was nearly as unlikely that a major artistic force could emerge from the English working class. Class and geographical prejudice, in place for nearly a millennium, still entirely held sway in the years immediately following the Second World War.

In the early 1950s, the media establishment and tastemakers in England considered the North an artless morass of uneducated, working-class people who had little impact on the cultural arbiters in London and the south of England. All media channels maintained this unfortunate perception. This was roughly analogous to the attitude a New Yorker in the 1950s might have had towards West Virginia or Arkansas. Likewise, in deeply class-entrenched mid-century English society, there was a near-universal belief that the British working class could produce little culture or art that was worthy of serious critical examination.

Circa 1950 — even as late as 1955 — it wasn't just unthinkable that a group of artists could emerge from the working class in the north of England, accrue respect and achieve a massive economic and cultural impact; it was more or less impossible. But that changed…

In the 1950s, Kitchen Sink Realism begins to puncture holes in the traditional ways of portraying the English working class.

Film, theater and literature in the late '50s — what came to be known as Kitchen Sink Realism — gave working-class England a unique and intelligent voice. As the decade progressed, the public image of the English working class and natives of the North began to change dramatically in a way that made acceptance of the Beatles, working-class Northerners, possible. This was especially evident in the work of film directors and playwrights like John Osborne, Lindsay Anderson and Tony Richardson and authors like Colin MacInnes and Alan Sillitoe.

The North gets its voice: Manchester's Granada Television goes on the air.

In 1956, the very first English television station outside of London went on the air. Granada Television was not only a pioneer in British independent television (prior to the mid-1950s, the state-run BBC controlled all television programming), but more pertinently to the future life of the Beatles, it brought a distinctly Northern flavor to culture and the news. For the first time, millions of television viewers in the United Kingdom were exposed to a cultural viewpoint that was not limited to or defined by a London perspective. Granada took its mission very seriously and determined, in virtually every program it aired, to reflect a distinctly Northern attitude and a positive reflection of the diversity of culture in the North. The appearance of Granada was a profound portent of the Beatles' emergence half a decade later. This culminated in 1960 with the debut of Granada's *Coronation Street*, a nighttime soap opera set in working-class Manchester, which became one of the most popular shows in British television history.

Granada and shows like *Coronation Street* profoundly changed the attitude of the nation regarding the intellectual and commercial potential of the North.

Comedy shapes the 1960s: The Goons give young England its own hip voice.

In America, Ginsberg, Kerouac and the Beats (not to mention Norman Mailer, J.D. Salinger and Tom Wolfe) set the tone for the 1960s by expanding the way language could be used and creating a private and anti-establishment lexicon for young America. In much the same way, in England the Goons (absurdist, Joycean sketch comedians whose wildly popular weekly radio show ran on the BBC from 1951 to 1960) and their surrealistic use of language and wordplay profoundly influenced the Beatles and an entire generation of young English men and women. The Goons created an environment where rabid, unfettered creativity — not to mention a near-constant sense of Dadaist absurdity and punning — could be used to both power sketch comedy and create a "private" language for the youth of post-war England. John Lennon was very open about the influence the Goons had on him (his lyrics and public persona are intensely indebted to them); he spoke about it frequently. Yet this debt still remains largely unknown to most American fans of the Beatles. Likewise, in his work with the Goons — 1959's *The Running Jumping & Standing Still Film* — director Richard Lester unveiled and developed the vocabulary of image and style that he would later use in *A Hard Day's Night* and *Help!* and would become inextricably identified with the Beatles.

Speaking of comedy... Four young men lounge about in front of the camera.

In 1963 and 1964, the Beatles stood in front of cameras for the black and white shots that would define their profile forever. They were cocky, slouching, confident, louche and vaguely uncomfortable in their new duds, utterly adorable but somehow rebellious. Yet two years before these era-defining shots, we find a remarkable, game-changing comedy team photographed in virtually the exact same poses, with the same half-grins on their face, also simultaneously mocking the establishment and welcoming it with open arms. These were the four young writer/actors of *Beyond the Fringe*, whose rebellious but user-friendly satire took the West End (and later Broadway) by storm in the years immediately before the Beatles. The visual precedent created by *Beyond the Fringe*, not to mention their spirit of user-friendly rebellion, both softened the landing for the Beatles and influenced the band's visual profile.

Last but far from least: Suez, and the end of mandatory military service.

On December 31, 1960, military conscription ended in the United Kingdom. Following the political humiliation in the Suez in 1958 (which underlined the loss of British colonial and overseas political power) and the destabilization of faith in government due to the extended rationing following the Second World War, the abandonment of conscription served to further underline a loss of trust in the "establishment" in the United Kingdom. Just as significantly, the door was now open for both productive cynicism and for young people to live a life free of the blind faith in authority, enforced deprivation and fear of military service that had haunted them since the Second World War. Think how differently the Beatles' story would have been written if their crucial years of gestation had been altered and abridged by military service (as Elvis Presley's had been). Free of that shadow of the draft, the Era of the Teenager could now come into full fruition … just in time for the Beatles.

By 1962, the Beatles were a reality, made possible by a nearly endless sequence of causes and conditions, some of which I have outlined above. On February 9, 1964, they changed everything about being young in America.

2021, *ROCK AND ROLL GLOBE*

Meet the Beatles' First Left-Handed Bassist

In 2020, I got it in my head to interview Chas Newby, who briefly played bass in the Beatles after Stuart Sutcliffe left and before Paul McCartney switched to the instrument. I reached out to the school where Newby had taught, and through a few different cheerful connections, finally reached the man himself.

Newby died in 2023; this piece was much cited — and linked — in many of his obituaries, as one of the definitive sources of information on his short career with the most famous band in history.

It's one of the most famous and exclusive clubs on earth. Historically, there are only ten members (and no new ones since 1964). Only six members are still alive.

Can you imagine being one of those six? Can you imagine puttering around your kitchen, making a big mug of tea, sitting down in a nice comfy chair in front of *The Great British Baking Show* and thinking, "Oh … I was in the Beatles. Yes, I was. How about that? Why, that's a different take on a Viennese tart! Oh, and I was in the Beatles. I think I'll have some biscuits. And, oh, that's right, I was in the Beatles."

There are ten men who performed multiple gigs as a member of a band called the Beatles. Their names are (in alphabetical order) Pete Best, George Harrison, Johnny Hutchinson, John Lennon, Paul McCartney, Tommy Moore, Chas Newby, Jimmy Nicol, Ringo Starr and Stuart Sutcliffe.

Chas Newby is a retired mathematics teacher who lives in Warwickshire, a county in the West Midlands of England probably best known as the birthplace of William Shakespeare. Exactly 60 years ago, in December 1960, Newby did four gigs as the bassist in the Beatles. He was six months shy of his 20th birthday. Notably, Newby was onstage for the Beatles' gig at Litherland Town Hall on December 27, 1960. This date is generally acknowledged as the start of Beatlemania, the first time a rapt, avid and responsive audience saw the Beatles display the energy, wit and wild abandon that they had learned playing six hours a night, six days a week, in the cellars of the Reeperbahn.

Unlike almost everyone on Earth (a big place, Earth), Chas Newby was actually asked to join the Beatles twice (!). The first time was in the autumn of 1960, when George Harrison was deported from West Germany for performing in Hamburg nightclubs while underage. Pete Best, who had played with Newby in Best's pre-Beatles band, the Blackjacks, reached out to Newby to replace Harrison on guitar for the remainder of the band's 1960 Hamburg dates.

Newby, who had just started his second year at St Helens College, studying chemistry and chemical engineering, turned Best and the Beatles down. However, Newby indicated that if the group still needed someone when they returned to Liverpool, he would be happy to help out (especially if the gigs coincided with his winter break from college).

As it happened, the Beatles never played Hamburg without Harrison. Due to a conflict with club owner Bruno Koschmider (who accused them of attempting to burn down the decrepit cinema where they were housed), the band's contract was cancelled prematurely, and John, Paul and Pete returned to Liverpool, shortly after George, in late November 1960. But this time they needed a bassist, not a guitarist: Stuart Sutcliffe had decided to stay behind in Hamburg. Once again, they reached out to Newby. This time, he said yes.

What do you ask someone who witnessed so much musical history, who actually stood onstage, in borrowed leather, and stomped alongside John, Paul, George and Pete? Newby seemed happy to answer anything I threw at him, though I deliberately tried to cover ground I had not necessarily seen written about in other pieces on the savage young Beatles, or in Mark Lewisohn's essential accounts of the period.

Can we go over the events that led to you performing with the Beatles, 60 years ago this month?

When the Beatles were playing their first gig in Hamburg I was starting my second year at college. I was in touch with Pete by post, and was vaguely aware of George's deportation, but there was no way I was going to give up my college place. When the band reunited in Liverpool mid-December, Pete organized a bass guitar for me and we had a couple of rehearsals, which must have gone okay. My overall memory was playing a right-handed bass upside down and playing with the best band in the world. Dave Bedford, a good friend from Liverpool, always reminds me that I was the first left-handed bass player in the Beatles.

There has been a lot written about the Litherland Hall gig, but I've seen very little about your other three shows with the Beatles in December of 1960. Can you tell us something about these?

The first of my four gigs was at the Casbah Club. This was a private members club, and all five of us were known by the punters, having played there before. However, they were not prepared for the power of the band, no doubt gained from long hours onstage in Germany. Everybody knew right away how much better they were. Neil Aspinall had prepared posters proclaiming, "Direct from Hamburg" which no doubt contributed to the excitement.

The next gig was at the Grosvenor Ballroom in Wallasey [a small town on the River Mersey, immediately to the north and west of Liverpool]. This was a ballroom open to the general public, with a reputation for violence. Also on the bill were Derry and the Seniors, also back from Hamburg. I honestly can't remember anything special about the gig. I was probably watching the audience for the first sign of trouble.

My last appearance was the New Year's Eve party at the Casbah. This was really a celebration of the return of the Beatles to Liverpool. On the 4th of January 1961 I was back at my desk in college, and my career as a rocker was over.

Where did you, John, Paul, George and Pete rehearse?

We did at least one rehearsal in the lounge of Pete's home, and probably one downstairs in the Casbah Club. The material that the

Beatles were playing at the end of 1960 was essentially the classic rock and roll tunes from the mid-to-late-'50s, i.e., Elvis, Little Richard, Carl Perkins, Buddy Holly. This was the same for most of the bands around the Liverpool scene, so it wasn't much of a stretch for me. Certainly, I was familiar with most of their repertoire from playing with Pete in the Blackjacks prior to him joining the Beatles.

It's been mentioned that you performed "Long Tall Sally" and "What'd I Say" in the December 1960 Beatles sets, but do you recall any of the other numbers you performed at Litherland or the other three shows?

Probably "Matchbox" and "Honey Don't" by Carl Perkins, "That'll Be the Day" by Buddy Holly, "Hallelujah, I Love Her So," which had been originally recorded by Ray Charles, but we did the Eddie Cochran version. Paul also sang a recent Elvis record, "Wooden Heart," and "Red Sails in the Sunset," which was a recent hit for Emile Ford. I'm sure we also did Chuck Berry songs.

Was there any chatter about doing original songs? Did you hear any fragments in rehearsal?

Although I now know that John and Paul had started to write their own material, I didn't hear anything at all, and it wasn't discussed.

Were you and Paul the only left-handed musicians on the Liverpool scene? Did you have a proper left-handed bass?

I don't remember any other lefties at the time. We just turned the strings around. For my four gigs with the Beatles, I borrowed a bass from a guy named Tom McGurk who was right-handed. I just played it upside down. I think the first time I saw a true left-handed instrument was when Paul bought his first Hofner later in 1961.

There's a well-known picture of you taken around that time — you appear to be playing a guitar, left-handed, in a front room. What was the setting and date of that picture?

This photograph was taken in the lounge of the Best home in December 1959. The photo was taken by Pete's younger brother Rory at one of the first practice sessions for the Blackjacks. Bill Barlow had just bought the first Burns guitar to arrive in Liverpool and so I felt I had to make an effort. Since left-handed instruments were not available, I decided to make one. I rescued a neck from an old acoustic guitar and screwed it to a piece of timber, shaped to look something like a left-handed Strat. The other pieces such as pickups, machine heads and controls were available at guitar shops. It lasted for about a year before collapsing, due to no rod in the neck.

Did you get the feeling at the time that Paul wanted to move over to bass or was under some pressure to do so?

It was probably Hobson's choice [*i.e., no choice*] for Paul. I had imagined that Stuart would return by the beginning of January 1961, and I got the idea that maybe they were under that impression, too. I do remember seeing Paul playing his Rosetti 7 with the six guitar strings replaced with three bass strings.

I have seen conflicting information on this, so I will just come out and ask. Did you choose to leave the Beatles? Were you actually asked to join? Was it always understood that your gig was temporary?

I was asked to play bass as a temporary replacement for Stuart. I knew it was short-term, and I also knew I would be back at college in January 1961. I had no desire to be a professional musician. When the subject originally came up, I think John was trying to get other people interested in going to Hamburg rather than replacing Stuart.

I have heard the Blackjacks' name a lot but have no real handle on what they might have sounded like. Can you describe them a little and compare them to other Mersey acts?

When Ken Brown left the Quarrymen in October 1959, he convinced Pete to start another band with Pete playing drums. Pete brought in Bill Barlow and myself, both school friends of Pete and Casbah members from the opening night. Bill and I had played together in a skiffle group at school, but this new band, the Blackjacks, was our first experience of playing amplified rock and roll. Ken was the most experienced, and the three of us picked it up as we went along. The Blackjacks were much the same as many of the other amateur bands of the period. The set list would have been much the same as Quarrymen or Searchers. Mid-'50s American rock and roll. Of the other bands around at the same time, Rory Storm and the Hurricanes, Cass and the Casanovas and the Bluegenes were playing professionally [*the Bluegenes were a higher-end skiffle group who evolved into the Swinging Blue Jeans*]. The Blackjacks played with three guitar players. Bill [Barlow] played lead, intros and guitar breaks. Ken [Brown] played rhythm, and I played the bass parts. Imagine Jerry Lee Lewis left-hand piano or guitar boogie-type scales. I never played bass until I played with the Beatles.

NOTE: *Let's address a little band-name muddle-up here. There is some small evidence that the Quarrymen, the skiffle group that eventually contained Lennon, McCartney and Harrison and evolved into the Beatles, may have also briefly performed under the name the Blackjacks. But that Blackjacks is unrelated to the band formed a little later with Best and Newby, despite the fact that Ken Brown and Bill Barlow were in both the Quarrymen and the Best/Newby Blackjacks. The overlap in names appears to be more or less coincidental, and the Quarrymen were not an early form of the Blackjacks, despite the duplicated moniker and the overlap in members. This has, understandably, caused some confusion over the years.*

At that time you played with the Beatles, Pete Best had only been in the band a few months. Did you get the feeling he was on solid ground as a member, and, either socially or musically, did he feel fully integrated into the group?

At the time I thought that they were like the Four Musketeers, all for one and one for all. I guess that came from sharing what was a new experience for them all, long hours of playing to a non-English audience in Hamburg.

I have always thought Mona Best, Pete's mother and the creator of the Casbah, was the unsung hero of this entire story, and it is possible the Beatles would never have happened without her. Would you agree with this?

I would also include Ken Brown in that comment. When Mrs. Best opened the Casbah Club in August 1959, it was Ken Brown and George who brought John and Paul back together to play the opening night as the Quarrymen. When the Beatles returned to Liverpool in December 1960, it was Mrs. Best who provided them with a base and the first and subsequent gigs before Brian [Epstein] took over the management role at the end of 1961.

Can you give me your impressions of Pete as a drummer? I have always sensed he got the short end of the stick. All the Beatles' recordings with him are very primitive, so it's hard to tell, but I assume that in order to drive a pure rock band like the Beatles, he had to be pretty good.

At the time, Johnny Hutchinson of the Casanovas and then the Big Three was acknowledged as supreme, but the rest of the drummers in the area bands were much the same. As you say, he was certainly good enough to get the Beatles to the start of their fame.

Were you surprised when Pete was booted from the Beatles? Did you guys talk about it at the time?

Along with almost everybody else in Liverpool at the time, the replacement of Pete by Ringo came as a shock. I was well out of the music scene by then and had lost touch with people.

I know you still have a relationship with Pete, but did you ever run into John, Paul or George again after they became well known?

I saw the band perform in Liverpool prior to 1962, but I lost contact when the guys moved to London.

In his remarkable book, Roots, Radicals and Rockers: How Skiffle Changed the World, *Billy Bragg makes the case that skiffle was a form that developed independently from American rockabilly, that it must be taken seriously as a completely independent, powerful and influential form of rock and not an "aside" or an interstitial. Would you agree? Can you say a few words about how skiffle rocked your world?*

I would agree with Billy Bragg that they were separate strains of music that coexisted side by side during the late '50s. You could make a good case for saying that they both emerged from the same source of American music, combining elements of blues, gospel, folk and country music. We were certainly listening to Lonnie Donegan at the same time as Elvis, Carl Perkins and Chuck Berry. I think everybody started with skiffle because it was accessible: acoustic guitars and washboards with tea chest basses. I remember thinking "I can do that." The gradual change to rock and roll occurred as electric instruments became available in the UK. The Quarrymen still play a mixture of both, to showcase the music that influenced the Beatles.

The mania for traditional New Orleans jazz and ragtime — "trad" — was something that existed alongside the early skiffle scene and seems to have been fairly present in the Mersey music scene in the late 1950s. When you knew the Beatles, was there any trad influence lingering within them? Some of their earliest recordings were songs that were borderline trad, like "Summertime" and "Ain't She Sweet."

I think Paul used elements of show music all the time. George was also interested in a wide range of guitar players, including jazz player Barney Kessel and country virtuoso Chet Atkins.

My understanding is that, in its earliest days, the Cavern favored trad bands. Was there any tension between the trad scene, the musicians who came from a trad background, and the young rockers?

I think the prejudice was from the owners rather than the performers. The Cavern opened in 1957 as a jazz club, and it wasn't until 1961 that the first rock and roll bands started playing lunchtime sessions. I think it was Rory Storm who made the breakthrough. The wider appeal of jazz began to wane in the '60s and the ownership of the Cavern needed to bring in a wider audience.

I have always thought that Americans vastly underrate the influence of Spike Milligan and the Goons on the sensibility of the Beatles specifically and Mersey rock in general. Do you have any thoughts on this?

The Goons were compulsory listening on BBC radio. I always thought that American interviewers had a "sense of humor failure" when talking to the Beatles, and I think the guys played that to their advantage.

Okay...it's January of 1961, and you are back at college and no longer a Beatle. Want to give us a rough guide to what happened next in your life?

If I was to describe myself now, could I suggest "Aging Liverpool Rocker"?

After December 1960, my career as a rock star was over. For the next 40 years I concentrated on family and professional career. I worked as a professional engineer until 1990 and then as a teacher of mathematics until I retired in 1998. Pete Best and his brothers, Rory and Roag, decided to reopen the Casbah Club in 1999 to celebrate the 40th anniversary of the opening of the original. Bill Barlow, Ken Brown and myself were dragged out of obscurity to reform the Blackjacks, and we played a short set of our '50s repertoire on the Casbah stage. Having reawoken our playing urge, Bill and I formed a band called Blue Suede Feet, playing mostly in the area around Bedford. At about the same time, I joined a local band here in Warwickshire called the Racketts. But the biggest influence on my musical output was joining our local Male Voice Choir. We have sung in some really notable places, including the Royal Albert Hall, Symphony Hall, Birmingham and many of the foremost cathedrals in the UK. However, the jam, the cream and everything else on the cake must be singing the six o'clock mass at the Duomo in Florence during a tour of Italy in 2004.

In August 2013, Bill and I were at the Casbah Club, playing a couple of tunes with the Pete Best Band. On the bill that night were the Quarrymen. We got chatting about old times and the result was that I started playing bass with the Quarrymen in 2016. [*The present-day Quarrymen still contain three members who played alongside McCartney, Lennon and Harrison.*] Since then, I have played in the Czech Republic, Hungary, Spain; a year ago we were in Mexico City. 2020 has been quiet due to the Covid outbreak, but we did manage to do a gig in Germany at the beginning of October, celebrating what would have been John's 80th birthday.

I am constantly amazed that people attend Beatles festivals to see four old age pensioners performing the music of our youth. We try to emphasize that we are not a Beatles tribute band but simply perform the music that influenced them 60 years ago. So far, we have avoided banging into the microphone stands with our Zimmer frames.

2020, *ROCK AND ROLL GLOBE*

NOTE: *Chas Newby died in May 2023, shortly before his 82nd birthday.*

The Beatles' Last Secret: The Real Reason Pete Best Was Fired

I stand by what I wrote here, back in 2021: there is pretty goddamn compelling circumstantial evidence that we have never been told the real reason Pete Best was fired from the Beatles. (There is also the possibility that the Beatles themselves never actually knew, though it would be hard to believe they didn't have their suspicions.) Considering the (literal) millions of words written about the Beatles, I remain surprised that more people haven't picked up on the plethora of clues that were left for us pointing to a radically different version of one of the most important moments in the story of the world's most famous band.

Is it possible that we may not know the truth about the most famous firing in the history of pop music?

There have been millions of words written about the Beatles. These luscious characters, briny stories and brothy myths are possibly the most recounted and retold legends of our era. Yet one of the remarkable things about the Beatles hagiography (a word I do not use lightly) is that one of its most interesting chapters may remain obscured.

I am fairly convinced we have been lied to about the real reason drummer Pete Best was ousted from the Beatles on August 16, 1962, five weeks before they recorded their debut album for Parlophone.

What follows is just a theory. But I think the circumstantial evidence is pretty compelling.

Circa mid-1962, the Beatles were about to break into the mainstream music industry. Although their manager, Brian Epstein, wasn't that much older than John, Paul, George and Pete, he was of an entirely different class and social strata than the band. Brian Epstein never was one of the gang, not even close, and he was most certainly aware of this. But Neil Aspinall, the Beatles' day-to-day manager and roadie/driver, was both the same age as the group and an active part of their inner circle.

In addition, since the inception of the Beatles, Mona Best had been exerting a powerful influence on the group. More than any Beatle parent (by far), she was involved in the band's life and supported their dreams in every way she could. Mona Best felt such a strong connection with the young musicians of Liverpool that she started a venue in her basement. The Casbah Club, opened in the coal cellar underneath the Bests' Victorian house at 8 Hayman's Green in the autumn of 1959, would become the first real showcase room for the nascent Beatles; in addition, it was their home away from home where they regularly met, rehearsed and wrote songs when they wanted to get out of their front rooms. Mona's son, Pete, would join the Beatles in August of 1960, on the eve of their first trip to Hamburg (we note that Pete was not a novice drummer at this point, and had regularly been gigging with a combo called the Blackjacks).

In the early spring of 1962, John, Paul, George and Pete signed a record deal with Parlophone, a subsidiary of EMI. A few months before the deal was signed, Aspinall had begun an affair with Mona Best. As the Beatles prepared to go into the recording studio to make their first major label recordings, Mona Best was pregnant with Aspinall's child.

I believe that Brian Epstein was so threatened by the potential of an Aspinall/Best alliance that he stage-managed Pete Best's dismissal from the band. Pete Best was fired on August 16, only 25 days after the birth of Vincent "Roag" Best, the son of Neil Aspinall and Mona Best.

This is important: I want you to stop for a second and try to forget everything you know about the Beatles myth and everything you've read about them, and really think about what this means:

It is midsummer 1962. The Beatles are on the cusp of the big time. Manager Brian Epstein's right-hand man, who is far closer to the band than he is, has just had a child with the mother of the band's drummer. In addition, this mother is someone who the band likes and respects and has always been close to their dreams.

Look at this from Epstein's perspective. He had to have been worried that Neil Aspinall, Mona Best and Pete Best were going to form an alliance that could jeopardize his control over the band at exactly the time when they had the golden ring within their sight. (Or, more charitably, he was worried about what would happen to the social, political and practical dynamics of the band unit if Mona and Neil broke up, or what kind of tension might be created on the road if Pete saw his mother's boyfriend flirting with another girl — that sort of thing.) Picture Brian Epstein: paranoid, pill-taking, insecure, on the verge of making a lifelong dream come true and making a splash down south in London; the idea of an Aspinall/Best alliance had to have made his head explode. Even if we take Mona out of the picture (unlikely, considering the band rehearsed in her basement), Epstein had to have been acutely aware that the Beatles' day-to-day manager was the father of the drummer's half-brother, creating an organic alliance that was bound to change the power dynamic.

Epstein also likely sensed that the Beatles, pragmatic young men who wanted success as much as he did, would side with him if he attempted a power play (he surely remembered how quickly they had dumped their first manager, Alan Williams, when a better opportunity presented itself). Likewise, we also must assume (and yes, I know there's a pile of assumptions here) that Epstein knew Aspinall would likely side with John, Paul and George over Pete, Mona and changing nappies, and this shows Epstein's calculated brilliance at work (or his willingness to take a high-stakes risk).

Now let us talk about some of the oft-repeated stories attached to Pete Best's departure from the Beatles. The most common one is that he wasn't good enough for the Beatles and/or George Martin. I'm calling bullshit on this, and there's a pile of solid reasons why.

By mid-1962, Pete Best had played hundreds of gigs with the Beatles. He had provided the backbeat for their rise to domination over Liverpool's ballrooms and Hamburg's nightclubs, and he was plenty good enough to do that. Not one single contemporary account says anything about Best being a crappy drummer. If Best had been as shitty as myth has made him out to be, he would have been out of the Beatles halfway through their first Hamburg run, not a year and a half later. There is also some convincing aural evidence testifying to Pete's competency. By far, the best and most representative recordings of Pete Best with the Beatles are their two appearances on BBC's *Saturday Club*, recorded in Manchester on March 7, 1962 and June 11, 1962. (The two better-known recordings of Best and the Beatles, the Tony Sheridan sessions from June of 1961 and the Decca audition on January 1, 1962, both lack the high energy and spontaneity of the Manchester sessions and aren't nearly as well-recorded.) The six songs taped at the two Manchester sessions display that Best played strong and tight, with a significantly harder kick drum and much louder snare-hand than Ringo Starr. Although Best certainly lacks Starr's finesse, he makes up for that with raw but accurate energy. He truly pumps and drives the band, playing with a whacking Memphis-meets-military style somewhere between D.J. Fontana, Bobby Graham (more about him shortly) and Tony Meehan of the Shadows … which is all to say that on the March 7 and June 11 sessions, Best sounds like a cross between Tommy Ramone and Don Powell of Slade. What Pete most decidedly does NOT sound like on the two *Saturday Club* sessions is someone who couldn't keep a beat or couldn't play the drums; in fact, quite the opposite. (I will note that Best has a distinctive habit of doing a pick-up with the kick right before the snare hit on the second beat — think of it as the Chiffons/Shirelles beat — which gives all the material a fairly pronounced swing, not unlike what Charlie Watts gave to the Stones; it is somewhat alien to the Beatles style we have become used to.) More than any other evidence, those two recordings show that the myth of Best being an inferior or insufficient player is complete bullshit. I will also mention that the March 7 recording was made roughly 36 hours after I was born, so there's that.

Next, and perhaps more significantly, we contend with the oft-told story that George Martin rejected Pete Best and/or encouraged the Beatles to engage a better drummer. I am going to concretely disprove that myth and toss it out of the window for all eternity in seven syllables: Bobby Graham (and) Clem Cattini.

This idea may seem supremely foreign to any band that came of age in the 1970s, '80s, '90s and beyond: when a self-contained pop/rock combo arrived at a major London recording studio for a session in the early and mid-1960s, there was virtually zero expectation that the drummer they walked in with would be playing on the finished record. This is the reason that Graham and Cattini play on almost every pop, rock and beat record of the era. (Even a cursory list would double the length of this article; suffice to say that Graham, in particular, is *the* sound of the British Invasion; the snap and oomph he brings to nearly all of the early hits of the Kinks, Them, the Dave Clark 5, the Pretty Things, the Animals, Herman's Hermits et al. helped define the sound of the genre itself.) It would have been extremely unlikely that an experienced producer like George Martin, working for a gigantic company like Parlophone, would consider using an unproven drummer on a session. Nor would Martin have ever used that as the basis to fire a band's existing drummer. What bands did in the studio and what they did onstage were considered entirely different parishes; the studio was the concern of Parlophone and its staff producers and engineers; live performances were the domain of the band, their management, their booking agent and promoters.

Seriously: If the Beatles had walked in with Paul's granny on bongos, George Martin wouldn't have asked them to fire her; he would have just said, let's bring in a session bongo player. As stated, it's very likely a contemporary ('62–'65) record producer probably would not have given the primary drummer a chance to sit on the stool. They would have already had a session drummer in place, as was the case when the Beatles recorded "Love Me Do." The presence of session drummer Andy White at minute one of the very first Beatles recording session is plenty of evidence that neither the Beatles, Brian Epstein, George Martin or Ron Richards used "competence" as an excuse to fire Best, since there was no expectation he would perform in the studio anyway. Regardless of the fact that there is no doubt Ringo Starr was a better drummer than Pete Best, I simply do not and cannot believe Best was ousted for this reason. There's just not enough contemporary evidence to support this.

Is it possible there were other reasons, either due to personality or musicality, which made John, Paul and George say, "Oh, Ringo, that's the one we want"? Oh, absolutely. But the circumstantial evidence that Epstein engineered Pete's ouster because he feared a Best/Best/Aspinall alliance (or, as noted earlier, he was wary of or unhappy about the personal complications caused within the band dynamic by the Mona Best/Aspinall relationship) is at *least* compelling enough to make us wonder why it has never been thoroughly investigated. I mean, come on! Are you telling me that when Brian Epstein found out the Beatles' day-to-day manager was going to have a baby with the drummer's mother, HIS BRAIN DIDN'T START TO LEAK OUT OF HIS EARS?!? It is ludicrous that this theory hasn't been widely discussed or investigated.

Now, none of this — not a word, truly — is intended to diminish the considerable skills and charms of Ringo Starr; and none of this, not a word, is to say that the Beatles weren't possibly, or even likely, better off with Ringo. It is simply to say that there's a very significant chance that the real story regarding why Pete Best was suddenly ousted from the Beatles has never been told.

2021, *ROCK AND ROLL GLOBE*

"Your Mother Should Know" Is a Turd

No one is infallible, not even the Beatles. That is a desperately important lesson.

"Your Mother Should Know" by the Beatles came on the radio. I have heard this song perhaps as many times as there are grains of sand in the River Ganges; yet for the first time I realized THIS SONG IS A TURD.

This Mento-flavored infusion of over-clever hookery (bereft of edge or even the bile-colored rainbow of irony) defies the spirit of discovery and adventure that defined 1967, but *not* in a rebellious or prescient way (as similar exercises by the Kinks did); instead, "Your Mother Should Know" is an asinine prodigy's shriek to be liked and to be admired, to be seen as *timeless*, in other words, *better than its time.*

"Your Mother Should Know" utterly lacks the thorny point of view or originality that, say, the spectacular Bonzo Dog Band would have brought to the proceedings. The Bonzos trafficked in revisiting and reinventing the 1920s tropes that McCartney explored here, but the Bonzos brought a true dose of adventure, invention, Dada and near-revolutionary fervor to the proceedings. The Bonzos did this kind of thing and waved the flag of Tristan Tzara; McCartney does it and waves the flag of Ukulele Ike. The Bonzos would have approached a song like this the way Magritte would have approached an apple or Picasso would have approached a woman's profile; they would have seen it from all sides, including dimensions that defied normal vision. Likewise, the Kinks (or the Small Faces, who also dabbled in faux-archaic material) would have tackled it as a musical adventure, attempting to construct an emotionally rich piece in an antiquated style using contemporary instruments and production techniques. But Paul McCartney, on the other hand, does none of that; not only is he JUST trying to reproduce the sound of a bygone era, he is also INSISTING we be impressed by how well he does it.

And that's exactly what McCartney is doing here: he is trying to impress the adults.

Conversely, with something like "Yesterday," I genuinely think he was trying to impress his peers; in other words, with "Yesterday" McCartney was saying "I can reach you via a different palette than the one we — the *generational* we — might normally use"; he was also likely referencing a somewhat underground (for UK and U.S. listeners) tradition of hyper-emotional French balladry. So, hooray for "Yesterday." See, believe it or not, "Yesterday" actually had an edge and a point of view that "Your Mother Should Know" completely lacks. "Your Mother Should Know" is an edgeless exercise (and a well-executed one, too, which actually makes it *worse* — that's why I prefer the similar but utterly ham-fisted "Winchester Cathedral"), and it is most loathsomely and criminally committed to tape NOT to emotionally reach or move the listener (as "Yesterday" or even the inferior but delightful "Michelle" did), BUT JUST TO IMPRESS US BY SHOWING US HOW WELL HE DOES THIS THING. McCartney is precisely like one of those moon-faced children you see in supermarkets who pick up a box of cereal and loudly announce "Mother, I hear excellent things about this product and suggest you buy it." And everyone within hearing thinks "Awww, isn't that *darling*, he sounds *so adult*!"

By the way, this piece is only indirectly about the mewling, faux-velvet-covered piss-puddle of forced smiles called "Your Mother Should Know."

It is really about infallibility.

Even the Beatles sucked sometimes. Their very vulnerability was essential to their genius, made them experiment and invent fearlessly, made them strive for the delicious angles of mortality instead of the boring ecru shades of mediocrity. Somehow, over the years the idea has developed that if you love the Beatles, you have to insist on their infallibility; you have to believe that *every* instance of Paul's establishment-pleasing musical pleas for immortality is *perfect*, *every* expression of John's angry sexism is *perfect, every* time George Harrison steals a sliding riff from Peter Green it is *perfect, every* time Ringo inelegantly whacks the crash-cymbal in a musically meaningless way that does nothing to enhance the song it is *perfect.* Kill your fucking idols, man. If you really love the Beatles, embrace the idea that they were real people who made mistakes, and did things for contaminated motives. Because I never could trust anyone who did not believe that all beauty comes with infallibility. I mean, shit, the first Boston album is pretty much perfect, but not one single person would accuse them of being the Beatles. There is no great art that *boasts* infallibility; this is why Warhol and Picasso will be remembered long after Rockwell.

Somehow, we set the Beatles apart; we consider them the one group exempt from the essential law of infallibility. Just stop it. It does them no honor, and lessens the magic of extraordinary, nearly flawless achievements like the *White Album* and *Abbey Road*. The magic of the Beatles *evolved*, and like anything subject to the laws of nature, evolution and impermanence, it is bound to be ridden with imperfection. And along the way, mistakes were made. And I proudly announce, as a huge admirer, fan and student of the Beatles, that calling "Your Mother Should Know" a turd does not in any way make me less of a lover of the music or the achievements of the Beatles.

2014, *BROOKLYN BUGLE*

Where Are Our War Beatles? How Current Events Highlight the Utter Impotence of Rock and Pop

Although it was written during the opening salvos of Russia's invasion of Ukraine, this piece seems more relevant than ever. I sometimes try to imagine what would have happened if rock and pop had been able to recognize that the right to piss off your parents by growing your hair long or dying it pink does not necessarily equate with genuine activism, and shouting "Give Peace a Chance" in a burning theater doesn't actually save any lives.

The crisis in Ukraine underlines the complete and total impotence of American rock and pop. We are speechless at the horror and heroism we see on television and our phones, this apocalypse that reduces lives and freedom to rubble, restart and Armageddon reckoning. Nevertheless, we have no actual expectation that music, the force that defined our own social evolution, will actually play any part in rallying resources or resistance. We've given up on that, haven't we?

We grew up under the mistaken belief that rock somehow fought for our rights, or would do so in a crisis, anyway. Think of all those fist-pumping songs we wagged our jaws to! This was always a leaky shelter, wallpapered with easily reproduced anarchy signs and peace symbols, doodled naïvely on notebooks. Thanks to the process of utterly idiotic magical thinking, we believed that chanting "Give Peace a Chance" would actually increase the chances for peace one-one-thousandth of one eyelash width. The real world laughed at us and went about its cruel business.

Unmasking this paper tiger, this impotent liar we grew up believing in, barely makes any difference. After all, any real activism now is being motivated, fueled and informed by social media. We no longer even pretend that rock and pop can change the world. That myth, on life support for a generation or three, was declared dead when the Talent Show Era began during the first decade of this century. That's when pop finally admitted it was nothing at all but a platform for imitation, cheap emotion and instafame.

Rock and roll, you were born of such promise. You were the sound of America's disenfranchised made electric. You were the melody and rhythm of slaves and their descendants, tenement dwellers and coal miners, the creation of willing and unwilling immigrants. Those who had nothing summoned and shaped you, and you shook the world. But we ultimately learned that it was easier to draw anarchy signs and shout slogans than it was to actually put this extraordinary object to work, to use these extraordinary songs, this extraordinary energy and this extraordinary legacy to inspire picket lines, voting rights, free elections. Why use this amazing electric art form to fight gerrymandering when we can use it to sell a T-shirt and make Jimmy Fallon giggle? Who needs Woody Guthrie, Jon Langford and Chuck D when we've got Dave Grohl? After all, for our entire lives, rock and roll has caused generation after generation to confuse the right to piss off your parents and annoy that guy/girl who likes that other type of music with the right to fight for anything actually meaningful.

It was not always this way. There was a moment when it changed.

On August 28, 1963, a quarter of a million Americans gathered at the Lincoln Memorial to advocate, with volume and grace, for the civil and economic rights of African-Americans. A number of major pop stars appeared at this event, making a strong statement, saying I am with you, and my generation is with you. Bob Dylan sang. Peter, Paul and Mary (major hitmakers at the time) sang. Joan Baez sang. Marian Anderson, Mahalia Jackson and Odetta sang. And this was not necessarily an extraordinary moment. In many ways these performers were just continuing a tradition of activism and awareness that was built into the DNA of rock and pop music. It was implied in its roots; it had been used by Woody Guthrie, Paul Robeson, Pete Seeger, the Carter Family, Josh White, Jimmie Rodgers and many others to tell the news (think of all those old country songs about floods, fires, illness and strikes). Three chords and the truth, and all the news that's fit to sing. Rock and roll was born of discrimination and segregation, social, economic and political exclusion. That is the parents, the aunts and uncles, of even the most superficial pop bullshit. This is why even when the Treniers sing about cough syrup, or the Rivingtons howl "Papa Oom Mow Mow," it's political. "Ba-dang-a-dang-dang Ba-ding-a-dong-ding Blue Moon" is sung by people who would have been murdered if they sat at the wrong lunch counter, and *that* makes it a political song, dammit.

Fast forward to 1969: Half a million young Americans gather in Bethel, New York for the *Woodstock Music and Art Fair*. At this same moment, 250 Americans, Americans who were the same age as the people flopping around in the mud in Bethel, were dying every week in Vietnam. With that in the news, on their minds, in their hearts, did the performers in Bethel make use of this army of youth in front of them? Did they put down their damp acoustic guitars long enough to convince half a million boys and girls to march to nearby Albany and take over the state capitol building and burn every draft card? No. They played them songs about fucking Animal Crackers and Lady Finger's fucking sunlight splatters. Truth: At *Woodstock*, Woody Guthrie's son sat in front of this amazing mob and sang them a song about smuggling pot.

A few months later the Rolling Stones played at Altamont. Six years after the March on Washington, at a massively attended counterculture event, security hired by the Rolling Stones murdered an African-American man because his girlfriend was white. (Important note: The Stones hired that security on the advice of the Grateful Dead, an act that regularly assembled armies of young people to do absolutely nothing but congratulate each other on how rebellious they were.)

What the hell happened? I'll tell you what the hell happened, and you are not going to like the answer.

The Beatles happened.

Undeniably, the Beatles absolutely reset the template for the sound and the look of rock and pop music. The industry was reshaped by the Beatles; the profile and idea of rock and pop was reshaped by the Beatles; the whole idea of what it meant to be a band and what young people, as listeners and artists, aspired to was reshaped by the Beatles. They became the template for multiple generations' concept of what pop music was and how a band and a career could be shaped. An entire industry and an entire gigantic army of consumers stepped into the model created by the Beatles.

But here's the problem: the Beatles did not have any skin in the game. Through no fault of their own, using music to promote a political and socially activist agenda was not on their radar. Changing the cultural landscape (and, to some degree, the concept of class mobility in the United Kingdom) was one of their targets and achievements, but the social and political matters that were dramatically impacting America in the 1960s were not in any way their concern.

Because the Beatles did not have to contend with the draft, because they did not have to reckon with their (literal) brothers or best mates dying overseas in a morally specious war, they were able to retreat into the dilettantism of spiritualism, the navel-gazing of psychedelia and the utterly empty nostalgia of music hall. Every now and then they punctuated this highly accomplished and amusing fluffery with a completely meaningless statement about the furor of youth. Can you imagine being the most famous band of the century in the most socially contentious decade of the century and not making one single relevant statement about the chaos, colonialism and sexual and racial battlegrounds of the 1960s? (And the only possible meaning of "Revolution" is that revolution means nothing to the Beatles). *Can you imagine?* My God, even the Beach Boys played in Prague at the height of the revolution there, and had a member choose jail over conscription.

The Beatles' only fight was with culture and class; race and illegal overseas intervention was of only marginal interest to them (the UK's crises in Algeria and Suez had passed into history when they were just children, and conscription had ended in the UK in 1960, 13 long and bloody years before it ended in the United States). The Beatles only needed to fight prejudice against long hair, northern accents and the idea that the English working classes needed to know their place. True, these were significant foes — and the Beatles' role in combatting them cannot be underestimated — but it was a very, very different catalog of battles than those challenging young people in the United States. But because the Beatles reset the pop landscape so profoundly on both sides of the Atlantic, they virtually erased the idea that rock and pop could — or should — be used to actively combat political and social ills. America needed its own Beatles. America needed a War Beatles.

The Beatles recast rock and pop as a tool of culture wars, not as a tool that could inform, inspire or enlighten the genuinely disenfranchised or those fearing for their life or freedom. Under their tutelage, fighting for the right to vote became entirely secondary to the fight for the right to grow your hair and take drugs. And rock and pop never really shook off that template.

Even punk, for the most part, underlined this split. As socially important as punk was, as necessary as it was for music to go through a reduction of form and the adoption of a fashion and look that a new generation could call their own, it was largely defined by style, not action (though at least people were singing about their anger again, often quite specifically — consider all the songs by UK bands inspired by events like the 1976 riots at the Notting Hill Carnival, the Sus laws which allowed police to detain and arrest people without proof of offense, or the death while in police custody of Liddle Towers, also in 1976).

Regardless of these exceptions (and, notably, the rise of the Rock Against Racism movement in the UK in the late 1970s), by and large punk's revolution — especially in the United States — was the revolution of pissing off your parents and the grannies on the street, and that's not a fucking revolution, that's just being 16. As a person largely shaped by that era, it pains me to say this, but fighting for the right to dye your hair pink and hate Kansas is vastly different from fighting for a right that really matters. We were taught, from the first moments that the Pistols told us that "giving the wrong time" was actually a political act, that the middle finger was the same as the loaded gun or the picket line. It's not, it's not, it's not.

From 1964 on, rock and pop affirmed, again and again, its role as a flag-waver for stylistic rebellion and attitude, and nearly completely ignored any connection to actual activism.

Certainly, some events contradicted this generality: the 1979 *No Nukes* concert and film was a rare, shining example of musicians aligning themselves with activism in a real and meaningful way; the same can probably be said of *Live Aid* and certainly the English Rock Against Racism and Red Wedge movements. But for every RAR or *No Nukes*, there were ten dozen examples of musicians who shouted rebellion in order to sell T-shirts and records and did next to nothing to effect change.

This is the house we built, where we have absolutely lost the ability to distinguish between slogan and action. We are fucking idiots, numbed by style. And now we expect nothing of rock and pop, aside from distraction and a flag underneath which we can find our peers. We needed a War Beatles but got *Woodstock*'s army of eunuchs instead.

2022, *ROCK AND ROLL GLOBE*

The Little Big Horn of American Rock and Roll: "Wooly Bully" Is a Very Effing Heavy Song

"Wooly Bully" came on the radio.

I've been listening to it for a lifetime, but I never really *heard* it.

It is far, far too easy to dismiss this hopping, hollering, shrieking, stomping habanero'd hash-sling of a screech, *almost sinister in its hysterical simplicity*, as a glorious piece of garage trash, a novelty product of cough syrup and too many late nights playing greasy covers in VFW halls.

But it is so very, very much more.

"Wooly Bully" by Sam the Sham and the Pharaohs is a radical repudiation of the strings, baroque influences, minor chords and maudlin grace sneaking into pop music circa 1965. Just as the Beatles were confirming their interpolation of the influence of Broadway/Tin Pan Alley pop — REAL music with bridges and modulations an' everything! — into the rock mainstream, here comes "Wooly Bully," the lucid, luscious, ludicrous opposite, something BASHED and memorable and probably playable on the very first try by anyone with a few amps and a basement to put them into. At first, "Wooly Bully" appears to be AN ACT OF WAR, a barbarian pouring oil on the fairy dust of the gathering tribes of the soon-to-be-psychedelic '60s; *in fact,* it is the house bands of those tribes, those lovers of sitars, 12-strings, delicate tunings and fancy turnarounds and the studio-bound Beatle boys and their ilk who were waging the war: the war on the bolt of black and blood that was primitive and perfect American rock and roll.

But the aborigines, that is the FIRST SETTLERS, the children of Treniers and Moonglows and Dominoes and Big Mamas and Piano

Smiths, STILL HAD A FEW BOMBS LEFT IN THEM before the John Phillips and George Martins of the world made their kind of Dean Moriarty thug-joy dead forever; these last feral, fierce cries are the howls of Sam the Sham and the Pharaohs.

Got it?

In 1965, the Beatles were making gorgeous wedding cakes out of tape: they recorded "Yesterday," "It's Only Love," "You've Got to Hide Your Love Away," "I've Just Seen a Face" and other songs that would completely redefine what the teen soundtrack would and could sound like. That's brilliant stuff, it really is, but in that very same year, Sam the Sham stood on a pile of twisting grease and said, "*This is my Little Big Horn, I am American rock and roll, I am the sound of the disenfranchised disguised in the cloak of simplicity! Hear me, the story of America is the story of the disenfranchised, and I am going to tell it simple and proud, and Dick Clark will play it loud, and you will dance and need no cello or piccolo trumpet to do so. Sister Rosetta needed no oboe and neither do I to tell the American story of thump and grind and shout and bridges, we don't need no stinking bridges.*"

Your Beatles did a lot of beautiful, amazing, stunning things; perhaps most significantly, they formally, fruitfully and finally married American rock to American pop. By this, I mean that the rock and roll of Bo Diddley, Eddie Cochran, Jerry Lee Lewis, Little Richard, Leadbelly, Louis Jordan, Wynonie Harris and a hundred others had not been significantly infected — or to use a kinder word, influenced — by the songcraft of Tin Pan Alley and the subsequent Broadway and vaudeville tradition of wordplay and melody that spun off of that. (NB: I use "Tin Pan Alley" to stand for the idea of workmanlike, crafted American songs, full of wit and clever musical and lyrical devices tweaked to create an emotional response.) These aforementioned artists — Wynonie, Jerry Lee, etc. — were, to put it simply, *doing their own thing*, and what they did was a very goddamn natural growth from the sounds of Basin Street, Beale Street, Maxwell Street, Congo Square and Clarksdale; this "other" thing, the "thing" I am lumping under "Tin Pan Alley," this thing that was 108,000 miles from Congo Square, was the (also) thoroughly American music of Jolson and Rogers and Hart and Ukulele Ike and Crosby and Columbo and many, many others; and that (frequently spectacular) music was, well, something else entirely, not only a different branch of the species, but a different species entirely.

Artists had certainly experimented and even succeeded with marrying the two traditions, but the engagement was far, far from solidified in the early '60s. When the Beatles entered American consciousness, they did something so *giant* that it is almost overlooked, and *that* may be their most significant contribution to the culture: they cemented the relationship between rock and traditional Tin Pan Alley pop music, in essence *creating* pop rock and ensuring the *vast* majority of rock songs, British and American, that would surface in the public eye in the next decade would be based in Tin Pan Alley's lyrical, structural and melodic philosophy. By the way, if you want some hard, cold evidence of this shit, how about this trivia question: the first song the Beatles did on their world-changing debut appearance on *The Ed Sullivan Show* was "All My Loving" (which in transcription form would have been perfect for any of the old-school crooners like Crosby or Columbo or even Jolson), but *what was the second song they performed?* It was "Till There Was You," a fairly mawkish and hoary piece of pure Tin Pan Alley songcraft from the hit musical *The Music Man.* The Beatles started a revolution that night, but they also ended one.

I am not making any judgment on this, by the way. And I am most certainly not casting *any* aspersion on the extraordinary achievements of the Beatles and the two extraordinarily gifted songwriters who led the band. I am just pointing out that while *a lot* changed when the Beatles came to America, perhaps the most important change was the virtually complete integration of the Broadway/music hall/Tin Pan Alley approach to songcraft into a form, rock and roll (and/or rock-blues), that had previously largely been devoid of it. I mean, there are plenty of times when I find myself genuinely angry at the Beatlefication of American pop rock and the entire industry that sprang up to support this ringing, glorious, catchy, rhyming, familiar but new phenomenon; I try to imagine how American music would have evolved, how it would have grown, exploded, chilled, thrilled, shook, soothed, rattled, rasped and even relaxed us if the beautifully handsome sharpie that was Tin Pan Alley moon-in-June hadn't been inserted into American rock and roll. But then I remember how completely satisfying and enrapturing, to listeners of any age, experience and taste, the goddamn Beatles are, and all is forgiven. *Except* the part where they ruin the art of American rock forever.

So, "Wooly Bully" is a number of amazing things, it is *not* just a piece of beautiful trash:

It is a repudiation of the rapidly progressing developments in English and West Coast pop rock circa 1965, but in an uncontrived, unpretentious sort of way; instead of being a novelty, it's more of a glimpse of an alternative reality, one shared by the Sonics, the Troggs, even the Velvet Underground and many etceteras;

It is an insight to a secret alternative history of American rock and roll, a keyhole into a world that changed the night the Beatles arrived on our TV screens, when the simple, pile-driving, parade-rolling rhythms of Bo Diddley and Huey Piano Smith and Jerry Lee Lewis and even Hardrock Gunther and the plaintive, plain, plainly powerful words and god-simple melodies of the Louisiana Bayou Parishes and the Mississippi crossroads were displaced by the Lords of Clever;

It is a presaging of the market correction of '75–'77, when a pile of young bands on both sides of the Atlantic largely repudiated the baroque filigrees of Beatlism (and the all the layers of frosting that the 1970s had laid on top of *that*) and returned rock to the *pure* sound of '50s shave-and-a-haircut shimmers, '60s three-chord shrieks (the line between the Sonics and the Ramones is so very small indeed) and the melodic minimalism of Sam the Sham and Question Mark.

(Because, lest we forget, this was all punk was, a long craved and delicious market correction; very little of actual innovation was spilled or spelled in those heady days, instead it was a perfect bursting of morphed influences, pared and filleted, and a discarding of arena and studio tropes implied by the excesses of the Beatles, but which the Beatles had tastefully and gracefully avoided).

It is a very fucking heavy song, "Wooly Bully" is. It's what rock *could have* been, an artifact of the World Without Beatle, a survivor from before the Beatles made it safe to sing Broadway show tunes and call it revolution. You want revolution? You want the sound of America rebelling?

Uno Dos One Two Tres Quatro

2014, *BROOKLYN BUGLE*

Part 5: Interviews

I have interviewed hundreds of musicians over the years. The famous, the infamous, the soon-to-be-famous and those who vanished into the bony bosom of obscurity.

Each and every one of these chats contained some little (or larger) curious nugget, and/or resulted in an amusing anecdote that might make for interesting chatter over a beer or a yellowtail and jalapeno roll. Seriously, every single one. Even the unmemorable ones are interesting simply for the fact that they were not memorable. (On YouTube, I recently came across an interview I did with Jools Holland in 1982. I literally, and I mean literally, have no memory of doing this. Isn't that interesting?)

These were done for nearly every publication I ever worked for, going back to the *Great Neck South Southerner*, for which I interviewed Michael Palin and Paul Weller. (It was once as easy as calling the hotel and asking for the person or crashing the soundcheck and politely making your request. Strange to think that I learned to crash soundchecks before I even had a high school diploma … but that's another story, recounted in the *I Am a Teenage* section of this book.)

Regardless of legitimately fascinating interactions I have had with everyone from Cher to Yoko, Stevie Nicks to Brian Wilson, I very consciously decided that the only interviews I wanted to feature in this collection were the ones I believed had unique content and were clearly and genuinely distinct from the thousands of other interviews these particular artists had done. I had zero, zero, interest in piling on a lot of larger or hipper or weirder names to wave at you and say, "Oh, I talked with this person!" Instead, I just wanted to share conversations which left me feeling, "Oh, shit, that was interesting" or, "I didn't know that before."

Towards that end, there's relatively little in this section (and it's an admittedly curious group of bedfellows): deep chats with Dave Davies, Stuart "Woody" Wood and Mark E. Smith. Each of these, I believe, revealed something new or insightful about the artist's life, work and era.

Dave Davies: "The younger brother physically might be the older brother spiritually."

The following contains material from interviews in 2017 and 2019; the set-up is from the 2019 piece, written shortly after the release of Davies' extraordinary compilation of unreleased work from the 1970s, Decade. *I don't know why more people aren't aware of* Decade*; it's both a brilliant and important album.*

There are moments that break the spine of our cultural history. After these, nothing is quite the same. Dave Davies created one of these in July 1964, when he was just 17 years and five months old.

Until that day, the electric guitar had been, in essence, a rhythm instrument that accompanied a melody, or a place keeper, something that imitated (in compact form) the boogie-woogie figures of the bass fiddle, the left hand of the piano or the alto and bass horns. Its value was its utility, its efficiency, not its potential. True, there were blues masters who could wring a near harpsichord-like purity out of the acoustic guitar (Blind Blake comes to mind), but, by and large, the electric guitar was still an atom waiting to be split.

Although Bo Diddley and Eddie Cochran had both made enormous inroads into creating a modern mode for the electric guitar, using it to summon a horny, rhythmic teen rage that no other instrument could create, it was left to Dave Davies to really bring the instrument fully into the post-blues, post-jump blues, post-big band era. On "You Really Got Me," he used barre chords to create a slobber, a blur, a space-age rocket of stuttering lust, a sound that was the electric guitar doing something no other instrument could do: spit, soar, stammer, roar.

We all know what happened next (that is, in addition to the entire universe of golem-stomp rumble and riff that followed): the Kinks evolved. From that curious mixture of the feral and the fey they grew, magically and uniquely, into a band that translated the split in the seam between the pastoral heart and the soot of modern industry into song. We all know that story. But on *Decade*, an astounding collection released late in 2018, Dave Davies has rewritten the story of the Kinks, in turn rewriting the story of British rock.

Decade is not merely an odds-and-sods collection of unreleased tracks. It reveals that throughout the 1970s, David Russell Gordon Davies was doing (unreleased) work that was as good *or better* than what brother Ray was recording and releasing. These "hidden" tracks, this strange and magical secret history, reveals that Dave was writing and recording some of the most evocative and emotionally rich work of any artist of the entire decade.

The 13 tracks on *Decade* — all recorded and largely completed in the 1970s but dusted up recently by Dave and two of his adult sons, Martin and Simon — are so strong, such a staggering surprise, that even a pretentious sod like me finds words elusive. Inside *Decade*, you will find work that reminds you of Elliot Smith, Mike Nesmith, Nick Drake, John Cale, Robert Wyatt, Tim Buckley and every hero of the elegiac red-dusted sadhappy shimmering pink blues.

Not only this, but *Decade* reveals something that many of us had long suspected: Dave Davies, in his ability to use his voice and guitar to conjure the spirits of hope, loneliness and the mysteries of the universe, is, honestly, very much the equal of George Harrison. My first reaction, after repeated listenings to *Decade*, was this: my god, it's like they delayed the release of *All Things Must Pass* for 47 years.

(Why did these songs never see the light of day? This is a possible answer: aside from a moment here and there on *Lola Versus Powerman, Everybody's in Show-Biz* and *Misfits*, it's hard to picture work of this grace and delicate emotional affect fitting anywhere on Ray's often unsubtle, story-driven concept albums.)

Dave Davies, who is just about to turn 72, is one of my favorite people to interview. Smart, intuitive, intense, eager to listen and investigate, he respects each question and welcomes the chance to examine his own work, history and motivation.

I'll also note this: if you ask Dave about reuniting the Kinks, you get an interesting answer. But if you ask him about everything else, everything under the sky and anything that vibrates the chakras and the heart, you get *really* interesting answers.

Decade *is like finding a secret history. If this stuff had been released when it was recorded, I think it could have changed the whole narrative of the Kinks' story.*

That's quite a statement. You're probably right, but who knows what you're going through at the time, when you think back — all the different motions, emotions and dealings, everything that's going on around you. It's certainly easier to view it all from a distance and make a statement like that. We won't ever know, but it's an interesting thought.

I was going through a lot of change around that time, embarking on a spiritual inner life, and coming to terms with all these new ideas — or old ideas, but new to me — concepts about living a spiritual life. It was really inspiring, as well as daunting. Many of these songs, well, I wasn't sure how they would be accepted at the time. I certainly was very busy with the Kinks. Consider a project like *Soap Opera* — my writing is very different from anything like that. My writing is very internal, about trying to find solutions to my own problems, and my own spiritual questions.

"Strangers" (a Dave song on the Kinks' 1970 album, Lola Versus Powerman and the Moneygoround, Part One*) was always one of my very favorite Kinks songs. I find that a lot of the material on* Decade *shares much of the same emotional quality.*

"Strangers" really seeded a lot of the ideas that are on *Decade* — notions and emotions and whole kinds of situations that don't seem to work, but if you hook up with someone or meet someone, it can help you or you can help each other. We find that it is all better with collaboration and co-existing, moving this whole mess along *together* — trying to make some sense of it *together*. Sometimes it seems the only way forward is first to connect with each other … well, that seems to always have been a driving force behind everything I've done.

When I first saw you onstage at the Palladium in New York City in 1978, I remember seeing this top-hatted vision, just dancing around onstage, this grinning space urchin... Is he a stranger to you? What's your connection to that person?

The really important feelings stay with you; they're embedded in your soul. We all change our viewpoint as we grow older, but some experiences remain permanent, engrained or scarred on our soul, if you like. There are things that never really go away; we try to learn from them or move forward, but they are always part of us. I don't treat the past as a stranger at all. I try to treat it as a friend, to help me in the present and in the future.

Your sons are a big part of this new/old album, and of course you were in a band with your brother. Obviously, family is, was and always has been an enormous part of what you create.

Ray and I grew up in a family with six sisters. And my mum was really the boss, it was very matriarchal. My dad used to go out and get the money, but it was my mum that organized everything. I've always found great inspiration from growing up with these weird and wonderful characters. The women were more intuitive. Those feelings informed a lot of my own ways and the way I saw the world, and I'm sure they had a profound effect on Ray growing up as well. I had a great time as a young boy, always inspired. We never had any money, but we always were encouraged to get on with things, to do things, to experiment with music. Whereas a lot of my friends in school at the time had a lot of pressure to get a proper job, like their dad, we were encouraged to be more artistic. My sister Rene, who died in 1958 I think it was, she was an art painter and musician, and I think she passed on a bit of the legacy to Ray and also to me. It was a wonderful upbringing.

Do you think growing up in a matriarchal way encouraged your later spiritual voyages? Do you think there's a connection there?

A profound connection. I don't know how to say it, but I'll say it anyway: the contact with the feminine stuff in all of us is important for making the *other* stuff work. I don't think it's a sheer fluke that there's male and female, there may be at some point in our human history where we had one brain and where we'd been both man and female. One helps the other. When you're writing you can see how the interplay of these energies work.

You always seem to be exploring, investigating, moving forward. With this in mind, would the idea of going back to the Kinks seem like a step backwards?

That has occurred to me. If it felt emotionally sound to me, I'd do it. When we first started recording, all those years ago, Ray would play a little phrase on the piano, and I'd say, "Fuckin' great," or playing guitars together, *that* feeling, not knowing exactly where it's coming from but it feels *good*, that's something that helped me a lot. It's intangible, you can't measure it, but you *know* it's right. For instance, I knew that "Tired of Waiting" was going to be massive when we did that recording, we put that *heavy* guitar on it, and I just *knew*, I had that *feeling*. If there was a feeling like that again, with Ray, I'd definitely have a go. But that feeling has got to be there. If that feeling isn't there, it's kind of like ... ughhhhh ... how do you create that feeling? I just don't know.

There is this wonderful film of the Kinks at the Olympia in Paris in 1964 where you are doing these very pure but radically different interpretations of American music. And you are singing a lot of the lead vocals, and you're out front and center a lot. When I listen to your very earliest records, and when I see that early film of you onstage, you seem like a co-leader of the band. That changed.

I agree. I was a big supporter of Ray's point of view, where he was coming from and what he was trying to create. I always felt I needed to be there for him, as he was going through change. Ray and I, we might be brothers and have a certain telepathy and closeness, but we're vastly different types of people. We work and function in totally different ways which I think are complementary. I was a young kid, enjoying the music so much.

Observing both your career (I mean the kind of stuff you were writing, especially as revealed on Decade*) and your spiritual and emotional life, it almost seems like you were the big brother in many ways.*

I've spoken at length to many people, brothers and siblings, and the effect they've had on each other. I've done a lot of research. In many cases — not every case, but many — the younger brother *physically* might be the older brother *spiritually*. I've seen it a lot in astrological charts of people. These hidden sides of life, like metaphysical and spiritual, are sometimes active in certain ways that uplift and encourage. Lots of charts of married couples, people that are close, you think, "How could these two people even be in the same room?" But on a deeper level you can see these people are really trying to help each other. Not by being the same, but by nurturing each other's differences.

Everyone talks a lot about getting back together with Ray, but do you feel like there is unfinished business with Mick Avory and John Gosling and John Dalton? [Kinks organist/keyboardist Gosling was still alive at the time; he died in 2023.]

I love those guys. They've got their own path. You can't go down the same path. Apart from it being desperately depressing and boring, spiritual energy doesn't work like that. They have to find their own way forward in their journey. There's a track called "The Journey" on *Decade.* I actually wrote it with the idea that it is like an overture for a movie. It wasn't to be, but I was glad to finally get it out there, mixed, to hopefully inspire people on their own journey.

That's one of my favorite songs on the record.

And it's full of the feelings I carry with me always. You know when you've got a great overture for a film? The expectation, the possibilities that lie ahead — it's something that's really deep within me.

"Trust Your Heart," off the Misfits *album, is a song that has followed me my whole life. It just tears through you. I think it's emblematic of the idea that you, Dave, are the emotional heart of the Kinks' music.*

I started to feel that in later years. Passion was always really important to me. I found early on that if it didn't feel right, it wasn't right. I've always been very governed by what I feel. Sometimes you can vanish off the face of the planet seeking some sort of perfection that, I think, does not exist. So, you get to a point, emotionally, where you feel inspired, and that's it — *that's* it.

Outside of writing within the voice of a character — which, of course, he did a lot — after 1965, Ray Davies didn't write a single true first-person love song. I thought to myself, Ray doesn't confess; he describes. You, however, confess.

There's a lot of truth in that. Ray finds it easier to write about someone else's problems than to confront his own. We all have something different to learn from — and about — life and our environment and our family. We all have different points of view and different ideas about how to work through things, and I think Ray has often struggled with confronting himself, whereas I have always found it to be a release and a relief to find out and explore what is really going on. I've never been shy about confronting things about myself that were problems to me. Getting out your emotions, tears — these are all tools that help us learn. Ray tends to use characters to come to terms with how he feels about himself. Which is like acting! It's what actors do.

In your music — especially in the last ten or 15 years or so — you seem to be engaging in a real and active quest to investigate who you are, and what more you can find out about yourself.

That's the most comfortable place for me to be. I feel safe there. It's not everyone's idea of a safe place, but it's definitely mine. I think coming into a big family, as a little boy, I'd see someone really upset, I'd see my auntie crying, and I'd always be the one who was trying to uplift people.

So, did you think of yourself as an empath? As someone who had to help other people reach and understand their emotions, their feelings?

I've always been like that. As a kid, even five or six, I was always concerned over how so-and-so was doing, or worried if my brother had sorted a problem out he was going through. My mother used to say, "David, you were born old." And I always got on really well with old people! I had a sensitivity to things — that's kind of a bit of a curse, a curse and a blessing, to be able to share people's feelings. At the same time, it can drag you down. We can't fix everyone we want to fix. It's not always a good idea to go there. If you're strong enough I think you should take on that responsibility, though.

I get the sense that you actively consider music a healing place.

That's what I'd like to think. With the right thought and feeling, maybe we can heal others. There's this character in [*Star Trek V: The Final Frontier*], he says he's a healer, "I can heal your pain, I can take it away," and Dr. McCoy falls for it, and of course Spock is very cynical about the whole thing, but he says to Captain Kirk, "Let me take your pain!" And Kirk says, "I need my pain!" [laughs] And that struck a chord with me. We have to accept our pain. You can't wave a magic wand and make people's misery and torment and anger go away. It's a process, and one we all have to work on. The way we interact with each other, as people, is the way forwards. I do believe in divine ideas and the cosmic and the oneness of the universe and all that, but we *are* on Earth, we have to keep our feet on Earth, and I think we have to use whatever tools we can muster within ourselves to help and support people. Sometimes, a smile at the right time with good intent can do wonders. To me, music has always been about healing, certainly, because even science has proved that everything is energy. I come from this place — some would call it mystical, or as my mum would call it, common sense. What we *think* can actually change our environment. We don't really know, science doesn't really know, but if you think it can, why not try it?

One of the first lyrics on the Open Road *album [2017] is, "In my heart I am just a boy" — and in several places you seem to be singing, or writing, from a child's perspective.*

[My son] Russ is responsible for a lot of that, too, it's a true collaboration. But "In my heart I am just a boy," that's a thing I've always had. I think it's important for us, somehow, to hold on to some kind of innocence. I think we should all give the innocent part of us a chance to explore. In my heart of hearts, I think it's how we learn. I've always tried to hold on to that innocence. Innocence is not the same as naïveté. It's wonder! When I was ill, years ago — 2004, when I got that stroke I had — I realized that none of us are in control of anything [laughs]. One minute you're out to conquer the world, the next minute you're flat on your back. I think that was important, to realize that we're at the mercy of the universe ... and I think the universe is compassionate.

Did your stroke lead you to a place where you were willing to take more creative chances?

It's quite possible. When I was ill, one of the first things that hit my consciousness was the fact that everybody seemed connected. They were all on the same set. The same film set. They had done rehearsal, now they were filming. This was it. That's it. It was like I had seen all these people before, I recognized them, and I felt a link to everybody involved in this "film." It was extraordinary. The past was overlapped with the present, and the future crept in as well.

I was always interested in alternative ideas. When my first son Martin was born, the first thing I did was study astrology and the Tarot. I wanted to find out who is this baby going to be? Why do people do the things they do? Astrology gave me a lot of ideas about the world, about people, how people interact or *don't* interact. I found it really helpful. I was really deeply interested in the Tarot, because all these symbols ... it's a language, and it's a language to me that is much more important than our verbal language. I think we need to find out how to tap these other languages. The human body is ancient.

When I was in hospital, I found out a lot about people talking to their bodies, people who had terrible illnesses, and they talked with their body in order to enlist its help. Our minds are young in comparison to our bodies. Our bodies have all the tools you need, really. It's connected to nature, and the Earth — there are all these links that we need to find out about, rather than try to *explain* everything. Modern man has to explain everything, chop everything up, and he still never finds out what it really is! Sometimes we just need to trust. You and I, we need to trust what's going on within ourselves, even if we can't articulate it or write about it. We need to trust each other emotionally and psychically, because we are psychic beings, really, whether we say we are or not. These are energies that science is starting to realize are real.

When you think of the Kinks, who do you visualize? Is it you and Ray and Mick Avory and Pete Quaife, or do you see Bob Henrit or John Dalton or Jim Rodford … who, or what, is the Kinks to you?

Good question, because there have been so many lives of the Kinks, every decade is different personnel. John Gosling in the '70s, Henrit in the '80s and '90s, and different bass players … but I suppose if I was being really honest, it all came from Ray, Pete and me. *That* feeling, *that* essence, what *that* is, or was … or is. I often think Pete has gotten written out of the story. But if you go back to when we were children, when this started, and observed the terrain, you can see Pete; it was kind of the balancing act, Ray on one side, me on the other side, Pete in the middle, balancing, he was so helpful to me as a kid growing up.

Many years ago, Ray told me that the Kinks, in essence, broke up when Pete left ... that it was never really the same after that.

I can see that. It's very valid to say that, it's certainly true in a sense. But we had the name, so we had to keep going.

When I listen to the early stuff, the classic early singles, I think one of the defining elements is [session drummer] Bobby Graham. I really hear him punching and driving those songs —

Kick ass. Kicking ass.

— in a way that, to be honest, I'm not sure Mick could have.

Bobby Graham really did do something for our music. That scruffy guitar sound that I had ... who *could* play with it? [laughs] Bobby Graham was a great guy. He was older, obviously, and he had some great stories, and I feel really privileged to have known him. We were just these scruffy kids — and he came in and glued these *feelings* and this wildness together; he *forced* it together in a sense. That's why those early records are extraordinary.

I feel Bobby Graham had the same effect with the Dave Clark Five.

He *was* the Dave Clark Five.

Were you aware that you, and I mean you personally, were inventing something on "You Really Got Me" and those early recordings?

I did! I felt more like an inventor with sound than a musician. I'm self-taught, so any attempt to "learn" music felt like school again, and that really put me off it, so I thought I'll do what I can with what I've got, I'd rather learn that way, and if it feels right, it must be right.

I think we were lucky, the people around us were fantastic. Growing up in that matriarchal system is very inspiring. You can try things! My mother or my sisters would say, "Oh, alright, David, try that!" It's not like that paternal, "Oh, David, you can't do that! It doesn't work that way!" It was a very transitional time in the 1960s; one of the first times when working class people could do a lot, the first era in which they were really taken seriously. None of that, "Oh, it's just working class boys, and they're just making pub songs." People were starting to take that culture seriously, in films, writers, poets. It was an interesting breakthrough time.

But I'll tell you this: as a young man, I always thought that me and Ray would last forever.

I keep on talking about these words, words like love and trust, but they're *energy*, it's magnetism, it's that sort of energy that helps you get out of and above problems, helps you do something new or try something you wouldn't have otherwise tried. I think *that's* what runs right through whatever the Kinks made, in the 1970s, the 1990s, 1964. I think the beauty of it is that we'll never really know *how*. Maybe it's ended. Maybe it did all end when Pete left the band.

I feel like I'm going faster as I get older. It's funny. I feel like a guy in a space suit. It's like those great scenes in *2001* of going through time and space. Maybe it's an illusion. Maybe it's like a wheel, a wheel with spokes — the faster it goes, it begins to look like it's going backwards. Maybe that's happening.

2017 and 2019, *THE NEW YORK OBSERVER*

Mark E. Smith: "When you are it, you don't have to affect it."

There is only one Bob Dylan.

And the other one is Mark E. Smith.

I genuinely believe the late Mark E. Smith, who spun a dusty cyclone of magical and strange words, personal and supernatural, within the songs of the Fall for 40 years, is one of the few authentic geniuses rock and roll ever produced. Like Dylan, just behind the opaque and tumbling lyrics and the distinctive voice, there is great logic, an entire universe of meaning, drawn with extraordinary skill.

In the very early 1980s, Smith supported this unique genius with a band of great spontaneity and originality, playing a nearly feral form of skeletal, electric-fence rockabilly; I swear, to have seen the Fall between, say, 1980 and 1983 was to have seen one of the greatest rock and roll bands of all time, a spitting, sparking, snapping, stomping mixture of noise, magic and emotion. I remember standing in front of the stage on several occasions — notably at Peppermint Lounge in 1981 and at White Columns in 1983 — and literally thinking it ("it" being the very idea of rock and roll) couldn't possibly get any better.

For evidence of Smith's skill as a sui generis lyricist and storyteller, start with "The N.W.R.A.," a song from 1980's Grotesque *album, in which Smith brilliantly weaves different voices, perspective, urgency, conversation and characters, combining science fiction with everyday interaction; somehow, "The N.W.R.A." has always reminded me of two of Dylan's greatest lyrical works, "Isis" and "Tangled Up in Blue." For evidence of what a remarkable, utterly shit-hot band the Fall were — I'd suggest listening to* Totale's Turns, *a live album from 1980, which is full of indescribable joy, tension and spontaneity, all in service of an utterly unique and poetic peeing-on-an-electric-socket noise-a-billy.*

I interviewed Mark E. Smith for WNYU radio in 1981. This interview — which appears here in print for the first time — has a peculiar reputation amongst the legions of Fall devotees; some consider it the best interview Smith ever did.

Contrary to his well-earned reputation, Smith was expansive, earnest, funny and considered and answered each question in depth. (And he did actually say "uh" at the end of a lot of words, as he does when he sings — I've deleted most of these from the transcript but left a few in for fun.)

Even though I had no idea at the time that Smith was supposed to be "difficult," I did sense, even at age 19, that this was a special interview. After we were done, as Smith climbed back into his van, he hugged me and the engineer (WNYU DJ Naomi Regelson), and his last words to us were, "We should have coffee sometime! Isn't that what Americans say when they like each other?"

Perhaps — or perhaps not — there was some astrological alliance; though I did not know this at the time, Smith and I shared a birthday (though he was five years older).

You've just released Slates, *which is a 10-inch EP on American Rough Trade. Before that you released* Grotesque, *also on American Rough Trade, and* Live at the Witch Trials, *which came out on IRS. What brings you to America right now and how long are you here for?*

Oh, we're here for about six weeks. We're doing the east, the west and the south. But the reason we're here is to hone in our act a bit more, sort of get across to a few more people. Britain was boring us for a while, so we decided not to play any gigs. So, the best alternative was to go. We went to Germany and now we're in America.

And what was it about Britain that made it boring?

It just became very safe. I mean, that's where our root support is, of course. But there's very sort of, uh, a lot of, uh, rubbish going down now. In Britain, our only choice was to go out and play to people who know the Fall inside out or not play at all.

And that was too safe?

Yeah. I mean it's, uh, nothing to sort of criticize, but I thought a change was needed for the band to keep it interesting.

I was trying to describe the evolution of the Fall approach to a friend, saying that you sort of play music as if you invented it. It's almost a pure stream of consciousness type thing. And it seems to have really come into focus in the last couple of albums, where it was less focused in Live at the Witch Trials.

Yeah, I agree with that. When I formed the Fall the ultimate goal was to have a group that was organic, that can just go up there and do various things and sort of cope with another discipline as well. I wanted it to be freeform with discipline, which is sort of an easy thing to say. Most bands have claimed to be that, but in fact they're not, you know. It's just getting a balance.

You formed the band in Manchester, yes? About how long ago?

It was about three years ago, four years ago. About, uh, beginning of, uh, '77.

And the personnel has pretty much shifted —

— completely since then. It's not as big a deal as everybody makes out, but we had a high turnover because of financial problems, things like that.

I've read that you fire members at age 20, but that's not quite true, is it?

Well, that is a lie. It just so happened that most of 'em left when they're around that age. And they started wanting to be in "bands" as opposed to wanting to be in "the Fall." [laughs] I think that might be a lot of why you're saying the music sounds different, a lot might be to do with the fact that we are all non-musicians. I write a lot of the music, and I can't play a lot of chords or anything. Obviously, I think most people write from what is in the head, and that's why it's become more honed. *Slates* is exactly as it sounded in my head when we were writing it.

Is it difficult getting a unity of thinking amongst the members?

It's not now. I had thought it would be an impossible thing to attain, but I think we're nearly there.

There seemed to be a real unspoken communication between the band onstage. It's not like anyone directly looks over at each other, but it's very together when you tumble from one song into another. Yet there doesn't seem to be anyone taking charge or anyone gesturing.

The Fall was never like that. Years ago, it was, uh, if one person was having a good night the rest of the band followed him or her.

What was going on musically in Manchester about the time the Fall came together?

There was nothing, really. It was just about things like the Buzzcocks and that, so pop bands?

Was Steve Garvey of the Buzzcocks once in the Fall?

No, he was our roadie. [laughs] You get to find, after a bit, that with rock press most of the things they print are wrong. It is not, uh, evilly wrong. It's just incompetence wrong. [laughs]

On stage you seem almost totally egoless. And it doesn't seem to be an affected ego-lessness. Some bands pretend to be aloof, but the Fall seem to have almost no onstage ego at all. Yet you still have a tremendous amount of stage presence.

Well, when you *are* it, you don't have to affect it. It always just happens. I must take responsibility for that, 'cause I select the people who go in the band, and that is one of the prerogatives of the group, you know? That's why we had a high turnover, because I'm a bit conservative like that. I just get very annoyed when people start prancing about and acting like jumped-up minstrels, you know? It's sort of a pack of shit and should have been altered a long time ago. I'm not saying all bands should be like that, but if you're trying to communicate, there's no way you can get into dancing about and stuff like that. Though if you just wanna make people dance, that's okay, I suppose.

The Fall seem to have perfected this idea of, well, unlearning. It's like you're taught to act a certain way when you think about what it means to be in a band, and then it takes a long time to unlearn that.

So true. It's really sort of a weird paradox. That's one of the philosophies of the Fall: never take it for granted and anything that is obvious will be the exact opposite.

I sort of relate what you do to what Wire was doing on Pink Flag *— a purity of noise and sound, like not listening to anyone, a sound out of nowhere. But it's hard to maintain that, either because of exposure or getting more expertise or getting more popular —*

— or boredom. You know, there's a lot of bands that attempt to do something novel 'cause they're bored or they live in the past, but then they sort of reiterate what they've already said and they're getting insecure if something they do sounds different from what they've done. Record company pressure and all that sort of stuff comes into that, too. And the bands themselves, too, they're not believing in what you've got to do, not believing that what you've got to say is right. I've heard a lot of records by bands who are obviously trying to change, but the producers tried to make it like the last record. I noticed that in a lot of groups. But I don't find it hard to retain it, because I know what I like.

That's the basis of the Fall as well. We do what we like and that is pretty good … without condescending. That's the important thing that a lot of experimental bands forget. They're still condescending. A lot of experimental bands go out and sort of say, "Look, you won't understand this." And if you say audiences are stupid, the audience picks that up straight away. Which is why audiences prefer, like, rock and roll bands. But what I'm trying to do with the Fall is get the pure parts out of both, because there are pure parts. That's a good part in discipline: knowing what you're gonna do — well, actually, *not* knowing what you're gonna do, but not sort of losing your nerve and things like that. Because it's not rehearsed.

The Fall seem pretty adamant in trying to avoid being pigeonholed. How have you avoided the industry and gig promoters or record companies, etcetera, from getting in your way? Isn't that usually what ruins the dream or something like that?

Well, we're a bit strange, in a way, 'cause we're from the north of England, you see, and we've got a very sort of... it sounds like a cliché, but we have got a very working-class attitude whereby we don't take crap for the sake of it. We don't think it is a big deal to be in a band, because in the north of England, you know, "stars" and that thing are sort of looked down on because it is so far away from the average sort of day-to-day existence.

There was a time when the Beatles were disliked in the north of England, people just couldn't handle that four Liverpudlians did that. It's strange, and I don't think you understand it unless you live there.

And I think that's a great advantage of us. We stay in Manchester, and I like it, for some reason. I think that's a lot to do with that.

I hate to ask about your influences because they're either obvious or irrelevant. But there's a more rockabilly feel to the recent stuff [as of 1981] then there was to, say, anything on Live at the Witch Trials. *What did that come out of?*

That came out of, um, country and western music. What you've got to remember is the north of England has a very big country scene. A lot of folk songs — like northern folk, not like the English folk — it's very similar to rockabilly. It's stuff about work and that. So, we've sort of always been into that anyway. There is a lot of stuff on *Witch Trials* which is very sort of, uh, northern folk. It's in your system somehow.

I was getting really into Johnny Cash. It's a totally accidental thing. We weren't aiming for a rockabilly sound. We were aiming for, um, a Johnny Cash sound. [laughs] It sounds incredible now because, I mean, we were the first English band to do rockabilly, or what the music press thought was rockabilly. When it came out in England, all the press said was that we were trying to be like fucking doo wop, that's how unaware the press was. I've always been sort of into rock and roll of the Gene Vincent variety. Anyway, how the rockabilly thing started was that I was writing a lot of stories, and that's a good medium to get them over. Country and western music, we all know that it's a fantastic medium for storytelling. That whole medium is storytelling. And the conventional rock scene never does that. Never tries to stimulate people with stories of anything, you know?

And so that was a good medium for us, 'cause I found I was just writing songs that would just sound like avant-garde messes with me telling the story over the top. And we found we could solve all that by playing straight rockabilly beneath it, right? But it's not rockabilly, really, to me. To me, the sound I go for is a Johnny Cash sound, or like a northern cabaret sound, which is like [taps out thumping Fall beat], like you're in a club with an organist and some guy is doing "My Way" or something. It's really weird to see a guy in a Manchester pub doing "My Way." [laughs] It's hilarious.

In a sense, it's sort of like pop art, how Warhol's idea of art was to take all of the art out of art and then it becomes art. Which sounds absurd, but that's what I think of when you describe a guy in a Manchester pub doing "My Way," or how that might translate into the Fall's sensibility.

Yeah, exactly. A lot of what keeps the originality of the Fall, strangely enough, is that I am very into trash music. I'm very into badly produced records. You could go on forever about it, but that's the thing that's wrong with rock music. All the interest has gone out to the point where all this stuff I listen to is considered "bad" stuff, 'cause you can usually sort of figure out that it's gonna be good. [laughs]

How do you keep it fresh every night, since obviously that's a very, very important part of the Fall? Especially when you're doing something as extensive as the 30 dates or so that you're playing in America. I do notice you vary your set list, but how do you get to the mic and not just say the same things again and again? Or do you?

No, I don't. That is important. I really work to make it different every night. Or I just wouldn't go on. I have a sort of a neurotic state before we go on where I try and compile a set that's different and think of things to do and say that's different. *That's* where I do my work. I've got to do the work; it doesn't matter how many people are there. But, also, we've got a very large repertoire of songs — like 40 songs we could do of just old material in there. So, there's never any, uh, danger of becoming bored. I mean, sometimes it doesn't work. On some nights, you know, like one in every ten, I'll compile a set of numbers that we haven't done for a bit and it just doesn't gel.

Here in New York, I've seen you do "How I Wrote Elastic Man" and "Fit and Working Again," but you didn't do "Fiery Jack," which is probably your best-known piece. I haven't seen you do that song yet.

When you do things just to do them they just become crap. That's how it becomes rubbish. I even fall into it, you know; sometimes I think these particular songs have got to be in the set every night. But if you do that more than two or three times, you notice they're getting crap. I've noticed it with bands I've seen, big bands. They just go and play what they think is a good number to communicate. And when I notice that I just drop the song, however popular it is. It's just not important. And not in the snobbish way where I think you should not do anything that is popular or anything like that. I never think that way. But if the band isn't into it, or the band is stale and played it a lot … I've seen so many bands run through their fucking hits, and they'd be sharper, better off, not doing that.

You mentioned that you do some writing … has your writing appeared outside of the form of music?

Yeah, I've had stuff published in magazines. I write a lot. I write a bit of prose, but, uh, I find that very sort of constrictive scene, and it's very class-ridden. In England, a lot of these magazines, if you write for them, there is no payment, so they assume you have a private income. If I had a private income I could probably write loads of books, you know? I'm starting to write books. I've got loads of books in my head.

I thought your Christmas message in the NME *was the most fantastic thing I'd ever read in that paper. ["Message From the Fall" reads like a very barbed Professor Irwin Corey meets Mark E. Smith: "This is the year the precincts filled up with young crims who hate the Dexys even though they're the people being searched for … this was the year of* SHUT YOUR TRAP LAD DON'T YOU KNOW THESE ARE HARD TIMES?!? *And after doubting whether I was in the right media decided to rid myself of vamps, patronisers of the 'wee kids,' and well-fed cult creeps…"]*

Thank you very much. [laughs] Nobody's ever said that to me about it. I've got lots of, "What the fuck was that about?" [laughs] That's how I'd love to write. I could write lots of stuff like that.

Like I was saying before, it's unintelligible until you stop thinking about it, then it becomes intelligible, you know?

That's true, that, Yeah. And that is what we're about. Which is what my main sort of message is. You know, there's too many people who have got preconceived ideas before they approach anything. Music, ironically, it's like one of the most impacted by that thinking, and it's just ironic that the Fall is in music, you know?

1981, *previously unpublished*

Never Mind the Bollocks, Here's the Rollers

There are a whole pile of reasons that I have long been fascinated by the Bay City Rollers and believe their music, their career, and their influence ought to be taken more seriously than it has been.

First of all, when they were good — I especially point the reader to 1979's Elevator *album — they were very good, one of the greatest power pop groups of all time. In addition, in the mid-1970s, with their spiky hair, ringing guitars and condensed-glitter-lite thumping pop rock, their music and image served as a major gateway drug for teenage and tweenage fans who would later seed the punk movement and beyond; there's the unique and often frightening experience they had as one of the very biggest bands in the world between 1975 and 1977; oh, there's the tragedy of the financial and sexual abuse they suffered, due to usurious record industry practices and a predatory manager; and there's the rather wondrous return they staged in (very) recent years, returning to make first-rate dynamic guitar-based power pop.*

But this interview — one of a handful I have done over the years with Rollers bassist/guitarist Stuart "Woody" Wood — went deep on a very fascinating subject: the peculiar connection between the Bay City Rollers and the Sex Pistols. (In fact, some of the revelations in this piece were considered so novel that they were picked up by the English tabloids and have since been cited in the English music press.) This article begins by discussing Danny Boyle's (just then-released) Sex Pistols bio-pic, Pistol, *which had tipped its hat in multiple places, subtly and not so subtly, to the Bay City Rollers ... references I did not think were remotely accidental.*

Do you remember when punk rock was just a rumor?

It is 1976 or 1977. You are 14 or 15. You live in Great Neck or a place very much like it. You dream of a world where you walk on streets seen in *Million Dollar Movie* openings and *That Girl* reruns. You know you don't belong where you spend your days (except maybe with the theater kids, or in line at *Rocky Horror*). And punk rock is just a rumor.

In the age before instant connectivity, rumors, sometimes, were as powerful as facts. And the rumor of punk rock, just the idea that it was a possibility, changed our lives, gave us hope.

Danny Boyle's *Pistol* honored that rumor. It really did. True, facts were all over the place or just plain invented out of whole cloth, but it was an accurate portrayal not only of how and why young people form a band, but also why we are driven to listen, engage and join the strange fray, alien yet so familiar. One of the primary functions of music — both from the perspective of the listener/fan and creator — is that it is a flag under which we meet our tribes. *Pistol* told that story and told it so well that, despite the fact that I am a legendary punk rock nerd, I forgave the errors, blatant as they were.

I also utterly loved the fact that *Pistol* honored the Bay City Rollers. The Bay City Rollers are an undeniable presence in *Pistol*: a key scene features the Pistols and their friends stomping around to the proto-punk glitter anthem "Shang-a-Lang." The same episode concludes with a carousel/playground version of the same BCR song. Thomas Brodie-Sangster, as Malcolm McLaren, refers to the Rollers multiple times and mentions his desire to incorporate elements of their imaging and marketing into the Sex Pistols; a (slightly) keener eye will note the appearance of magazine photos of the Rollers displayed in multiple places, from the bedrooms of the Huddersfield girls to the Pistols' office.

This wasn't just artistic license. Circa 1975, the Bay City Rollers were a ubiquitous part of British pop culture. They literally dominated the British charts, television screens, tabloids and media as no other band had since the Beatles (we quickly note an enormous difference between Beatles and Rollers: one manager encouraged the band to achieve creative independence, adventurism and growth; the other was terrified of deviating from formula and therefore locked the band into a suicidal stasis of image and artistry). But the pure constancy of the Rollers' visibility in the UK isn't the only reason they impacted McLaren and the nascent Sex Pistols: the Rollers may have been a bizarro-world model for the Sex Pistols themselves.

Pistol (and, to a slightly lesser degree, the Steve Jones memoir it is based on, *Lonely Boy*) stressed that McLaren genuinely saw the Pistols as the dark side of the Rollers and consciously modeled them in this image. After all, the Bay City Rollers were sexy, tartan-clad (very) young men with rooster haircuts, playing utterly simple music that drove teenagers crazy and caused them to destroy venues and defy their parents. The Rollers were as much the anti-Floyd as the Pistols were, only they were there first.

Stuart Wood is 65 years old. He joined the Bay City Rollers in 1974 when he was 17 (alternating between guitar and bass) and was one of their most recognizable members during their glory years. Wood still tours and records with a version of the Rollers that he leads.

Stuart told me about an encounter he had with Malcolm McLaren at a party in London in 1975 which speaks directly to McLaren's interest in Woody's band.

"It was a wee while ago, so I don't recall the exact date," Wood remembers, speaking to me from Edinburgh. "We chatted, and he asked me all sorts of questions about the Rollers, the image, the tartan, the fans, how we did our hair … [guitarist Eric Faulkner] and myself had the spiky hair. We didn't think it was such a big deal: Bowie had the spiky hair; it was just something you did back then. Eric would cut my hair and his own hair himself; we never had a professional do it. And it certainly looked like we cut it ourselves. Malcolm seemed interested in that."

(It is worth noting that, around this same time, McLaren attempted to recruit another Scottish lad, Midge Ure — then 22 and fronting a moderately popular Rollers-wannabe band called Slik — as the Pistols' vocalist. It has been rumored that McLaren was interested in approaching Wood himself for the Pistols job — he certainly looked the part — though Wood doesn't know anything about this.)

When the Sex Pistols and punk rock emerged, Wood and the Rollers did feel some kinship.

"Back in '77, we had heard from various people that a lot of the punks liked the Rollers. I suppose we always had a certain affinity with the punk movement.

"When people would ask me what I thought of punk, I would respond that it wasn't necessarily my cup of tea, but I very much appreciated that it brought music right back to the basics again. You didn't have to be the world's best musician. The Rollers weren't great musicians, but we had something that other bands didn't have, and punk had a rawer version of that. The Rollers had the tartan; we would sometimes use safety pins to hold our trousers and clothes together onstage — these funny wee bits and pieces I flashed back on when I watched [*Pistol*] — the punks took those things and roughed it up. 'Shang-a-Lang,' look at it, there's nothing fancy about it. You just bang out the chords. It starts in A. It goes down a fret. It goes down another fret. Then right back up again.

"I never heard a punk slag the Rollers. I never heard a punk say a derogatory word about us. And we certainly never put it down, when asked. Eric, especially, was very vocal about the fact that music had gotten very complicated, and it was time to return to something that was rough and full of energy."

What did Woody think when he saw the big scene in *Pistol* where the Pistols and their mates are stomping around to "Shang-a-Lang"?

"That was quite an accolade to the Rollers, it was great that they did that. The UK can be quite funny towards the Bay City Rollers — I sense that most of the establishment music industry would like to pretend we didn't exist. But you can't keep it down. I sense that's because of the songs, and that we had so many fans. They can slag us all they want, but when you do that, you're just slagging the people who spent their hard-earned money on our records and concerts. That's who they're slagging, because we just played it and enjoyed playing it."

The Pistols and the Rollers had something else in common, something quite a few shades darker: both bands had controversial and controlling managers whose personal and business style may have negatively impacted the naïve young men they represented. When Stuart watched *Pistol* and its portrayal of McLaren's manipulation of the Sex Pistols, did it give him any flashbacks of the Rollers' relationship with their manager, Tam Paton?

"In my opinion, Tam was the only manager who could have managed the Rollers," Stuart says. "What happened to him later was disgusting, but in the early days if Tam hadn't been managing us and keeping such a close watch on us, there probably would have been 50 to 50,000 lawsuits and babies … Baby City Rollers. I mean, I was 16, 17, during the height of all the Rollers stuff; if I hadn't been watched carefully, kept under control, I would have been out all the time, drunk all the time and likely getting myself into massive trouble. So (and I know this is hard to imagine now), it wasn't necessarily a bad thing that Tam was as heavy-handed, as laying-down-the-laws, as he was."

There's one other aspect of the *Pistol* saga that reminded me of the Bay City Rollers' story. John Lydon sued, unsuccessfully, to block the making of the show, creating a significant rupture in his relationship with the other living members of the Sex Pistols. A little over a year ago, the Rollers' best-known vocalist, Les McKeown, died. At the time of his death, Wood and McKeown were estranged (both were, essentially, fronting competing versions of the band). We discussed Lydon's break with the Pistols, and I wanted to know if Wood has wished, in hindsight, that he had made peace with McKeown before his death.

"I think it would have happened, and I think we both wanted to take that extra step. One of the last things I heard about him was that he was looking into the possibility of putting together another reunion. I read that in the paper. And I had heard that Les was in a much better place, health-wise and emotionally. But it's a shame we never came together again. It wasn't meant to be, which is quite sad. Al [Roller founder Alan Longmuir], who was my best pal, obviously he died, and not much later Ian Mitchell, who was another one of the good guys, he died. With those three gone, there's no chance of a proper reunion, that died with them. My main objective now is to keep this band going. I know that people still want to hear it, they still want to see it, they still want to love it, and they do love it, and I want to keep that going as long as I can."

The experience of being in the Rollers, these fishbowl situations with dominating managers, makes me feel that these bands would understand each other.

"I think that's probably true. I was watching the show with Denise, my wife, and you know at the end of the second episode where they play 'Shang-a-Lang,' but it's a carnival-type version — like the kind of thing you'd hear on a carousel? And she noted that it signified that the Sex Pistols had become part of the same thing that we were part of, the same machine that we were part of, the carousel of the music business, here we go, join the circus. During the same show they had played our version of 'Shang-a-Lang,' and it was really a joyous moment; but they ended the show by playing this version that signified that the Pistols had joined the circus. They were saying that the Sex Pistols were now part of the same carousel that we had been on."

2022, *ROCK AND ROLL GLOBE*

Part 6: Not Politics (but Not *Not* Politics)

The pieces in this section do not, I suppose, deal with politics in any conventional sense. Instead, they consistently underline two of my core beliefs:

First, since rock and roll is, essentially, the sound of America's disenfranchised made electric, all rock and roll is, essentially, political. Secondly, the public face of rock and roll has, by and large, been conformity and cowardice dressed up in rebel's clothing. It has encouraged us, again and again, to think that pissing off our parents is the same as taking a utile stand on something meaningful, and that dying our hair pink actually changes something.

I also think recent history has borne out something I wrote in one of the pieces in this section: "The right was not a viper in our midst. We were a paper tiger in theirs."

How sad it is that an artform and a tool born of such struggle and promise basically screams "Black jeans!" in a crowded theater and tells us that is meaningful.

In other words… "But we sang 'Kumbaya' and 'Imagine' over and over! How did we wind up here?"

Notes From a Small Town Called Rock and Roll

This was another quickly written piece (quickly, not hastily); honestly, I often think my best writing is the stuff I dash off.

This was written in response to the release of Jason Aldean's "Try That in a Small Town." That got me thinking. Regardless of where I have lived — suburb, city or bayou — I've always lived in a small town.

That's because I am a citizen of a small town called Rock and Roll.

Before you injure yourself laughing at the pretension and naïveté of that statement, please read this. I thank you. I mean that.

We recognize that rock and roll is the most beautiful thing to happen in our lives. It gave words to our hopes, feelings, fears and dreams when we did not have the words ourselves. It invented and described love for us when we were unloved, and it was the soundtrack for love when we were loved. It found us friends when we were friendless, and it was the fuel for friendship when we found it. It told us stories of freedom when our world was small and square. It comforted us on nights scarred with rejection, fear and acne. It was big when we felt small, and it was intimate when the world was too big.

Some of us even plugged in and marched across the world's stages like an army of happy conquerors, and it made our dreams come true. Every night, we waved this banner: I just want to give you the same feeling rock and roll gave to me.

Even if you never played a note, it inspired you and distracted you and was the landmark for all the remarkable and trivial moments of your life. And we recognized that banner; and we ran to that banner; and we wrapped ourselves in that banner; and it felt like home. And it was our friend. And it created a town without borders, where all over America we could recognize a friend just because we shared rock and roll. Once we were outside; now we had friends. Welcome to our dream of inclusion, our dream made by the outsider, for the outsider, to bring them inside our tent. Now you have a friend.

Rock and Roll is our small town. We carry it in our hearts wherever we go.

We recognize that rock and roll is the sound of America's disenfranchised made electric.

We recognize that rock and roll was created by America's unwilling and willing immigrants and their children and grandchildren; by the sons and daughters of sharecroppers, tenant farmers and freed slaves; by the sons and daughters of coal miners and hard rocks; by the sons and daughters of the great northern migration and the sons and daughters of the veterans of Johnston's First Mississippi Infantry; by the sons and daughters of Pullman porters and those who grew up under the Third Avenue El; by the sons and daughters of those who played the bent blues on Rampart Street and those who sang celebratory schottisches in dusty west Texas towns.

Find the names of those who were meant to be excluded from the American dream and you will find the names of those who invented your music, your rock and roll, your country, your pop.

They were in every small town and every city and every place in between: the outsiders, the excluded, who found a forever voice in music, who turned their experience and their suffering into the beat and melody of work and play and who live in every guitar chord played yesterday, today, tomorrow. Do not keep them from your town, because they built your town. They are the bricks and mortar, the heart and tears, of your town.

And in our times, in the cathode ray dust of the last century and the buzz-less ether of this one, we were also the other, the excluded: we were the greasers and the stoners, the geeks and the sullen and brilliant; we were those who were called faggot and dyke and who learned to wear those labels proudly, and we called it rock and roll. We recognize each other because we love rock and roll and how it made us all princes and princesses in the Kingdom of Outsiders.

Everywhere you look, there is a small town that is a cloud kingdom, and it is a kingdom of outsiders. Everywhere you look, rock and roll is a town called inclusion. Rock and roll is inclusion, and rock and roll is our small town.

We recognize that rock and roll not only celebrates our differences, it is also a creation of our differences. It was made by those who sat in the back of the bus because they had to, and those who sat in the back of the bus because they wanted to. It was made by those who had no choice but to be different, and those who were told over and over they were different; and those who used rock and roll to find the door to a world that welcomed them, a town of the spirit where they could fly a flag which said, "Freaks, geeks, you are welcome here; those who love noise that is too quiet or too loud, you are welcome here; those who have more questions than answers, you are welcome here; the beautiful refused of high school hallway cliques, you are welcome here: I am rock and roll, I am inclusive, I welcome you, Skynyrd fan and Bauhaus fan alike, you are home."

We found our small town under that flag. It was a land scattered with pretty boys and handsome girls, the strange who seemed instantly familiar, those within whom we finally recognized ourselves, who sang in a language which we instantly recognized. We carry the freedom of that small town with us, wherever we go. We really do. My feet are on this floor, in this zip code, but my heart will always be in a small town called rock and roll.

We recognize that Jason Aldean can say and sing whatever he wants. This is important. We celebrate freedom and inclusivity, even the freedom to state an opinion that we find distasteful. Freedom of speech is ours; we share it. But your fear of the outsider, your fear of the other, that is something we do not share. We adamantly do not censor it, but we are compelled and committed to announce that we reject it. Your idea of a small town is not ours. We believe the foundation and framework of the music of our lives was built on the lives and the creative invention of the outsider, the other. That is our small town.

We choose to say our house is inclusive. In fact, it is not a choice. It is a fact. It was built by outcasts, the disenfranchised, the bullied, by those economically and socially disenfranchised from the American dream, who claimed a stake in the dream via sound, rhythm, melody and art. Our house, our dream, was built out of wood scarred by prejudice and rejection, made into something so powerful we gathered within it, and found a home.

We are Rock and Roll. Rock and roll is inclusion, and rock and roll is our small town. 2020, *ROCK AND ROLL GLOBE*

Is Music Ready for the Apocalypse?

Let's just say this 2015 piece seems, oh, prescient. ("Prescient," much like "defenestration," is a word that must be used at least once in any book.)

America, I am a member of your luckiest generation.

Those of us born between (roughly) 1956 and 1975 were born into an era pregnant with prosperity and endless invitations to escapism, and we came of age in a time when this nation's penchant for invention and daydreaming soared without the clouds of impending disaster and involuntary conscription. We are the luckiest generation: we have lived the rough bulk of our life in the downy-soft years after the threat of Vietnam yet before the apocalyptic Goliath of the caliphate wars and environmental catastrophe. Personally: I was nine when the shadow of the draft ended, and it is likely I will live most — and perhaps all — of my active life before things become really dark, both figuratively and literally. Our children, our grandchildren and you (if *you* are under a certain age) are going to grow up and grow old in a very, very different world than the dynamically inventive and often wonderfully trivial era that is ending.

Every freedom we have taken for granted, whether it is the freedom to practice our religion, the freedom not to practice any religion or the freedom to drink fresh water, will be assaulted.

Will your music, your art and your culture rise to the task?

From Chapel Hill, North Carolina to Raqqa, Syria; from the West Bank to Paris; from Manhattan to your hometown; the corpses of those killed in the name of religion are going to pile high in the streets. The bodies of 88,000 and more children, slaughtered hysterically because of the country or creed of their birth, will be laid at the feet of 88,000 mothers; hysterical statesmen, waving testaments old and new, will demand allegiance to a holy land; weapons created by cold-blooded scientists in the last century to *defend* freedom will be used by hot-blooded hysterics in this century to *end* freedom; the flashing, shattering scythes of the middle ages and the darkness of the Toba Extinction will return to our world, grim twin revelators riding the pale horses of virulence and deprivation.

Will you be watching the Kardashians?

It is entirely feasible that we will soon find ourselves returning to the constant state of religious war that existed throughout most of history (remember, as recently as 1683 Ottoman troops were at the gates of Vienna); simultaneously, assaults to the environment will force our children and grandchildren to radically alter the way they live and ration things their ancestors took for granted. Continuous breaches of internet security will compel us to redefine the word privacy and, even more likely, force a sizable portion of the wise men and women of this planet off the grid, into an existence that both denies and combats progress.

This is our future.

Will music meet the challenges of this new world? Will music motivate the people of raped Gaia to fight for positive change? Will music mobilize armies to stand up for the disenfranchised, the hungry, the frightened, the abused? Will music provide amiable distraction that somehow creates joy but avoids numbing? Will music incite courageous and productive dissent? Will music underline atrocity and suggest solutions? Will music rouse brotherhood and combat ignorance?

The model for a utile, user-friendly, informative and provocative pop has existed in the past, and must be recalled and implemented again. Let us consider Phil Ochs and the MC5, performing in Lincoln Park in Chicago during the protests at the 1968 Democratic Convention; let us recall the theories, screeds, pranks and radical distribution models of Penny Rimbaud, Crass, Woody Guthrie, Will Geer, Billy Childish, Allen Ginsberg, Paul Krassner, the Mekons and everyone else who thought that art could inform, balm, spotlight the truth, highlight hypocrisy and witlessness, provide facts and inspire accord.

In the future, entertainment can continue to feed escapism and act as the clown distracting children on the way to the death camps; or it can be a utility, a bridge to unity, information and power. From the shtetls of the Pale of Settlement to the cotton fields of the old South, from Welsh mines to lunch counters in Mississippi, from Lincoln Park to Compton, the story of music and the story of activism is inseparable. And the story of every single aspect of our pop, whether you listen to country, death metal or rap, is synonymous with the story of America's disenfranchised.

Seriously, friends: the DNA of every goddamn thing you listen to can be found on slave ships and in the hollers of Appalachia. American music is the sound of those who had less, the sound of those who had to fight to be heard, fight to eat, fight to vote, fight to survive. Whether you're Jack White or Lightning Bolt or Bon Jovi or Paul Simon, when you make music, you are echoing the noise of America's disenfranchised screaming to be heard, or seeking joy in their toil, or setting a melody to the fight for equality.

Our music is a talking drum, passed down from the disenfranchised of the past for the use of the desperate of the future.

And that future is near. Our children, our grandchildren, ourselves, will need the utility of music more than ever. Music must mean something, say something, fight for something, take risks, announce agendas, denounce lies and tell the truth. Music is beauty and power. Do not fucking forget it. Honor it. Playtime is over. Rock and roll is just beginning.

Be Woody Guthrie. Be Crass. Be Phil Ochs. Be Jon Langford. Be Victor Jara.

You owe it to the future.

2015, *THE BROOKLYN BUGLE*

When You Mistake the Beatles for Che, You Get What You Deserve

Context, friends: Written in the run-up to the 2020 presidential election.

We are people of the older generation, raised in suburbs and educated in universities where the hallways echoed with Joy Division and Springsteen, looking uncomfortably to the world we gave our children to inherit.

We are the people who fought our parents over haircuts and mistook that for an actual war.

The wars we fought in the name of rock and roll made us think of ourselves as rebels, as people who took a stance. All around us, the evidence that we were grotesquely mistaken roars.

We are Americans. Therefore, we love personalities and we love stars to the exclusion of common sense. This, along with the fact that we came of age and were indoctrinated in what we perceived, mistakenly, as a continual upward slope of social, cultural and spiritual realization, led us to ignore this fact: Trump was a symptom, not a disease. The America he electrified and empowered was always there; we just chose to ignore it, because we were too busy fighting the wrong wars.

The story of my generation is the extension of teenage vulnerabilities and insecurities into adulthood and mistaking that for a political and cultural stance. We deny this, and we may not even be aware of this, but we respond to the world through the same cultural lens we looked through when we were 14: "I am rock and roll, that in itself is a statement, and that is enough. Rock and roll is not only my distraction but also my political party, my union, my army, my flag." We may not even be aware of this, but it is a fact. We mistook our culture for our weapon, for our shield, for our dogma. By believing that singing about working for the clampdown was the same as working against the clampdown, we worked for the clampdown.

Loving attitudinal music and art is not a stance; it is just a pastime. My god, we confused the two until it was too bloody late. The story of my generation is a profound selfishness, an unwillingness to be inconvenienced and a sucker's sensibility that invited us to con ourselves into thinking the world and a slogan or a song could save the Republic. These factors made us so extremely vulnerable to fascism.

Our generation wasted our time thinking style was rebellion. We thought listening to the Clash was enough. (Yes, I mean you. Yes, I mean us.) The entire motherfucking trip we have been on since *Woodstock*, when we began to mistake drugs and sex and the crowds that congregated to do them and hear people sing songs about them for things that had actual fucking meaning, is an invitation to fascism. *Woodstock* was our Pearl Harbor, only we surrendered immediately. Our rock and roll culture was a motherfucking paper tiger. Educated white people mistook style for action again and again and again until it was too fucking late. Again, Trump is a symptom, not a disease, and when the disease was spreading we thought it was enough to listen to and quote Public Enemy; we misunderstood, again and again, that simply singing from the "man of the people" perspective is NOT the same as dispensing advice or taking risk.

In other words, ladies and gentlemen, when you mistake the Beatles for Che, you get what you deserve.

We not only left this door ajar but wrote a note on the fucking door with our bank codes on it due to this thing I shall call Seinfeld-ish. When television reflects your values back at you (as it did for much of the last quarter of the 20th century), it's easy to think everything is hunky dory A-Okay! How bad can things be, man, if *Seinfeld* sounds just like us?!?

Seinfeld was motherfucking opium, man, it kept you quiet and made you think winning the culture wars was enough. It wasn't. You retreated to your cities, to your cars, to rooms full of songs that made you feel both safe and engaged.

Recently, I was driving away from the sunset, and the car was full of a golden, dusky light, like my happiest memories from the crib. And at that moment, "Waterloo Sunset" came on the radio, and I thought, "If something like 'Waterloo Sunset' exists, how bad can things be?"

AND THAT IS EXACTLY WHAT IS MOTHERFUCKING WRONG WITH MY GENERATION.

We thought because a song could save us, a song could save the world.

A song can elate us, even inspire us, and provide us with a mnemonic for our emotions and our empathy. But the moments of grace they provide, however personally profound they may be, did not save our world. Loving rock and roll, even rock and roll that shouted all the right slogans and supported all the correct issues, did not save our world.

The best thing a song can do is provide genuine instruction; that is, a song can be the focal point for a rally, it can provide specific information. But most of the songs our generation loved were statements, descriptions or complaints, not instructions.

I'm not saying we all should have been storming the ramparts, but we have to recognize that the cultural hills we chose to die on were beyond meaningless: beautiful, entertaining, distracting, but of absolutely no consequence (or very, very little) politically. Think of a singer or a song you absolutely adore, or think of 18 of them; then tell me, did that song change someone's vote? Did that song strengthen a union? Did that song pass a law that made it harder to abuse a transgender person? Did that song remind you, in a way that stirred you to action, that there were three bodies buried in the Mississippi mud?

Look at rock and rollers, look at us. Our ambitions and goals were so childish, so based in teenage fantasy, that we chose to remain virtually inert and powerless when the streaming revolution chose to cut the artist out of the economic chain. In any other business, the supplier of the material being purchased would have figured out a way to get paid, and/or gone on strike, and/or engaged a powerful union to demand that they get a fair share of the profits. But for musicians, oh, it was enough just to be heard. It was enough just to scrape a little dust off the soapstone of fame. So, it is no wonder that an entire effing generation that perceives itself via the platform of rock and roll and its cultural and stylistic symbols should also settle for such powerlessness.

Because we declared victory in the cultural wars, we abdicated from assuming any greater risk. Even worse, we confused being a spectator with being an actor. We have grown extraordinarily and sadly accustomed to our stars shouting, singing or tweeting slogans that are grabbed lustily by the outstretched hands of the already converted, and somehow thinking that the performer has "taken a stance." A stance, a slogan, is meaningless unless it either comes from a source that the unconverted might actually respect or is taken by someone willing to withstand the ire of the unconverted.

And here I note what I fear is inevitable in this sort of rant: there are, likely, half a dozen (or possibly less) pop stars who could actually shift public opinion in this coming election. And, let us assert and underline, shouting or tweeting a slogan that affirms the opinion of the left half of your followers is absolutely, positively not the same as taking an action. A great artist demands the chance to preach to the UNconverted, regardless of the risk. To do anything less is to be either complicit or cowardly.

There was once a time, honestly not terribly long ago in rock'n'pop terms (where we still luxuriate avidly in thrall of albums made 30, 40, 50, 60 years ago), when artists who leaned left or artists who believed that there were statements worth making regularly risked not only their careers but their lives to do so. The Weavers, Paul Robeson, Phil Ochs, even the MC5, not to mention the Fugs, they said, go ahead, send in the goons, send us death threats, blackball us, redline us; we still sing.

Even Elvis, this emblem of the mainstream, emerged as such a radical bisection of influences drawn from different races that his very existence has to be seen as profoundly challenging and physically dangerous. And this is even without detailing those genuinely willing to lose their freedom and their lives for their songs, like Victor Jara, or those who put the "active" in activism and actually walk the walk, like Billy Bragg and Gerry Hannah of the Subhumans. (The bassist in this influential Vancouver punk band was a member of a small environmental and social radical activist group in British Columbia called Direct Action who publicly came to be known as the Squamish Five; throughout 1982, they set off explosive devices at nuclear power plants, factories doing munitions work and pornographic bookstores. After the arrest of some of their members in early 1983, Hannah served five years in prison.)

Although this species isn't quite as rare today as it was just a few years ago, the fact that it was relatively uncommon at a time when the Republic and the electorate could really have benefited from very famous voices speaking very loudly is worth noting. Around the time the Flower Children bloomed and *Woodstock*, uh, stocked, we began to accept slogans about action instead of genuine action and the appearance of risk instead of actual risk. The pop industry burst into full bloom, creating a fantasy that did not exist when Seeger, Guthrie, Geer or Robeson were young men. Future "rebel" musicians fulfilled rock star fantasies first, the needs of a cause second (this model did not exist when Seeger and Guthrie emerged; they were drawing on the balladeer tradition, which was based around using song to tell a story or communicate news and information).

And honestly, though this may sound extreme, I think one of the reasons the American left lost the American white working class is because we no longer had performers who risked their tails to stand up and sing in defense of their unions, their wages, their jobs. Universally, we happily and idiotically and destructively mistook songs that described working class life — say, your average Springsteen or Mellencamp song — for songs that advocated for the rights and dignity of the working man. Once again, empathy is all well an' good, but it should not be confused with empowerment, or with risk.

One need only to look at what happened in the world since August of 1969 (another half decade of the Vietnam War, the reelection of Nixon, the twice-election of Reagan, the willingness of those in power to ignore the AIDS crisis, the rise and rise of the right and on and on and on — all long before Trump) to know that *Woodstock*-ism, punk rock and the plastic soul of rock and roll itself (which allowed us to dress as rebels while reinforcing the status quo) was not only a paper tiger, but actually something worse: it made us think that action was being taken, that change was underfoot, when none actually was. It created the impression of change because we mistook cultural and stylistic change — the right to grow hair, dye hair and tattoo our bodies — for actual change. And because we looked out into our world and we saw *Seinfeld* and the Clash, we thought, ah, all is well, we must have won.

The right has to love rock and roll because it sapped us of our power. It was an utter time-waster, a distraction; like *Seinfeld*, the prevalence of good rock and roll fooled us into thinking the world was like us, and the world had changed.

It didn't. That's why we are in this mess.

Because we grew up under the stinking shadow of *Woodstock*, a million flowers without the poison of power, we grew up thinking winning the cultural wars was the same as winning the war for America's egalitarian soul.

We were wrong.

The right was not a viper in our midst. We were a paper tiger in theirs.

2020, *ROCK AND ROLL GLOBE*

We Are at War: All Free Men Are Citizens of Music

Every now and again, you stop and realize what a gigantic role music plays in our life. The harmony constant and forever mnemonic, it is in our life and our days and our work and our play. You stop to think, if only for just a moment, what if all that energy could somehow be harnessed for positive change?

Towards the end of the first Trump administration, I was trying to imagine how music might change our fates and improve our world.

We are at war. Deep down you know this.

Who will lead our army?

I want you to imagine an army of millions. For their entire lives, they have been told that they are ugly, that they are worthless, that their life has no consequence, that their brief and troubled time on Earth will leave no impression.

Now, imagine a great rebel leader standing in front of this army.

This leader tells these people that their lives and their thoughts have value, and that the legacy of memories and wisdom they will pass on to their children is a kind of gold. This great leader holds up a mirror in front of this army and says, look at you, you are beautiful! Your flaws, your lisps, your limps, your jaws too soft or too sharp, they are all beautiful!

The greatest rebel leader makes those who have never felt beautiful feel beautiful.

You already know this rebel leader.

Her name is music.

We are an army! You will know us by the trail of our song.

Protest music, as it came to be defined through much of the 20th century, is no longer necessary. In 1964, Phil Ochs released an album called *All the News That's Fit to Sing.* He wasn't merely punning on the famous motto of the *New York Times.* He was also saying, "Here is where you will get your news." This was once a very, very important function of music: consider the (literal) broadsides of Bob Dylan, Woody Guthrie, Pete Seeger or Phil Ochs. They passed on information, in the form of poetry and song, about racism, imperialism, war, the union movement and so forth. Protest songs, subtle and severe, from men like Joe Hill to bands like Crass, consistently served as a source of information and a platform for discussion and discovery.

But we no longer need music to incite rage or impart data or intelligence. The ubiquity and accessibility of the internet essentially renders our need to hear news via songs irrelevant. This is not a good or bad thing; it is just evolution.

However, I do very much believe in music's ability to be a locus for identity, a pin on the map of who we are and what we believe in. And identity has the ability to incite rage. Identity has the ability to invite enemies and attract friends. Identity has the ability to provide comfort and shelter.

If you identify, either by birth or choice, as anything other than a heterosexual white male, you are under attack as you have been at no time in the last 50 years. Maybe the battle is not yet on your doorstep — or maybe it is. In any event, it will be soon.

You can pretend otherwise, but you are fooling yourself.

At this moment, core aspects of identity of you or someone you love are under assault. It is extremely likely that these aspects of identity were initially formed by music, were supported by a community you found via music and continue to be felt and underlined when you engage with music.

Music is inseparable from identity.

We are music.

It is our homeland. We are the nation of music. It welcomed us when we were lonely, bullied, frightened, chased and harassed, and it said *you are now one of us.*

We found ourselves through Bowie or Jerry, or maybe even *Company.* You saw that slash of color on an album cover or T-shirt, and you were *never* the same; suddenly, the polo shirt from Korvettes and the haircut from Adam West seemed inadequate — not just inadequate, but *wrong.* Ray Davies, Patti Smith, Rotten, Bolan, Stipe, Morrissey … we are not just talking fashion or music, we are talking *identity.* We are talking about the warpaint we wore to find our tribe, as we wandered, the diaspora of the strange, through high school's conformist halls.

More importantly, music was a way for us to declare, "We are not our parents." It was also a way for us to say, "We are not *that* group sitting at *that* cafeteria table. True, for a few moments I wanted to be them, but then I knew that I absolutely could not. I had to be someone else. I looked for a flag. I looked for shelter. I found it under music."

Music has always said *this is who I am.*

Today you may think *I am a parent.* A lawyer. An uncle. A publicist. A psychologist. A teacher. A nurse practitioner. An accountant.

But before you were *any* of those things, you were a punk. A mod. A Deadhead. A Bay City Roller fanatic. A metalhead. A folkie. You knew every word to *Rocky Horror.* You knew every lyric to *Ziggy Stardust and the Spiders From Mars*, or *Lola Versus Powerman,* or *Tyranny and Mutation.*

Music was your first portal to identity when you were old enough to choose for yourself. And it has stayed with you, still somewhere inside of you, hasn't it?

After all, you could not forever identify yourself as someone who loved dinosaurs, someone who loved astronauts, someone who loved stickers. You had to move on. You probably went through a stage of trying to "just" fit in or trying to "just" not be picked on. But when that didn't quite work, you started looking for a tribe. You searched, perhaps unknowingly, for a tribe that would welcome you and even protect you; a tribe that would make you feel like, well, *you.* You didn't necessarily know what that tribe was, or where it could be found. You did not know where the signs were, where the map was.

And then came music. Music made it easy. Music made identity joyous. When you were lost or lonely, music said, "Stand under this flag."

I want you to recall those first weeks when you had to find out absolutely everything about the Beatles, and that was *all* you could talk about. You are *still* shaped by that week! And then, remember that weekend you first heard the Kinks or the Velvet Underground? You found out a little more about who you were, who you were not, and who you might become. These discoveries were transitions as real as puberty, or your first solo voyage on the subway, or the death of a beloved bubbe, or your first kiss. These discoveries didn't just accompany life's big events (though of course they often did); they *were* life's big events.

Music was not just a soundtrack. It was also a magnet. It was a flag to fly, a flag to seek.

Our experience with music, for the most part, is absolutely inseparable from identity with an outsider culture. Sometimes this was an outsider culture that presented itself in an extreme way, other times in a relatively passive way; but music culture is inseparable from outsider culture.

And outsider culture is under assault. This means that the homeland of music is under assault. Many of us, arrogantly but understandably, could not imagine a time when human dignity, freedom of the press and basic issues of gender and racial equality would again be threatened.

But that time has come.

And although we no longer need protest music to tell us the news, music may still be the greatest and most dramatic way to establish identity. And we can *fight* with identity, nearly as surely — and more pervasively — as we can fight with bullets. The frontline of this war is identity. And the doorway to identity is music.

I absolutely reject any musician who does not use the power and the gift of their platform to advocate for the rights of identity. Every musician, whose art was absolutely born of the discovery of identity, must say, "I stand here because I once chose not to conform. I will defend your right to do the same."

We are at war. And you will know us by the trail of our song.

I am a citizen of the Free Republic of Music. It has made me open-minded. It has made me contrary. It has made me compassionate. It has made me ridiculous, and it has made me serious. It has made me find grace in noise and dissonance in grace. It has made me curious. It has made me welcome those who wave the flag of nonconformity. It has made me believe that beneath the flag of nonconformity, we may find invention, success and happiness.

Let me paraphrase John F. Kennedy, as he stood in front of a wall, as he stood literally at the gates of freedom, as he stood at the frontline of the fight for the right of men and women to seek an economic and social identity of their own choosing. And I say:

All free men and women, wherever they may live, are citizens of Music. And, therefore, as a free man, I take pride in the words: "I am Music."

2019, *REAL CLEAR LIFE*

How Kent State Helped Create the Template for American Indie Rock

During the 2010s, I formed friendships with two important American musicians: Chris Butler of Tin Huey and the Waitresses and Gerald Casale of Devo. They had something very remarkable in common: both were (close) witnesses to the Kent State shootings on May 4, 1970. Not only that, both had felt compelled to channel the frustration, anger, activism and cynicism inspired by what they saw that day into something creative.

You are 20 years old. You are a student protesting on an American college campus. You are armed only with your voice and your ire.

"I remember it the way you remember a terrible car accident. Time kind of suspends itself. The soldiers formed two lines. They had the bayonets of their rifles pointed towards us, so we thought, okay, they're going to scare us with the bayonets and march us down the hill into the student-teacher parking lot. That's when they just *shot* … the last thing in the world you could even anticipate."

These are the words of Gerald Casale of Devo. He recalls, with adamantine clarity, a horrifying spring day in 1970 at Kent State University in Ohio.

"I remember hearing somebody screaming 'Allison!' and I turned around and it was Allison Krause, she's laying there, and I see the effects of a fucking M1 rifle, the reality of what a bullet does. And I felt like I was going to barf, like I was going to pass out. And that's when I saw the people kneeling around Jeffrey [Miller]. I knew how he was dressed that day, so I knew it was him. And the blood, which is running down the sidewalk in the noonday sun, like bright red and glistening, and … I lay down in the grass. Shaking. And it seemed like everything was in slow motion, and nothing was real, and then suddenly it crashes like an edit — boom! — and now you're hearing everybody, the chaos, the screaming, the crying, the desperation, the panic and these teachers with armbands on — they were like monitors for the protest — screaming and begging students not to move, don't do anything, don't move."

On May 4, 1970, at Kent State, members of the Ohio National Guard opened fire on unarmed demonstrators protesting the bombing of Cambodia. 67 rounds were fired in 13 seconds, killing four students and seriously wounding nine. The incident had a profound effect on the national psyche: within one week, millions of college and high school students went on strike, and over 100,000 young people marched on the Capitol.

Remarkably, this tragedy was also the impetus for a groundbreaking local music scene that would serve as the prototype for DIY rock movements all over the United States.

"I don't think I would have started Devo had that not happened," says Gerald Casale. "It's that simple."

"It was a government-sponsored school shooting, and I didn't get any grief therapy afterwards, let's put it that way," notes Bob Lewis, one of the protesters and the co-founder of Devo. "May 4th derailed a lot of people from the track they were on, so they were looking around for alternative ways, and creativity is one of the ways you can keep your sanity."

"It's the day I realized there was no place for me in the uber culture," states Chris Butler, another Kent State student who witnessed the shootings. He went on to form Tin Huey and, later, the Waitresses. "You looked at the world and said, 'I can't be a part of this uber culture that tried to kill me, I'm going to have to create a clean space for myself because there is no room for me in the culture.' Thankfully there was a musical outlet."

Although it is less well known than the better publicized indie rock scenes that were to follow, the template for the DIY spirit in American alternative music was forged in Akron, Ohio in the early and mid-1970s. Here, parallel with the earliest days of CBGB and long before the explosion of small-label punk and college rock in Los Angeles,

Washington DC, Athens, Georgia and Seattle, we find inventive bands making non-mainstream music and creating an autonomous system to record, release and promote their work.

These pioneering groups included the quirky, bar-band-via-Beefheart/punk-via-Monk 15-60-75 (also known as The Numbers Band); Devo (who began in the early 1970s as pop-art agitators/media satirists); the seriously proto-punk King Cobra (who shortly changed their name to the Rubber City Rebels); and, a little later in the decade, Tin Huey and the Bizarros.

Many of the veterans of the Akron scene will tell you that this burst of vitality was a direct response to 5/4/70.

"The likelihood is that both Gerald Casale and I would have stayed on our career tracks," says Lewis, who left Devo in 1977, shortly before they attained national prominence. "We were pissed off, and we wanted to take the energy that comes from that anger and channel it, and it happened to be into the concept of Devo."

Casale: "Bob Lewis and I began to develop a very cynical frame of mind, and the idea of devolution came up. We thought about what was going on in society and what we all sensed about the military industrial complex and centralization and fascism, and this *wasn't* progress: devolution was happening for real. This future we had been promised, this concept of linear progress and the idea that things were getting better, and the notion that there was a humane society developing with more and more people informed — we didn't see that."

By the late 1970s, the strange and fierce spirit of Akron, born of tragedy and fueled by necessity, began to spread its tentacles out through the world. Devo developed into one of the archetypal bands of the new wave era (and continues to represent the pinnacle of a certain kind of purely American quirkiness and invention); Tin Huey's Chris Butler wrote and recorded a number of massively familiar songs with the Waitresses; and Chrissie Hynde, another witness to the Kent State shootings, became one of the most respected artists of her generation.

"Places like Athens, Georgia didn't have the trauma," notes Butler. "The trauma makes a difference, and it puts an edge on all the acts. The Waitresses, sure we had one little pop ditty, but those are fucking angry songs. It's not as direct as Devo, who mocked the established culture viciously — that's the angriest band in the world, the angriest band that's ever been."

"We were punk in the true sense of the word," adds Casale. "We challenged illegitimate authority and challenged politically correct thought, but from a base of *knowing* things and reading and looking at things and having new ideas. Our whole response was a response to the state of American culture."

Butler: "You give up on hippie, 'cos hippie has no clout, and you grab art and your ideas, and you become very self-reliant because there's no alternative."

At the start of May 1970, Chris Butler was three weeks shy of his 21st birthday.

"I was with Jeff Miller, who was a friend of mine. I had brought a little plastic bucket with me that I had found somewhere, the idea being that you would fill it with water and dip your bandana in it, and it would help against the tear gas. I was a dumb-ass hippie and didn't know that pepper gas was water-soluble, but it was a good attempt.

"So, Jeff and I are walking around with this little plastic bucket, and the tear gas started. I had run out of water, so I said, 'Jeff, I'll be back in a second.' There was a water fountain in the dorm that was next to the parking lot, so I ran in and I filled up my bucket. I left the building and was moving towards where I thought I had left Jeff. And that's when the shooting started. I heard someone shout, 'Ahhh, they're blanks, they couldn't really be shooting at us,' but just in case I ducked down behind a car that was in front of me, and the glass got shot out, and I was covered with safety glass. I'm glad I ducked.

"I realized later I was about 20 feet from where Allison Krause had been killed. I did not know at the time that Jeff had been killed until I saw the *CBS Evening News*. He was about 50 feet in front of me."

2018, *THE WASHINGTON POST*

Part 7: Tributes, Memorials and Memories

I very rarely write tribute pieces. But on a few select occasions — in most of the instances featured here, literally within minutes of when I became aware of a death — I felt compelled to peck out a few words. These were not necessarily about the greater or lesser deeds of the artists, or some list of their achievements (others can do that, and likely do it far better than I could), but rather about what these artists meant to me, how they moved me and changed me. I attempted to address the deep personal and cultural reasons we cared about someone famous or influential and made room for them in our lives and hearts. I find meaning and context more important than details of a life or career.

This section, like much of this book, is a record of why and how we were moved by the life and work of someone we probably never met. I wanted to write about what an artist felt like; how they reached through a stereo speaker or a TV screen to shift my tiny world.

Maybe, in the wake of loss, underneath a hailstorm of tributes, we can get so distracted recounting the details that we can't process what really mattered: how the unique souls of these artists changed, inspired us, saved us.

David Bowie: The King of Outsiders

We begin with a tribute to David Bowie, written (literally) in the hour after I heard of his death. I deliberately chose not to discuss Bowie's music in any depth; I thought it was far more important to say what he meant to those he saved, the beacon of hope and lighthouse that he provided as the King of Outsiders.

This was, incidentally, one of my most read pieces at the time it was published (both on the New York Observer *site and in its print edition). It was also fairly unique in the manner in which it was written: virtually spontaneous and, if memory serves, it didn't even receive a second draft. I just banged it out on the Mac in one sitting in the middle of the night, ran spellcheck and hit send.*

It may have also been the first appearance of the "Kingdom of Outsiders" phrase that appears again and again in my work.

He was the King of Outsiders.

To any of us, to all of us, to everyone who believed life was full of exclamation points and question marks and not just periods and the dull ellipses of the dreamless, he was our King, our guide, our Bodhisattva. He was not just a name but also a noun, not just a noun but also an adjective, not just an adjective, but also the one we all had in common. Each of us loved him, or was loved by someone who loved him, or fell in love, hopelessly or horrendously or even, rarely, happily, with someone who loved him.

It began in 7th or 8th grade with the feeling that you might be a little different.

You sensed that these weren't the best years of your life. You believed that somewhere out there was a great city, shimmering with golden lights and stinking with subways smelling of piss, where every corner held an over-lit diner where coffee could be snorted at sunrise after an evening of inconceivable and unnatural urban bliss, and that this glittering prize, this city, where you belonged, was just waiting for you. And in the hallways of your school, colored aqua green and Wonder Bread yellow, in the hallways of this shoebox of shame and staggering incivility where you were forced to live eight hours a day, these jocks didn't know your secret; those meat-headed bullies didn't know your secret; those satin-wrapped, peasant-bloused foxes who never returned your glances didn't know your secret; none of them knew your secret: one day you would be someone.

Faces scarred by acne, bodies and brains terrified by wave after wave of testosterone, we withstood gym shower horrors and bit our thumbs until we broke the skin to prevent heretical shouts in social studies class and, still, everyone told us these were the best years of our lives. But we knew, first deep down and then as close to the skin as the first fawny, tawny wires of secret hair, that they were wrong. We looked for our King, and along the way, found some boys and some girls, also looking, also heretics, also certain that we were being told lies. We needed *Breaking Bad* but got *The Brady Bunch*. Who was going to take us to our Kingdom, our future, where we would be fucked and famous and fulfilled and carry pens and paintbrushes and guitars into the 1980s and beyond?

And then one day, out of the corner of your eye, maybe a shock of orange on a stranger's locker, maybe a rooster red rumor on a T-shirt, there he was. He had been waiting for you. He was beckoning you.

The city lies outside your door. These sounds, these flames of hair and soaring chords and sullen sprays of keyboards, will take you there. We will be heroes. Yes, you too.

He made us realize there were enough of us to make a Kingdom. He would lead us across the moat, the middle school moat and the Middle Neck Road moat and the Middle America moat. You, too, can join me in the Kingdom of Outsiders, where we will all be Princes.

But I will be your King.

He was the King of Outsiders. He will always be the King. We, who believed life was full of question marks and exclamation points, will always be his subjects. A long, long time ago, when Gerald Ford was President, maybe even before that, when I first spied the louche beauty of Lance Loud, I began asking for directions to the Kingdom of Outsiders. The first time I saw his face, I knew I had found the Map.

Even if you didn't care for his music, which was full of rich, sassy headlines ripped from all the hip broadsides, you still knew he was the King of Outsiders; you still knew he was the up-all-night sun who smiled at us all, who would always be the constant touchstone and common ground for every Prince in the Kingdom. Let others step into elevators with strangers and speak of sports and the weather; we could stand or slouch or sashay into any room in the world and we would recognize another Prince, and we could speak of our Saint. There may have been others you loved more but no one you loved more often, and no one you loved more when you most needed someone to love.

I perceived his music as brilliant confabulations of his extraordinary influences; I could never hear a minute of his work without thinking of the Move, and Harmonia, Cluster, Neu! and La Dusseldorf, and Barrett, Pere Ubu, the Swans and the whole library of extraordinary outsiders, full of invention, harmony and attitude, he integrated into his music. Nor did I hold these most gentle, wise and luminously assimilated appropriations against him, not in the slightest way; for multiple generations, he was our greatest musical concierge.

I met him a few times over the years, professionally, politely. Circa 1988, he took a small interest in the avant-pop band I was in, Hugo Largo; in the early 1990s, myself and his guitarist, the endlessly talented and endlessly kind Reeves Gabrels, hatched a cunning plan to have him collaborate with Glenn Branca (this, sadly, never came to fruition; I think it anticipated the stunning Scott Walker/Sunn O))) project that emerged two decades later). In each encounter, Bowie was brilliant, brilliantined, cool and continental, and he seemed like an extraordinary man impersonating an ordinary man, and both of you were in on the joke that he could never be an ordinary man. He had the soft, adamant manners and delightful superficiality of an ambassador, and each of these times we spoke about Neu!, because it seemed as if he had a keen salesman's sense of saying the right words to make you believe he actually cared about you. Although he was both slighter and smaller in "real life," those incredible, essential mismatched eyes startled in person as they never did in any pictures.

When I heard the news so very early this morning, I did not think of these brief encounters with the coolest of cool customers; nor, frankly, did I recall the music, which you will be hearing so much of over the next few days. Instead, I instantly thought of his face on a T-shirt, glimpsed in an echoing and awful school hallway 40 years ago. I recalled how this sight was instantly a beacon of hope, a path to the possible, and knowing his name was a passport to other lands in the Kingdom of Outsiders. I recalled that, from that first moment, just the idea of Bowie was a gold-and-rust-colored torch lighting the way out of the dismal sameness that we somehow suspected was not inevitable.

Just the idea of Bowie told us that we were not alone.

2016, *THE NEW YORK OBSERVER*

Scott Weiland

Others will write of his darkness. I want to speak of his light, that Diamond Dog Astronomy Domine Mystery Tour light that was alive in his music and sometimes his eyes. I am not interested in cause of death, because I saw the lightning he was capable of in life.

He sits in a chair in my office. My office is on the eighth floor of a blunt white building that stands where Sunset makes a turn towards the sea, exactly at the bend where the strip ends and Beverly Hills begins. He sits across from me, all right angles creased and gathered into an office chair, sucking down Marlboros and stammering in anticipation.

I am an A&R person for a major label. It is 1997, and I am going to help Scott Weiland make his first solo album. He is here to play me his demos.

His body folds and unfolds, moving like a *Thunderbirds* puppet. His deeply alive rock star eyes stare through me, those eyes that sit so far back in their sockets that they seem to reveal all the possible combination of darkness and light behind them. With childish excitement he slides a cassette tape over my desk. It's contained in a hand-drawn sleeve, baroque and psychedelic.

I put it in and turn it loud; he turns it louder. The room fills with blue smoke and bright, amazing, silvery, slutty, psychedelic music. These could be the best demos I've ever heard. The sound and the songs are extraordinary, clumsy and precise high-pop that sounds like Neil Innes channeling the Move via Suicide, Mott the Hoople recording *Magical Mystery Tour*, Gavin Friday recording with Oasis, Redd Kross suffering on the Cross. Scott is reaching for some kind of strange space-age buzzing version of Beatles via Bowie, but he achieves something even more remarkable, more unique than he could ever have hoped. The demo sounds lo-fi and psychoplanetarium 3D all at the same time: soaring melodies, sizzling and strange guitar sounds and dark, almost Scott Walkerish splashes of mood and self-loathing.

These demos became *12 Bar Blues.* Scott's first solo album is a strange and wonderful excursion, but to be frank, not as good as those demos; some of the ecstatic, childish Beatlism was lost during the polishing/recording process; more significantly, a couple of fantastic-sounding songs had to be excised for legal reasons (the almost slavish joy Scott took in replicating the past had caused him to lift — likely unconsciously — some pre-existing melodies).

Nevertheless, in many ways, I think *12 Bar Blues* tells us what Scott hoped to be. I believe he was trying to develop a new vocabulary for his rock star language, somewhere between Ziggy Stardust and Nikki Sudden, somewhere between Brian Eno and Brian May. He was making twisted Britpop via Brecht via Malibu Beach, something that buzzed with the deeply British accent he heard in his heart and the Lite-Brite L.A. lights that surrounded him. My god, if only he had fully achieved this, what a magic rainbow fog he could have spread over the world.

Scott was also attempting to invent a new kind of millennial rock star. For all the extraordinary music of the 1990s, the decade still felt flannelled and mournful and fratful, and the era lacked a shameless rock star (Bono too holy; Stipe too conscious of the irony that went with the crown; Kurt too pure). Scott wanted to be *the* star, he understood that we needed Gaga but had Hootie.

And of course, perhaps most of all he wanted to be Bowie, but there was too much Black Flag and Kurt and Stipe in him to make his imitation pure. Yet, on *12 Bar Blues* he was so very, very close to inventing an explosive combination of the deeply artistic and the deeply decadent and the deeply feral. Ultimately, he was Bolan designed by Egon Schiele, or Michael Stipe pretending to be Brian Slade.

I think the salty pomp of Los Angeles strut-rock was essentially wrong for Weiland. If only he was raised in Hackney and not Huntington Beach he might have known that his musical soul belonged more to the world of Andy Partridge, Robyn Hitchcock and Syd Barrett than the Sunset Strippers. Maybe this miscasting caused some essential harm to his character, who knows? If he had born a Gallagher brother, I think it might have all made more sense. He was at his best, I think, not just on *12 Bar Blues* but also on STP's *Songs From the Vatican Gift Shop,* where he injected the springy, twisting riffs of the magnificent band with a high-British hyper-melodic whine.

He wanted to be Lennon and he insisted on being Jesus, crucifying himself for reasons I did not investigate. Both beauty and pain were visible in those impossible cheekbones, pinned eyes and Egon Schiele body, all right angles and vanishing waist and the rods of cigarettes he fed himself. Yet on those occasions when you heard that magic that he heard, that he aspired to, like that day in my office and a few moments when he struggled through the haze and recorded *12 Bar Blues*, you wanted to hold him tight, and say there was a truth in pop that was better than any drug,

(But who am I to say that? I did not know drugs the way he did, and not knowing drugs meant I did know what drove him to love them more than his own body and brilliance; I refuse to judge the drugs, and I will only note that he attracted some dreadful moths when he was on them).

His most recent album (with the Wildabouts), *Blaster*, found him once again channeling Bolan, but recasting him as the vocalist for Fu Manchu; it's an album I almost love, although his vocal clarity was dimmed (that thin but clarion-fierce high end that had infused his best work with a kind of bitter bubble-gum whine was largely gone), but I could still hear what he was going for. He was still hanging Union Jacks from his cheekbones while reaching for SoCal punk and Sunset Strip strut … which is all to say I wish he had grown old and become Michael Des Barres.

For a few moments 17/18 years ago, I was elated with him and celebrated his vision of a decadent electroshock Jellyfish music, but I could not stop him from the sad, shivering figures that recognized an addict and praised him only to take. We fought over that sometimes, but it was not a fight I could win, because I did not understand how the draw of the impossible dream of his windowpane-laced wedding-cake pop could not be as strong as the drug. Perhaps I failed him. But please buy *12 Bar Blues*, that celebration of light pop in dark colors, sounding like a yellow submarine sailing through green seas choked with algae, with a periscope reaching up to a beautiful Laurel Canyon sky choked with winter's crystal light.

I do not know why he died, but if you knew him at that moment in the late 1990s in an office high over Sunset Boulevard, you would know he was once alive, so very alive, and his dreams and future were so alive in the high, hissing, acid-drop feline pop music that was on that cassette, and it seemed everything and anything was possible. He was trying so desperately hard to light new electric fires, and true, those fires were muted by the addiction (and even more so by the weight of the sad, using moths who are drawn to the porch-light of an addicted star), but if you saw him in those moments when his deep eyes were fired by dreams and the even rarer moments when those dreams turned from lightning vapor to musical reality, you loved him.

Because, ultimately, let us not speak of potential unrealized, but just remember that he achieved so much. He did realize that potential, and it is selfish for us to say that we wanted more. Let us not remember that he faded away, but that he sparked so hot, so real, so full of a silvery, shimmering, slinky cosmonaut pop heat.

2015, *THE NEW YORK OBSERVER*

Mia Zapata 1965–1993

My liner notes for Sub Pop's 2024 reissue of the Gits' debut album, Frenching the Bully.

It is not the years we have had without her. (A lifetime now.)

It is the years we had with her. (The wobbly end of our adolescence, the half-remembered taxi-hunting heart of our hop-stinking, dayless youth.)

I refuse to tell this story through the lens of tragedy or sensationalism; she is not a story to be streamed; she is not the ending dwarfing the beginning and the middle. She was an artist full of sparks, wisdom; the usual mundane and spectacular damage that the great ones turn into exquisite noise and poetry, and the kind of voice and presence you might encounter once or twice in your life, if you're very lucky.

This story is legend, even without its sorry ending.

So, let us tell it like this: first, to celebrate what we saw that others did not have the gift of seeing; and secondly, to be thankful that we have very goddamn solid evidence of all this gorgeous, twisted, humid and beatific magnificence in living music, living memories, even living film. Mia Zapata was the greatest rock singer of her time.

She may have likely been the greatest singer in punk rock history, the woman who married the 78 and the '78.

Tragedy did not make this true. Mia Zapata made this true, and the ferocious, spring-loaded shrapnel frame that was built around her by Andy Kessler, Steve Moriarty and Matt Dresdner, made it true.

Anyone who swayed beneath her and gazed up at her while she worked, while she clawed at her soul, while she demanded eye contact, then insisted on looking only inside, knows how extraordinary she was. Anyone who held the neck of a rapidly warming beer and saw this fierce sack of elbows and knees who seemed to be wrestling with time and art and insecurity, all expressed in a voice that belonged as much to Beale Street or Frenchman Street as it did to silly old Seattle, knows they were witnessing a singular, generational talent.

Mia Zapata (1965–1993), the vocalist and frontperson for the Gits (1986–1993), did not have the type of voice one usually associates with a punk rock band. She had the sizzle, sass, shriek, grace, rasp and fury of a classic blues shouter (what if Janis Joplin had fronted Fugazi, we must ask?). Although there was a purity, an accuracy, to her voice, she could point it at the stars and scoop cigarette butts out of the venue floor all at the same time; it sounded like a voice on fire, it sounded desperate and angry and pleading and commanding, all at the same time (what if Amy Winehouse had fronted Fugazi, we must ask?).

Her onstage persona was utterly devoid of bullshit, as well: Mia Zapata was a rag doll, a stick figure, a sock puppet, alternately bent with sadness and arched with rage. Sometimes she looked like she was in pain, clawing at an ulcer; other times like a holy woman on a soapbox, testifying the joy of truth; still other times like someone draped in a bedtime T-shirt reading from the inner ramblings and confessions in the margins of her notebooks. The voice, the presence was extraordinary, there was nothing like it anywhere in punk — it was like finding the missing link between Nina Simone and Johnny Rotten (what if Joss Stone had fronted Fugazi, we must ask?)

Mia Zapata was a pure yet twisted soul singer with the heart of a gospel shouter, the gnashed teeth of a punk and the bleeding heart of a folkie. Her recordings (and the films of her twisting within herself as she rasped herself inside out, like the most sensitive artist you ever met trying to dig a sliced Sprite can out of the garbage disposal) display someone whose place in the world of music has never been filled, not even close. I can aver that every single person who heard Mia Zapata's voice, that voice that could peel the old green paint off barroom walls and summon us to Shambhala at the same time, was socked, throttled, moved and changed by it.

Now, much of this story takes place in Seattle, Seattle, blah blah

blah, and during, ohhh the strange night fog of the early 1990s, but did that matter? No. That didn't matter. The Gits were beyond era or place. Maybe that's why they were one of the most important acts to emerge from Seattle during that time. They were in that place, but not of it. They were bigger than we who trilled with the frisson of "scene." We came alive in university districts, in loud saloons with tin ceilings and shoebox nightclubs lit by Christmas lights. Under over-bright streetlights on the pavement outside, we begged for phone numbers and cigarettes. Mostly the music was an accessory or an excuse, but sometimes (almost never but sometimes) it was transcendent. But when it was, oh, it humbled us, it awed us, it made our childishness small, it turned an evening into a lifelong memory. And that was the Gits.

The Gits, who defied any categorizations (ferocious bluesy post-hardcore sideways-metal screw-propellor punk rockers?)made a sound most of us pretend artists could only aspire to. Certainly, they sounded (far) less like an archetypal Seattle band and more like the wonderful realization/destination of American/ Anglo-ized metallic an' fluid punk rock.

Ideally, what the Gits combusted should have been hardcore's magic apotheosis, where it combined art, heart, melody and fury, yet with an empathy and absolute arrow to the soul that evaded other progressives who tried to take hardcore to the next step. Essentially, the Gits never stopped thinking like a rock and roll band (in the true twisted BÖC or James Gang sense), even if their chopsticks-on-fire/too-tight braces attack resembled certain hardcore, punk or metal bands (I'm thinking Ruts, Minor Threat, even early/mid-Maiden). And this is worth noting, again and again: although Mia was a once-in-a-generation talent — a wrapped-tight urchin/ingenue/artist applying a shredded Bonnie Raitt blues-rasp perfect-pitched alto to thread-shredded screwed-tight punk rock — she was swaddled, supported, instigated and propelled by an extraordinary ensemble.

Without any doubt, the band matched and inspired Mia Zapata to double down. Andy Kessler (guitar, metronomic and furious), Matt Dresdner (bass, fluid, punching and melodic) and Steve Moriarty (drums, martial and explosive) wrote and performed with a jaw-tightened fury, a clenched soul that shrieked and stomped with precision. Andy, Matt and Steve matched Mia, pushed her, were the inbreath to her outbreath and the outbreath to her inbreath. The Gits tendered a hyper-musical kind of clenched metal; on a purely instrumental level, they were dime-tight and diamond-tough, a band that could have redefined both metal and punk (why "could have"? They did!); Mia was constantly pushed by their power and balmed by their subtlety. In every moment onstage, Andy, Mia, Steve and Matt displayed the discipline of ferocious restraint; theirs was the sound of the heart and the mind bursting, the sound of that fractioned inbreath before the fist goes through the wall. There is grace in that moment, y'see, because it contains both release and restraint, and that's what the Gits were: the fist through the wall, the shame and relief after the violence and the grace when you restrain your soul just before it goes to that place, all at once. Yeh, I swear it's all true: the Gits were an angry, inflamed slinky fully in tune with and tuned by the Bessie Patti Smith of her time, truly the only singer who could summon Joplin, Poly Styrene, Sam Cooke, Iggy Pop and Ian MacKaye all in the same goddamn song.

The Gits formed at Antioch College in Yellow Springs, Ohio in mid-1986, grabbing and swapping pieces of art, thrash, noise, punk rock, classic rock and all the sorts of magical silly and bookish jingle bells that an old-school liberal arts education handed you; for the next few years they worked on turning it all into something tough and sensitive, both brutal and kind. Andy, Matt, Mia and Steve moved to Seattle in middish 1989, landing in a house on Capitol Hill where they (and fellow travelers) woodshedded and rehearsed for the next few years. The Gits put out three EPs in 1990 and '91 before signing with C/Z Records and releasing their first full-length album, *Frenching the Bully*. Seattle quickly claimed the quartet as their own and embraced the Gits' blend of ferocious fangs and soft heart, the slug/slap of the guitars and the gorgeous, soft underbelly of the poetic emotions. These qualities not only fit in with the doe-eyed/sharp-clawed grunge ethos but earned the Gits the respect of their peers, including Nirvana, who tapped them to open a major local show in 1990.

Then other stuff happened, and their frantic, confessional barbed-heart snowball began rolling uphill very, very fast; the Gits "quickly" (hah! after half a decade learning to implode and explode hearts and stomping their boots on manifold beer-softened, Marlboro-weeded wood stages!) inspired rapture, awe and the levitation that happened when peak emotion meets peak grindage in front of amps spitting out something that sounded like the mad marriage of Bolan swagger and Dischord tension … all fronted by a genuinely incomparable woman who held her heart in her mouth and shared it, in all its celebration and fear, without hesitation.

Mia was a painter, too. Her canvases are full of broken, neurotic and aspiring figures caught in the midst of transmigration, captured in the middle of a silent scream; they look like her, and they look like she sounded, and they walk the sharp wire between joy and pain (Mia's painting consistently remind me of two of my favorite painters, Egon Schiele and Richard Gerstl, both of whom also died far too young). Like her music, her paintings remind me of this: do not speak of promise unfulfilled or what would have been: instead, say, joyously, she gave us this!

My name is Tim Sommer. It was my great good fortune to have witnessed, multiple times, what Andy, Mia, Matt and Steve could achieve, to have inhaled that extraordinary mixture of intent and effortlessness. Goddamn fire is what it was, fire fueled by ale, hard-inhaled smokes, casually discarded smokes and the un-arty desperation that only a true artist has. (Arty people make art because they can; true artists make art because they must, and my god, Mia and the Gits sounded like they were doing something they had to do. Yeh.)

In 1993, I was a newish A&R person for Atlantic Records, performing the strange job of trying to make the world listen to the same music I loved. I told the label I had found the missing link between Bonnie Raitt and Iggy Pop (a silly phrase that sold Mia short — she had more in common with Sam Cooke, Gene Vincent, Ma Rainey, Charlie Patton or my all-time favorite blues singer, Amédé Ardoin), and that I had to sign the Gits. They — specifically, my boss, the legendary Danny Goldberg — said I could, so I decided the Gits would be the first band I signed to Atlantic. In the first days of June 1993, I met with the Gits (over better-than-average Chinese food in a cream-colored room with high ceilings located on Sunset Boulevard at the crack of West Hollywood and Beverly Hills) and told them I wanted to sign them. They were excited to accept my offer.

Less than four weeks later, Mia died. We leave it at that, because this is not about death — I have zero interest in the creepy voyeurism of true crime — it's about an extraordinary life. I do not say, "You should have been there," I say, "We are lucky so many of us were, and I am so glad we have this extraordinary evidence of the power and gifts of Mia and the Gits that you now hold in your hands." And we note that *Frenching the Bully*, this extraordinary testament to the soul, shock, fury and feeling of the Gits, has been long out of print on vinyl, and this new collection joyfully rectifies that, and the Gits' entire recorded output is now within easy reach for the first time.

Although it is impossible to tell the story of the Gits without engaging the hues of tragedy, it is hugely possible to experience their music with awe and without shadow, and with the abandon, emotion and joy which it was created. So, friends, please listen to one of the greatest punk rock bands of all time, fronted by the greatest woman rock vocalist of the last half-century.

FRENCHING THE BULLY liner notes (Sub Pop, 2024)

Alan Vega

Alan Vega, who died July 16, 2016, at age 78, was deeply in touch with the darkness at the heart of our most euphoric music.

Alan Vega was not a rock star; he was the shadow behind every rock star, a brutal, bone-cutting burlesque of the rock star's desire, the entire animal reduced to stuttering incoherence and a few words about lust, love and violence.

Vega was one-half of the churning, whirring, maxim-minimalist future/past frightwig godband known as Suicide. Suicide's music was shimmering, vibrating, anxious — the noise of angels being eaten by the machine age. In its manic circular hum and tic, it was the sound of crazies sleeping on the subway and lonely, spit-dripping men in uptown SROs; it was the sound of aging men and women living in the 20th century but still sleeping in old slave shacks on South Carolina farms; it was even the sound of West German children trying to rebuild the future with electronic music. Behind the keyboards, Martin Rev conjured the sound of death at Christmastime, his machines spitting out TB coughs in the delivery room at the birth of the computer age.

This vastly original noisescape was complimented by Vega's extraordinary, angry, deeply terrified posture. He sang as if he was caught between the hum of beautiful love and the self-hate of angry lust. He sang of American dreamers drowning in death, debt and the pursuit of the dreams that drove them to both. He sang like a man unable to distinguish between death and love, between relief and eternity.

The sound of Suicide married the junkie red and gray of "Sister Ray" and the hiccupping velvet tremble of the purest rockahillbilly via means so modern that they virtually defy classification.

In the last 45 years, it's possible that only the Ramones and Neu! were so shatteringly original yet so vastly compelling. Suicide made music that was beyond blues, beneath the blues, yet I would not say it was beyond rock and roll; in fact, it was the most severe and affecting gut-scoops from the world of Sam Phillips and Alan Lomax. Only Suicide evoked this spirit with an incredibly original hot-wired modernism that escapes any reference (other than to say it alluded to the speed-freak raga hum of Terry Riley, the rudeness of grave rockabilly and the beat hysteria of Joe Meek).

The man born Boruch Alan Bermowitz refused to be blinded by the happy light of the frontman's sexdream; his cold, caged stare, prisoner flails and bubbling, hissing, pleading voice were kindling for the eternal flame he guarded of rock's dark roots and its stories of despair even as he fronted one of the more progressive and adventurous bands of our time.

Alan Vega wasn't just one of our greatest rock singers; a century of rock and its brutal and beautiful antecedents lived inside of him. For the last 45 years, he reminded us that behind the happy distraction of rock and roll was the howl of the frightened, the hungry, the desperate. Rock and roll was their sound, their voice — even before it had a name, rock and roll was the ecstatic messenger of the politically, economically and emotionally disenfranchised. Alan Vega understood this.

Alan Vega's rock and roll was not a route to Pink Cadillacs; it was a path to survival.

Alan Vega was Jim Morrison caught with a bloody knife in one hand, Elvis' Sun Sessions in the other and no alibi. Vega cut to the core of the American nightmare at the heart of rock and roll: the best of our music exists because something went very, very wrong, wrong with our history and our hearts. We are a damaged culture, we are damaged souls, so this is our sound.

"Frankie Teardrop," one of the greatest American songs of all time, functions like that: it is the story of the natural fantasy at the end of joblessness, the last nightmare when the dream is gone.

There is a lonely, hungry sound made by the greatest American artists; it reflects both the lightless tenement and the dry dirt-patch in an Appalachian hollow; it sings of the sorrows to be found both in loveless Parchman prison and on the street of an ashy city where puddles reflect Terminal Bar neon. Our greatest singers, singers who predate rock and roll and transcend genre, manifest this: Sid Hemphill, Fred Neil, Amédé Ardoin, these are saints stalked by hunger, fear and death, and their melodies remain as old as the heart and as fresh as the landlord's frown.

Vega matched this sound with one of the greatest live performance personas in our history. He was confrontational and disturbing in a way Iggy, Johnny Rotten or Nick Cave never could be, because Vega knew that to tell the American story, he had to stand unprotected, he had to not just receive the abuse but preempt it with self-abuse; there was no greater way to announce that rock music was so much more than the alcohol-fed soundtrack to a Sweet 16. Vega channeled the feral acrobatics of rock and roll's most frantic frontmen — doomed and sinewy geniuses like Gene Vincent and Vince Taylor — into clawing, psychotronic shadowboxing that laid bare all the paranoia and anger at the roots of the rock and roll star's psychodrama.

If all punk rock had been as shocking, as beautiful, as advanced, as naked as Suicide, it could have lived up to its promise and not just been a fashionable revamping of the Troggs.

Suicide provided an idealistic and deeply over-optimistic picture of what punk rock would become. The duo's music was truly new, it was an entirely new vocabulary to sing about America's old stories of death, deprivation, lust and fear (and macho collapsing in the face of it all). Instead, punk rock, with very, very few exceptions, just became a childish revisit to Ronson dreams and downsized-Roxy glamour, when it should have been this, the revolting, hypnotic, bluesbilly electric eel of Suicide.

2016, *THE NEW YORK OBSERVER*

Tony Kinman and the Secret History of Rock and Roll

There is a secret history of rock and roll.

It has been written by the road dogs, the roadies and red-eyed tour managers, white-knuckled from gripping a steering wheel for 16 hours straight; it has been written on battered basses scarred with decals and precious chipped acoustic guitars by the masters of odd tunings (and no tunings at all); it has been written by those who sleep on the hard benches of old vans and shit in doorless toilets of low-ceilinged nightclubs, the unbathed who invent genres and find new starlight in old pop; it has been written by the women and men who lived on grilled cheese and crackers and the worst bourbon, who came alive like God's children for 44 minutes every night under the blue lights and leaking roofs of Cradles and Milestones; it has been written by unhealthy adult children who played angels' music because they had no choice in hopeless rooms they filled with hope.

But most of all, it has been written by the pioneers of invention and conviction, creating the future not on the springy stages of enormodomes but at 1:18 a.m. in that corner of the bar to the left of the jukebox and in front of the big window; it has been written by those who looked through the cedar-colored glass of whiskey and the blue haze of Camel smoke and insisted rock and pop move forward by honoring a sound they heard in their head and their heart, while not chasing the radio or the charts; it has been written by those who were not humble in their heads but *were* humble in the hearts; it has been written by those who understand that America was the Waffle House, not West Hollywood; it has been written by those whose inventions were echoed months, years or even decades later in the mainstream, where we would hear a harmony that sounded just like them, or an E minor suspended between heaven and the bus stop that we first heard on a 45 they pasted together themselves.

The future is always written by those desperate to make noise, swallowed by those who desperately need it. We were invented by pioneers; we write because we read the unwritten history.

You know some of their names, but do you know that they breathed petrol so others could sip champagne? Peter Holsapple, R. Stevie Moore, Amy Rigby, Dayna Kurtz, Mitch Easter, Steve Wynn, Paul Sanchez and on and on … I cannot begin to create an adequate list of the giants who crawled through the diners and Motel 6's of this land so you could feel that there was one musician out there who understood you, who was talking to you, who made that one 45 you rushed home to hear, with the anticipation that made the heat of the packed PATH train invisible.

I honor the people who made that 45, who built the future, who write our secret history.

And today, please honor Tony Kinman, of the Dils, Rank & File and Blackbird, bassist and bass singer of sepia songs and revolutionary rocking. Tony has departed this incarnation, perhaps for another or perhaps for the simple nowhere at all; but as the work, soul and heart he left with us will continue to ring with art, energy, guts and harmony, so his long jaw and Lincoln eyes will remain with us.

Tony Kinman has a major role in our secret history.

Tony and his brother Chip sang every song as if their life, their art and their country depended on it. The music they wrote and recorded sounded as if it was made because it *had* to have been made, because the men behind the guitar and bass had no choice. Even at its most romantic, even when it was lifted with the sighs and twangs of another era, it resonated with a passion and anger that we heard in Johnny Cash and Crass, in Mekons and Faron Young, because who knew that we needed a cross between the Mekons and Faron Young? Tony and Chip Kinman knew.

I first became aware of Tony and Chip Kinman in the Dils, who, along with D.O.A. and Bad Brains, were almost certainly the best (non-Ramones) punk rock band North America ever produced.

The Dils anticipated the short, sharp shock of hardcore while also predicting the teeth-gnashed atonality of no wave. Emerging circa 1977, they somehow mixed the alienation of Southern California with the earnest beat artistry of the Bay Area, resulting in a brusque but emotional sound of great conviction, the sound of angry but life-loving young men attempting to turn guitar strings into feelings with as little distance as possible between electricity and emotion.

Not only are the Dils one of our best punk bands (in fact, when I first heard them, they were so very good and real that I assumed they had to be from Vancouver, because they had a reality to them that I had only seen in bands like D.O.A., Subhumans and Pointed Sticks), their 1977 45 "Class War" is one of the best punk rock singles of all time: a 100-second two-chord (plus modulation) call to arms that is both feral and catchy, melodic, memorable and urgent. Sung with an almost folkish, western lilt over thrashing, raw chords, it's damn close to being the missing link between Phil Ochs and the MC5.

Honestly, the Dils should have been our Clash, because the Clash merely pretended to be what the Dils came to honestly and completely: the love letter from Woody Guthrie to Wire. Their music was tough, spare and honest, eliminating all the bloated remains of Ronsonism and cock-rock sub-Springsteenism that the Clash virtually rolled around in. The Dils sang and snarled every song like they meant it, like they wouldn't turn in Gerry Hannah, no matter how big a record contract they were offered.

And, spectacularly, the Kinman brothers moved on; like all great artists, they were not afraid to grow: The second stage of the Dils' life saw them integrating a ringing, country-influenced 12-string and harmony-based palate to their powerful sound, anticipating the jangle of early R.E.M. and the deep, roots-loving sincerity of alternative and underground country artists. Fueled by a conviction and credibility that seemed to be in their blood and DNA, material like "Red Rockers" and "Sound of the Rain" jangle and roar as so very, very few records of the time do.

By the early 1980s, the Kinman brothers had relocated to Austin, joined forces with another future roots-rock hero, Alejandro Escovedo (formerly of the Nuns), and reformatted as Rank and File, who were to country punk what Gram Parsons or Mike Nesmith had been to country rock in the late 1960s: that is, they were a blueprint for so much that was to follow. Rank and File played their proto-Americana with an engaging effortlessness and a still palatable sense of their punk origin; their sound was shocking yet smooth, their sweet harmonies full of question marks and skepticism. As they had during the latter days of the Dils, they played with an absolutely unique but very audible mixture of desperation and joy, blending C&W-era Byrds with Rickenbacker-era Byrds with the Everlys with the Dream Syndicate; the result was something as pure and light as a West Virginia mountain stream and as rich and muddy as South Carolina barrier island marsh, something that felt like both college radio and the Ryman Auditorium.

There was more to the Kinmans' musical life — after Rank and File, they continued to move forward, refusing to replicate the sound of either of their earlier bands, emerging with Blackbird, who applied those deeply affecting western, folkie melodies to a leaner and more contemporary rhythm-driven musical palette. (I am sure there was more after that, too, but I am not a completist, and the shadows cast by these pioneers, the Dils and Rank and File, are more than enough.)

You and I, we have lived our lives in the shadow and sunlight of song. We have been on this voyage with a thousand and eight bands, and each of them stole a piece of our heart. These musicians who write the secret history, they looked in their record collections and couldn't find what they wanted to hear, so they had to make it themselves. Alternative saints like Tony Kinman are not only the authors of the secret history, but also the authors of a history only they could write.

Thank you, Tony Kinman, and have a safe and fascinating voyage.

2018, *INSIDEHOOK*

Greasy, Angelic, Ridiculous and Utterly Holy: Thank You, Huey "Piano" Smith

Rock and roll has many mothers and fathers and a million and more bastard sons and daughters — but only a small handful of true Queens and Kings. Huey "Piano" Smith — who died on February 13 at age 89 — was one of those Kings.

Huey "Piano" Smith leaves behind some of the most memorable and wonderful rock songs ever written and recorded, from "Rockin' Pneumonia and the Boogie Woogie Flu" to "Sea Cruise," from "Just a Lonely Clown" to "Don't You Just Know It," from "Little Chickie Wah Wah" to "Don't You Know Yockomo." Flying bop, that's what it is, smoggy angels with wings made of Mardi Gras Indian feathers fluttering the bottom edges of the low oyster shell-colored clouds above Canal Street, that's what I hear. It's Creole punk rock that has this strange, undeniable lightness to it. Huey "Piano" Smith made rock'n'punk'n'b that was charging and chugging yet somehow both silly and mysterious, as exotic as the steel-colored bayous, sinking sidewalks and humid, panting calliopes of New Orleans, yet somehow as fist-thumping as Eddie Cochran or Motörhead, because, man, did this cat make rock and roll the way it ought to be made.

Listen. We leave the details of his life to others (and I am sure some of that information is damn interesting, especially the mystery regarding why he essentially retired for the last 40 years of his life; for those details, I happily direct you to a first-rate biography, *Huey "Piano" Smith and the Rocking Pneumonia Blues* by John Wirt). I want to talk about how the work of his life feels: the nearly dissonant holler of the rhythm/against the space of the arrangements/

against the goofy masquerade and quadruple entendre of the lyrics/against the beat that goes up and down and a little sideways like a freight train running east and hard through Arabi; and mostly how it runs forward and backwards and in circles like it's inventing rock and roll while outrunning Mardi Gras Indians while inhaling completely synapse-separating weed, all at the same time (yes, I know that's the second reference to Mardi Gras Indians, but their rhythms, their language, their strange and beautiful legacy is, I think, essential to Huey's sound).

Huey "Piano" Smith's music is simultaneously silly and ecstatic, and it contains both space and urgency (sort of a cough syrup/coffee kind of thing). When I listen to Huey "Piano" Smith, I see the ley lines of all the rock and roll I love, from Star Club *mach schau* to Dusseldorf Rother-thump to Manchester Mark Smith billy-heat to Motörhead meatclubfoot to the swaying BOogie/DIDDLEY pulse of the bands marching down screaming Orleans Avenue in Endymion and all the Sonic psycho in between.

The music of Huey "Piano" Smith doesn't go straight to dinner bell hell, like say, Jerry Lee Lewis does (though it is a cousin); it sashays. It doesn't hang on for dear life as it scrapes the pads of its fingertips utterly raw trying to grab onto trucks flying fast down Airline Highway, like Little Richard does (though it is a brother). And it isn't totally lost in the Zulu Parade morning fog like Dr. John or Dave Bartholomew (though it is an uncle). The music of Huey "Piano" Smith breathes and tells jokes. It is an ace definition of tight but loose, maybe the first time we can apply that term to rock and roll. There's something delicate, almost feminine, about it, but at the same time it's a clear precursor to punk rock, especially the kind of screwed-tight/played loose punk of Dr. Feelgood, the Flamin' Groovies, Paul Revere & the Raiders, Sam the Sham & the Pharaohs, etcetera.

True, you can hear the very real connection to the bouncing, funky genius of Professor Longhair, Fats Domino and Jelly Roll Morton — all of whom played piano as if they were popping big fat poppy seeds into the loamy, over-wet Louisiana soil and the sidewalk they were standing on was on fire. But Huey took a pen knife to that piano and cut it down to its bare outline and straightened it out and made it something that a sassy skeleton could slide into. In doing so, he created something that somehow connects Tipitina's to *die Grosse Freiheit* and links "Shortnin' Bread" to "Wooly Bully" (a song that is, in fact, an ultra-reduced rewrite of Huey's "Don't You Just Know It").

A real fat and fierce vein of the indigenous and very goddamn distinct American post-Elvis/pre-Fabs rock and roll — such as the Sonics, Raiders and Wailers — appears to have been distinctly influenced by Huey and his tight but loose, simple but exotic sassy wallops. Huey also left an enormous thumbprint on Creedence and Fogerty ("Rockin' All Over the World" is a transparent attempt to write a Huey song), and a very real but more subtle influence on Dylan and the Band. I mean, it's all there, and if you've seen any of Dylan's rollicking, ecstatic, spontaneous and thumping rock revues over the last ten or 15 years, you know that he carries a lot of Huey "Piano" Smith with him wherever he goes.

The music of Huey "Piano" Smith bounces, sighs, pushes, stomps and tiptoes on the curb-edge of hysteria. It is likely the only sound instantly familiar to fans of both Motörhead and the Grateful Dead; which is to say it has a cough-syrup and absinthe time-hop, a purely weed-foam green weight on the temples, that the Dead repurposed as one of the primo signatures of their music (and, yes, the Dead covered Huey); at the same time, often on the same goddamn songs, Huey's music has a pure over-the-top satanic mill overdrive (the sound of beer drinkers rushing to the saloons after work, the sound of Fred Flintstone foot-pedaling his pedi-car on his way to buy condoms, the sound of a rusted-out out of control funicular whaddda-dadda-da-ing down a hill) that was taken as the basis of Motörhead's meatgrind.

Mostly, it just sounds like rock and roll, a furious funny ankle-bendy wobbly R&B punk rock set to a New Orleans parade beat; it's what the Reeperbahn would have sounded like if it was on Rampart Street. Which is also to say there's a very direct connection between Smith's bliss-nod Hadacol + chicory coffee nail-gunning and *Jerry Lee Lewis Live at the Star Club*, or, for that matter, the ballroom-shaking punk rock of the Sonics and two of Smith's most direct disciples, Joe Meek and the Dave Clark Five. Both Meek and the DC5 took Smith's hysteria, beat madness and absurdist point of view and made it the foundation of their inventions (one of the best Huey "Piano" Smith covers

— out of many — is Screaming Lord Sutch's "Don't You Just Know It," from 1963, produced by Meek).

In fact, virtually anyone who played post-1960 electric boogie hysterically, with a complete abandon that discarded finesse but held on to the beat for dear life and who had no problem descending into the madness of nonsensical lyrics and even dissonance, can trace their DNA to Huey "Piano" Smith. We cite, well, anyone from Slade to Status Quo (especially bloody Status Quo) to Dr. Feelgood to Rockpile to NRBQ, man, not to even mention the New Orleans-centric acts who owed him so much like Doctor John, Galactic or Cowboy Mouth. When you listen to Huey, you see a direct connection between his thumping hysteria, two chord vamps and 4:30 a.m. silliness — with elements of too-late nights and peekaboo games for waking toddlers — and the American garage punk sound of the very early 1960s, or even the bubblegum origins of the Velvets (it's hard not to notice how "Everybody's Whalin'," from 1956, frequently breaks into Velvets repetition and near-dissonance). Huey's creations have one foot in the high energy vaudeville-meets-meathammer bleats of the Treniers and the Rivingtons and one foot in the overdrive of the Sonics, all the while leaving a kind of stoned space for the brain to take leave of the senses. And that's probably one of the most remarkable things about Huey "Piano" Smith (I mean, alongside his utter and complete catchiness, and the way he compels one to instantly fall in love with his music): he leaves space in the chaos and throws us some serious joy.

To love rock and roll is to love Huey "Piano" Smith. It's greasy and angelic, ridiculous and utterly holy, it's a green fairy an' gage smoke-hacked two-beat that stutters in the lungs but stomps the mold-veined wooden floor as solid as any last-century motor; it's the head always trying to catch up with the soles of the shoes and the heart aligning near goddamn perfectly with the snare even if everything else flails its arms and elbows. Yessirmaam.

I cannot imagine how he invented this, this masculine/feminine wide open wild-time bayou-holler nonsense/total sense punk'n'b. While turning the corner on Rampart and Dumaine on a hot winter's day, did he think he could see the air, full of winter white and the palest blue? Or maybe he was just high. Was he floating on a pillow-fist mixture of codeine cough syrup, very light very strong coffee and cheap bourbon? And in his head, did he hear the sound of Louis Jordan, Junior Parker, the Treniers and the Coasters stripped down and opened up, mechanized and then melted, reduced to loose, louche, gage-hoppy lyrics skipping around a solid damn snare and kick, like a silly but goddamn serious elastic exoskeleton? Or maybe it was just Longhair's hopscotch bounce plugged in and Rocket 88'd?

Maybe. Probably not. But Huey "Piano" Smith leaves us with a relatively small but utterly extraordinary catalog of recordings that need to be incorporated into the dreams of everyone who loves rock and roll.

2023, *ROCK AND ROLL GLOBE*

Happy Voyages, Joe Franklin

This is one of the few pieces in this collection not about a musician.

When his city hummed with radio waves, autumn-colored incandescence heating up bakery brown Bakelite, he lived to be lit by the stars of the golden radio city, he lived to find relics in the smoky shade of the old Rialtos.

He lived to recall the pre-atomic radioactive shadow of Jolson.

Baby-faced in ballrooms actual and imagined, he had been bitten and beamed at by Banjo Eyes and found his one true church: Wintergardens, where the sacrament was the croon and cry of immigrant America, slippery with Yiddish and leaping with long Italian syllables.

And this was his world, the world created by Jews and minstrels and men of gossip and kings of jazz. On shellac and magic Philco, they were more perfect to the heart than sloppy reality. Life in newsprint was always better than the newsprint-colored world, and what truth, sepia sad, could compete with the cartoon curve of Dagmar's hip?

When the winter-white bathtub-colored sky above his city hummed with terrestrial television waves (and the bunny ears bent to catch them), the pictures from the Motorola fluttered and hissed, and he knew: there was no love, no laughter, no tears greater nor more authentic than those we would find when persistence of vision fooled our eyes and made us think the flicker was real.

When his city was full of Robert Moses modern, and the Zenith was tube-heated and so sexy-warm to the touch, and in the *TV Guide* there was a big C next to the talk shows and summertime fun hours; when the children sat Indian-style in Great Neck dens and overheated Chinatown flats and Grand Concourse kitchens, and Captain Jack taught us, all of us equal in his eyes whether we be belly-full or belly-empty, about Hal Roach and Moe Howard.

And behind a desk and a cool Canada Dry he reminded us, like a Buddha, that everything old was alive in the new and that Tony Pastor knew Weber & Fields and Weber & Fields knew Lillian Russell and Lillian Russell knew Ziegfeld and Ziegfeld knew Fanny Brice and it went on and on and eternally returned to the beginning and the middle and it could not be more beautiful.

When his city hummed with the slap and jaw of the three-card monte men in a Times Square shattered and burst and smelling of ammonia and weed, everything yellow like old Scratch's stucco and the vials crunching crisply underneath hurried feet, he insisted we make time for King Vidor and Johnny Ray and a self-published author from Tuckahoe, and it could not be more beautiful.

I looked through a window in his building once (true), a building full of Bialystocks and tragic hopefuls and hope-nots huddled by dairy-creamer-creased coffee machines, and I squinted through wired windows dark with soot at any time of the day out to the Deuceland below; if you looked through half-closed/half-happy eyes you could see *his* city, as *he* saw it, clocks clicked back and El Morocco black and white, a pigeon-colored world turned at dusk to Roxy Rainbow lightfogged by Camel smoke rings and a Canadian Club just within reach.

I looked into his eyes once, true, and saw Phil Silvers and Eddie Cantor and even sweet Veronica Lake in the shark's teeth tick of the sassy iris. Pass me your world, dear friend of so many nights, of every age of my life; give me your century, your hungry, sassy Jews, your prat-falling Irish, your Midwestern Cleopatras and Neopatras curved of plenty, your crooners, your jugglers, your tin pan beggars and boastful losers, your soon-to-bes and once-weres; give me your century, the last century, when the arclights were high and the overture started at 8:05, sing me the song of your century, give me the paint with which you touched up tense reality and made it tender and alive with song and silent film.

And he is the last of this world, and I love him so.

And to love him without irony is to love the hope felt when you were a child and you lost a breath when the blue lights caught the star onstage.

Joe Franklin March 9, 1926 – January 24, 2015

Sui Generis

2015, *THE BROOKLYN BUGLE*

New Orleans, Before and After the Flood: An Excerpt From Exile on Dumaine Street, a Work in Progress.

I love to write about cities.

This is the thing about cities: They are constantly reborn in the minds, hearts and imagination of every young person who claims them as their own. (That's why every New Yorker thinks "their" New York City was the best New York City.)

I am including this piece in this Tributes section because, well, it feels a little like — no, it certainly is — an obituary to a place I lived for a sizable chunk of the first decade of this century and a time in my life. Like all cities, it stops being "that" place once you leave it, grow out of it, grow away from it. It then becomes "that" place for someone else. All great cities are eternal that way.

The first part of this was written shortly before Hurricane Katrina. It is an attempt to describe an extraordinarily unique place and its definitive, wonderfully dysfunctional mindset. The postscript was written shortly after Hurricane Katrina.

It was the summer of rain, and the rain was so frequent that it made you wonder if there ever could be a summer without rain. In New Orleans, wet was always hiding beyond the next corner, and if it wasn't raining there was always a rumor of rain, and even on a purely sunny day there were ten million curtains of damp air to be parted every time you left the cool suck of the air conditioning. But this time it was different. The dog-curtains had fallen, and the skies fell with it; the constancy of the rain had become an event in and of itself, like the Blitz or Chernobyl. You no longer thought about when it might stop raining; instead, you wondered if it had ever not rained.

"Oh, it is raining now, look how it is raining." You no longer even bothered to say this. That would be boring, and the rain was not boring. It was just there like the sky, and we all know that the sky is anything but boring. It was as if rain had found its homeland; its long diaspora in all the other moist vales and hills of the earth was finally over. In New Orleans, we recognized that sooner or later this might happen, and we, the settlers who were not made of rain, were prepared to coexist until the inevitable moment when we would have to move on.

New Orleans was no place to stay dry, and New Orleans was no place to be famous, and New Orleans was no place to dream big dreams: both the sleepy, lazy hopers and the desperately poor people here could barely muster the energy to consume the famous, much less create them — and the famous need to be created and consumed, often by the same hands. And we here in New Orleans are mostly too lazy or too truly poor to bother with the famous, and their bitchy, itchy, firecracker dreams. Anyway, the lazy dreams of this place were too ill-defined for an ambitious person to even form the gravel of hope.

Or oyster shells of hope. How strange it is to live in a place without rocks. What kind of freakish, Third World town is this? It is a splendid time to recall that we are built on a swamp, and rocks don't exist here (you do know that nature is such a complex, brilliant and stunningly diverse and gorgeous thing that if you really were to spend any amount of time at all thinking about it, you would probably be compelled to crawl into one corner of a room and live on ice chips).

But in so many ways, New Orleans was already a lazy dream come true, a dream where the leaning buildings are the colors of the chalks of a sidewalk artist and the money is damp and largely meaningless and you sip beer and listen to junkie chatter to the sound of the chee-cheep-chirp of the video poker machine and you know you might do this until you die and every second (colored with the vague pink of pleasure) ticks and you can hear it ticking and you know nothing is going to happen until you or someone else you know or love dies. Change is for the ambitious, you, you, but you are still subject to the sloppy rules and dumb, repetitive pleasures of the dorm room, but the dorm room is 20, 30, 40 years ago. Did you hear what I said? The dorm room was a generation ago, indie rock superstars have been born and died in the time since I stumbled amidst the cinder blocks and low dull ceilings of a college dorm. Yet here is a city, here is New Orleans, full of the self-conscious half-smiles and wisps of plans and whispers of crashing romance that marked your first days free of the dorm. But you are 40, 45, 50, 52, 63 years old; you have found the lazy Boho which wants nothing of you, and you deliver.

All my life I had wondered if there was any reality behind a certain expression; now, indeed, I found myself living in a place where life was cheap. This was a very strange place even before the rain, believe me. Someone on television (incidentally, a word we shall never abbreviate) just referred to a certain service that was available only east of the Mississippi. Despite the fact that I live close enough to the Mississippi that I can hear the raspy, desperate, asthmatic hoot of the riverboats, I couldn't immediately cite whether I live east or west of the river. In fact, I think I live north of it, but that barely seems applicable, even if it is wholly possible. I think I live on the East Bank, though, but let me just say that east of here is a part of town known as the West Bank. So, despite the fact that I live north of the river and west of the West Bank, I am going to tell you that I live east of the Mississippi, and this would be the truth, at least until the day comes when I live underneath the Mississippi.

Nonetheless, New Orleans is a strange and happy tomb.

I wake up every day with the corny wonder and eye-snapping awe of a visitor, the same as I might wake up in Vienna, or Vancouver, or Helsinki. Can you do that in New York City, or are you too busy looking over your shoulder, or over the shoulder of the person you are speaking with? Did someone from the Strokes just walk into the room?

Now, under the rain, there is a motley collection of lo-fi Peter Pans, still hipster thin, still clutching whatever dog-eared boho bibles that they have not yet sold off or left behind, still mastering artful and eccentric forms of facial hair, still believing in irony and guitars as we once all did. If they suffer because of unrealized dreams, I can't tell, because they glow with the gladness of someone who has realized at least a form of a dream — if I were rich, they might suppose, certainly the beer and the girls would taste the same and hardly be more plentiful? And they raise their beer bottles even higher than a striver, who always looks out of the corner of his eye for someone who might be judging him. There are few judges here, and I refuse to say that these people aren't living their dream. Only their suitors seem frightened, as they slowly realize they must adapt to life amongst the forever boyish.

I do not want to be harsh to these people. If these people seem very familiar, and they should, it's because they were all the hippest people in the dorm, and once again, I ask you to recall this time, whether you are living it now or whether you lived it 40 years ago; I ask you, for a moment, to think of the hippest people in your dorm.

Not all of them became great screenwriters or internet mavens or television directors or record company executives or studio development people or stock brokers or the sort of people you read about in the *NY Times* or *Jane* magazine, the sort of people who write and assemble the *NY Times* or *Jane* magazine, the sort of people you see on *Sex and the City* or the sort of people who work on *Sex and the City*.

For a long time, I was convinced that this is what we all became. Achievers. Doers. Shapers of Culture and Owners of Things. This is what we are supposed to think. (Now, I am fairly convinced that a similar displacement has occurred with desire: what we are told is "sexy" has become far removed from what our bodies and our hearts find attractive. Those Mesozoic types created those pear and eggplant shape fertility icons for a reason, you know. There is a feral, primitive base for our sexuality, our music, our love of living, our fear of death, our joy at the idea of the unknown; all the structure the 20th century attempted to apply to these things cannot make the graceful drone of Real Gone Music or the soft, round curves of Real Sex go away; our efforts to dim the gorgeous primitive are only temporary, you know).

But the sun is going to burn into a cinder on everyone, whether you're Mao or Morrissey. Take your well-toned asses out of New York or Los Angeles and you see that very few people, indeed, write screenplays, and very few of them live a life written about in screenplays. But some of us thought we were going to become something, and it didn't quite work out the way we imagined. Instead of remaining in New Yos Angeles, instead of walking in shadows of our failures, we founded a kingdom in exile.

Welcome to New Orleans.

We: the Exiles. Slightly underachieving bohemians, screenwriters, painters and punkers, mostly unwilling to admit our disappointments, large and small insults which New York, Los Angeles and even *Woodstock* might wave in our faces. We: resistant to change, unable to cope with the first earth-groan of pain associated with any change while reveling in the small, dependable shifts of a shabby, pastel-colored burg seemingly fixed in the imagination of the dreamer of small dreams fed by thick books. We: fighting boredom with the same noise with which we yelled that we were young, when it was truly work to yell that we were young, but now those yells just distract us from work that needs to be done. We all came to New Orleans to write novels; instead, we just bitterly critiqued the ones being written in a world that was not afraid of change.

Without a doubt, it was beautiful.

The record collectors, the self-hating parishioners of irony, the no longer young jobless hip, the coffee shop poets, the writers of forever partial screenplays, the makers of adamantly lo-fi music, the still smoking, the still drinking, those who refuse to lie to commit and commit and then lie; there is, of course, an absolute beauty to our lack of shame. In Los Angeles, there was a simple word for anyone half a century old (or nearly) who poured cocktails in hotel bars or sold books at Barnes & Noble; this hateful word "failure" implied that there was something better that these people should be doing.

No one uses that word here, and it took me only a few months to recognize that there was likely nothing better we ought to be doing. Fame and wealth are both truly well and good; the artlessness of chasing it makes dogs and whores out of some very fine people, people whose actions and hypocrisy give a bad name to whores and dogs.

Of course, there is another city, which the ghost ship full of aging achievement-free dreamers passes through, largely unnoticed; perhaps our failure gives us both a certain empathy with and anonymity amongst those from whom we were always separate, because if the great ambition Meccas of New York and Los Angeles do any one thing exceptionally well, it is to segregate classes with an almost medieval efficiency. But This City, which is not the second city nor a hidden city, but the primary city, is poor and largely African-American.

We are guests here, guests who see whimsy where they see reality.

We left the Lazy Susan of ambition; unable to replicate the great emigration of our parents and grandparents, and refusing to move to a shadow city like Williamsburg or Silver Lake (pretend all you want that you are exiles; you are still trying to cut into line in the BigTown salad bar, still chasing the dream already realized by the guy or girl who lived down the hall in the dorm). We left for a place where we would not be judged by our inability to make those dreams of mammon and fame come true. This was now our life, you half-smiling adult children, still vibrating with the lusts and dreams of Bard and Barnard, NYU and UCLA. First, you are a refugee; then you will change the world; then you are a failure; then you are a stoic and reconciled failure; then you are a proud failure.

Welcome to New Orleans.

Postscript: New Orleans, October 2005

The city is an alien landscape, far from the wolf whistles of the stacked bar cars of the French Quarter and the polite little Creole manses, all of which looks simply splendid on television. But outside of the Quarter and the still-neat aisles of St. Charles Avenue the city is smashed, dreary, gruesome, twisted; every space of sidewalk covered by piles of life left molded and useless. Two-thirds of the trees are down and nearly all of the plants and grass — and not just dead but baked parchment toxic brown. Imagine the worst thing you ever saw in the back of the cheese or vegetable drawer in the refrigerator you had in your first East Village bachelor(ette) apartment, then recall that rotted, tire-razored dog you saw last week on the side of the road, smoosh the two images together, then times that by ten million: this is the filth and decay and destruction piled in New Orleans. But we would take the filth, we would, it can be washed away (or, this being New Orleans, just forgotten; we will march around it to grip and grin with our neighbors), but what we can't take is the neighborhoods that have been washed off the map; entire swaths of the city, gone, gone, gone, brown and ripped and bombed out block after block after block. Yet most of us recognize that this isn't even what we mourn. We miss the death of the Exile Kingdom, the death of a deep and poor and rhythmic city. We understand that the future of New

Orleans will be very different, full of hale wide boys and contractors with true Southern accents (everyone who has heard a New Orleans accent knows that it has far more in common with Coney Island or Summit, New Jersey than the rest of the Confederacy) and gamblers and hoteliers and all the giggling and tottering white boys from all over America. New Orleans will be rebuilt on the backs of the poor for the pleasure of the rich — we feel resolved to that. It will no longer be a shelter for the aimless and income-erratic who lived alongside — in some kind of grim compliance and occasional mutual admiration — with the poor, the poor, the desperately poor, whose numbers and whose desperation was apparently a secret to everyone but those of us who lived here year round. You couldn't live in these crazy and crazily named buckling and pitted streets without the knowledge that the city was desperately poor and had the infrastructure of a rotten Mexican republic; this was bloody obvious to everyone here, but now everyone knows our secret. New Orleans, you brilliant dusty rouged-up dowager, you barely worked, you were a mess, an anarchic keg of ill-aimed gunpowder simply awaiting some kind of ignition; in the future you will work, you will work well, but without the flavor of the exile, the idle dreamer, the record collector, the lo-fi Peter Pan, the desperate and the poor who gave this city its rhythm. I may return, one day, to the Disneyland Storyville this place will become, but the Haiti/Prague by the Gulf that drew us here is gone forever, trust me on that. This town will look fine through beer goggles, but the beautiful hallelujah sunsets, just as beautiful when seen sober, and the lazy dream that did not need either Mardi Gras or Bourbon Street to fuel it, is gone.

2005, *THE BIG TAKEOVER*

Afterword

From Anywhere to Anywhere

John S. Hall

Having read the book, it occurs to me that what Tim Sommer does incessantly is go from anywhere to anywhere:

And in doing this, he invites us to do the same. I am guilty, sometimes, as most of us are, from staying in one place for a while, then moving elsewhere and then staying there for a while. But Sommer's mind doesn't seem to work that way, as if he is trying to capture and convey everything everywhere all at once. From a lesser talent, the effect could be disorienting, annoying or just plain wrong. But Tim Sommer is right. Even when he is wrong (as I believe he might be about MTV), he is right.

If I were less religious, I would refrain from suggesting that Tim connects to the single source from which everything emerges in timeless, simultaneous oneness and perfection. When reading him, I get the same feeling that I got from reading David Foster Wallace's essays: that of someone grabbing you by the shoulders and staring deep into your eyes and not letting go or looking aways until EVERYTHING has been explained, described and opined upon. To read Sommer is to ride a roller coaster of emotions and facts. It is to be shoved into the back seat and driven 110 miles an hour on Route 66 or the Autobahn.

But this is an afterword, not a foreword. These words come at the end. They come afterwards. After you have read the book. So, I shouldn't be telling you what it's like to read Tim Sommer. Instead, I guess, I should be trying to describe what it's like to have read him. Except that if you've read the book, then you already know. So what am I doing here?

I guess it's like those times when you would all go to see a new band, or a band you all loved but have never seen before, and then you go to a diner afterwards and commiserate about great how it was. So: wasn't that great? Isn't *Dispatches From the Kingdom* wonderful?

For example: when was the last time anyone you know mentioned Lance Loud, or the Mumps? How many people even saw the Mumps? I did, and so did Tim. Tim and I were also both at the Public Image Ltd. show at the Ritz, although we didn't know each other at the time. And Tim's perspective on that show is more or less the same as mine. Tim believes it was irresponsible of PiL and the Ritz not to warn people of what was to take place, but he may have been more in the line of fire when the riot ensued. My perspective (naïve at the time, I acknowledge) was that it was a drag that I didn't see a real PiL show. In retrospect, I saw the most real PiL show that there ever was.

I'm also with Tim on Taylor Swift. I think it's so odd how many people complain about the unoriginality of her music, when it is clear that what virtually all of her fans are responding to is the lyrics, which, as Sommer says, "give words to the thoughts, fears, hopes and heartbreaks" of teens and tweens, but that also reach far beyond that demographic.

Tim is also right when he says that R.E.M. "altered the landscape immensely." My own band, King Missile, never would have been signed to a major label had it not been for R.E.M. I was told this directly by people at the label who explained that Atlantic Records had wanted to sign them but was rejected because they didn't have an alternative music department and had signed no college radio bands. At that time, my band had a number-one college radio song, which would have meant nothing to the majors a year before, and wouldn't have meant much more a year or two later. So, R.E.M certainly changed the landscape for me, and I know I'm not the only one.

Random thought: Are Tim Sommer and I the only people who remember the Bay City Rollers album *Elevator*? Are we the only ones who like it? I see that *AllMusic* gave it four stars (out of five), so maybe not. And the connections he makes between the Rollers and the Sex Pistols (and punk rock generally) are yet another revelation in a book full of revelations. If the name had not already been taken, this book could been called *The Book of Revelations.*

Less random thought: Tim's view that those who say rock and roll is dead are perpetrating "an ugly myth created by people who are unable to distinguish music from the music industry" reminds me of an article I read recently that proclaimed that film was dead, making a similar mistake of failing to discern between the great films that are being made today and the floundering film industry. Tim's concerns are rarely if ever with the monumental or insignificant sales of any given artist, let alone their performance on the charts or the number of awards they've won.

Rather, Tim writes about the music, and what the music does to the listener. Although he is a musician with some serious credentials (Glenn Branca, Hugo Largo and almost the Beastie Boys), Tim's takes on music are not from the perspective of an artist or musician or a critic — he rarely gets into the weeds about theory, or melody, or rhythm, or the mechanics of writing or performing. He doesn't even purport to act as a gatekeeper — he doesn't aim to promote the obscure (with occasional exceptions, such as Sinatra's *Watertown*) or denigrate the popular. Tim writes as a fan, as a listener, as a consumer.

I love Tim's "compare and contrast" piece on *Tusk* and *Sandinista!* I didn't listen to *Sandinista!* enough times at the time of its release or since to be in a position to fully agree on what Sommer says about it, but I suspect he's 100% spot on. As for *Tusk*, that album is easily in my top ten albums of the 1970s (were I to compile such a list, which I would never do), for many of the same reasons Tim lays out.

I also love this, about Weezer's cover of "Africa": "This is a record that thinks it is smarter than you. This is a record that hates you." That encapsulates what I dislike about Weezer and a whole bunch of other bands that I won't list, because who cares what I think? But I will say that Weezer's "Africa" is so Weezer that I almost appreciate it.

It occurs to me to suggest that overreach may be a good strategy for coming to the truth. For example, it seems like almost scandalous overreach to suggest a "direct connection" between Sha Na Na's performance at *Woodstock* and Phil Ochs' *Gunfight at Carnegie Hall* seven months later. But I think it's true. And Tim seems to arrive at truths like this the same way that penicillin occurred to Alexander Fleming — by accident. There is this sense, when reading Sommer (and again, I get this sense with David Foster Wallace and few others) that the ideas that come to him are coming to him as he is writing them, as if the process of writing is a way of "thinking out loud" (though, obviously, not out loud). When a mind like Tim Sommer starts spitballing, genius ensues.

I'm still reeling from the history lessons in Tim's piece on the Streisand-Dylan duet, "The Very Thought of You." To whom else on Earth would it occur to take note of the fact that at the time the two singers were born there were hundreds of men who had fought in the Civil War? Or to note that the day after Bob Dylan's first New York appearance, humans entered space for the first time? Or to tell us that Zita of Bourbon-Parma, the last Hapsburg Empress, "died the same year the Pixies released 'Here Comes My Man' and the B-52s put out 'Love Shack'"?

I've almost reached my word count, and I feel as though I've barely scratched the surface. I haven't even mentioned the essays about the Beatles, which are so full of insight and factoids that I don't even know where to begin.

But I must ask: what am I doing here? Am I trying to remind you of what you have just read, or am I just geeking out over a book that gives me chills of nostalgia, and of recognition, and of being recognized. When Tim points out that we are a palimpsest, not only do we immediately recognize this to be true, we also feel the impressions of the past written on us in a smudged underlayer of our ancestors' memories. This, in a book that purports to be a collection of essays about music (mostly rock music), but aims to be, and is, so much more.

I can't take you on the wild ride that Tim has taken us on — I wouldn't even attempt such a thing. I'll just say that he has reminded us of what it was like to be 12, or 14, or thereabouts, and to hear music that you know will define and shape you. In so doing, he reminds us what art is for: to connect ourselves to ourselves, and to everything else. He also reminds us that writing about music or art is also an art. And Tim is a consummate artist.

Acknowledgments

We writers all stand on the shoulders of our editors.

We may work alone, but never without their ropes, their nets, their extended hands. Whether they are engaged, silent or somewhere in between, these are the people who provide access, encouragement and insight. Every journalist must admit this: as brilliant or unique as we might sometimes think that we are, we don't exist without their patronage. Period.

I am loath to single out any of the editors who have tendered their wisdom and kindness to me over the last (nearly) half-century or set any of them above the others, but veracity demands that I must, and five names demand, loudly, to be spotlighted. Sometimes you go, "Huh, if it wasn't for that person, I might not be doing this at all" (or, just as powerfully, I might not *still* be doing this). My debt to this small group of people is incalculable.

Let's start with these two: First and foremost, Ira Robbins for giving me a shot, when I was 16 and when I was 63; in addition, Ira and the *Trouser Press* crew gave me a university level education in alternative music that largely complemented, and ultimately supplanted, my actual college matriculation. Next: Robert Christgau not only brought me into the then-Everest-like music section at the *Village Voice* when I was still in my teens, he taught me that editing was an engaged, even aggressive process. When it came to being a hands-on editor who was determined to make your point clearer, your words more utile and your pieces better than you ever thought they could be, Christgau was non-pareil.

Three other names are nearly as integral to my life as a journalist, and I am genuinely delighted to honor their remarkable roles in my strange sort-of career.

In 2013, a random encounter on an otherwise remarkably unremarkable side street in Brooklyn Heights with an old college radio chum resuscitated an interest in music/culture journalism that had, at the time, been largely dormant for nearly thirty years. John Loscalzo, if I had to dedicate this book to only two people, it would be you and Ira Robbins. I am so very sorry John and his wife, the wonderful Tracy Zamot, are not here to read these words. Because of my involvement with John's site, *The Brooklyn Bugle*, my somewhat loud and unconventional work came to the attention of the two other people who played manifestly crucial roles in my journalistic reverse-defenestration: Cole Garner Hill and Ken Kurson. Not only did both of these gentlemen see something in me that seemed to pleasurably addle their pates (and which, for some reason, encouraged them to go out of their way to publish and highlight my work in *The New York Observer*), they both were extraordinary, gorgeously hands-on editors (in fact, for the record, alongside Christgau I would rate Cole as the best nuts-and-bolts editor I ever worked with). I could never thank them enough for their support, wisdom and friendship.

Saying "on to the rest" profoundly demeans the support, camaraderie and editorial acumen of everyone else on this list. I am proud to have written for each and every one of these people. I also apologize for the (many) names that have been lost in the deep white fog of memory; this list is far, far smaller than it ought to be, and I look forward to it being amended. The only way to make this (remotely) fair is to do this in (sort of) alphabetical order, so here goes: Garry Bushell, Georgia Christgau, Mitchell Cohen, Danny Eccleston, Geoff Edgers, Caryn Ganz, Drew Grant, Ron Hart, Andy Hermann, Mark Kemp, Jack Rabid, Ben Robinson, Doug Simmons, the late Lou Stathis … and a special non-alphabetical shout-out to Robert Polner, who commissioned and edited my very first printed pieces, which appeared long, long ago in *The Great Neck South Southerner* (a review of Wire's *Pink Flag* and a "think piece" about Barrett-era Floyd. Can I just say, quickly, that I hate the term "think piece"? Does that make all other printed musings "thoughtless pieces"?).

Some other important figures didn't edit me in the context of a magazine, newspaper or online site, but shaped, slashed and honed the work I did during my not-so-infrequent forays into radio and television. Since every one of these people made me more aware of the best way to use words and how to make a point with grace and impact, they deserve to be noted. So let me thank (again, alphabetically) Barbara Barna, the late Alisa Bellettini, Stu Cohn, Linda Corradina, Merle Ginsberg, Doug Herzog, Jackie Sharp, Michael Shore, Michael Simon and Dave Sirulnick.

This is also a fitting time to acknowledge the people who, with great enthusiasm and even greater patience, taught me about the vast, magical world of music and music culture. Especially in the era before the internet and social media, you relied on The Wise and The Excited to tell you about things you might be interested in (especially if these things were off the radar of commercial radio and mainstream music publications). In no particular order (and without any doubt, this is a horrifically incomplete list): Dorian Beslity Cope, Paul Sherman, Arthur Brennan, Tanya Seeman, Dave Schulps, Scott Isler, Jim Green, Jefferson Holt, Ken Sitz, Ed Bahlman, the late Katherine Kahn, Binky Philips, Sue Cummings, Karen Schoemer, Steve Fallon, Katherine Dieckmann, Laura Levine, Thurston Moore, Sal Lo Curto, Michael Dugan, Naomi Regelson, Danny Goldberg, Michael Stipe, Peter Holsapple, Rosemary Carroll, Hahn Rowe, John Neilson (who has the peculiar and extraordinary honor of having introduced me to my two all-time favorite bands, Neu! and Hawkwind), Paul Sanchez, Eddie Ecker, Bob Giordano (who turned me on to the Beach Boys) and last (but maybe even first), Matthew Goodman and Andrew Cutrofello, who were there, literally, when the obsession began, and I realized that I was far, far more interested in Phil Ochs, the Beatles, and the Kinks than anything going on in 8th or 9th grade.

Enormous thanks to Afterword author John S. Hall. John, you are a prince and a treasure of the city, the scion of Ferlinghetti and Carroll and possibly even Professor Irwin Corey, and I hope your name is long remembered. Kristina Juzaitis, thank you so much for your patience and grace in creating an attractive and readable template, cover and package for my occasionally attractive and readable words. And, my god, an enormous bow of gratitude to Gregory Crewdson for the extraordinary, beautiful, moving and appropriate cover image; your gifts — and your generosity — leave me awed. I have literally known

Gregory for as long as I have been writing professionally, and it gives me such genuine pleasure that we are still in each other's lives.

For continued support and counsel as I stumble my way through the literary world, I humbly thank Rick Richter, Laura Albert, Mahinder Kingra, David Menconi, Louis Maistros and Michael McGandy.

Finally, this book — both this compilation and the nascence of its contents over the past 47 years — would not have been possible without seven people: Jennifer Brout, Emily Brout, Bo Brout, Madeline Brout, Kay Kasperhauser, Peter Sommer and Cathy Iselin. If my words stand on the shoulders of my editors and the friends who shaped my tastes, my heart is held in the hands of this group of sages.

www.ingramcontent.com/pod-product-compliance
Lightning Source LLC
Jackson TN
JSHW082147150526
102460JS00002B/2

* 9 7 9 8 9 9 9 0 4 8 7 3 8 *